Global Issues in Language, Education and Development

LINGUISTIC DIVERSITY AND LANGUAGE RIGHTS
Series Editor: Dr Tove Skutnabb-Kangas, *Roskilde University, Denmark*

Consulting Advisory Board:
François Grin, *Université de Genève, Switzerland*
Kathleen Heugh, *Human Services Research Council, South Africa*
Miklós Kontra, *Linguistics Institute, Hungarian Academy of Sciences,Budapest*
Masaki Oda, *Tamagawa University, Japan*

The series seeks to promote multilingualism as a resource, the maintenance of linguistic diversity, and development of and respect for linguistic human rights worldwide through the dissemination of theoretical and empirical research. The series encourages interdisciplinary approaches to language policy, drawing on sociolinguistics, education, sociology, economics, human rights law, political science, as well as anthropology, psychology, and applied language studies.

Other Books in the Series
Medium or Message? Language and Faith in Ethnic Churches
Anya Woods
Imagining Multilingual Schools: Language in Education and Glocalization
Ofelia García, Tove Skutnabb-Kangas and María Torres-Guzmán (eds)
Minority Languages and Cultural Diversity in Europe
Konstanze Glaser

Other Books of Interest
English in Africa: After the Cold War
Alamin M. Mazrui
Ideology and Image: Britain and Language
Dennis Ager
Language and Society in a Changing Italy
Arturo Tosi
Language Attitudes in Sub-Saharan Africa
Efurosibina Adegbija
Language, Ethnicity and Education
Peter Broeder and Guus Extra
Linguistic Minorities in Central and Eastern Europe
Christina Bratt Paulston and Donald Peckham (eds)
Multilingualism in Spain
M. Teresa Turell (ed.)
Negotiating of Identities in Multilingual Contexts
Aneta Pavlenko and Adrian Blackledge (eds)
Quebec's Aboriginal Languages
Jacques Maurais (ed.)
The Other Languages of Europe
Guus Extra and Durk Gorter (eds)
Where East Looks West: Success in English in Goa and on the Konkan Coast
Dennis Kurzon
Understanding Deaf Culture: In Search of Deafhood
Paddy Ladd

For more details of these or any other of our publications, please contact:
Multilingual Matters, Frankfurt Lodge, Clevedon Hall,
Victoria Road, Clevedon, BS21 7HH, England
http://www.multilingual-matters.com

LINGUISTIC DIVERSITY AND LANGUAGE RIGHTS 4
Series Editor: Tove Skutnabb-Kangas, *Roskilde University, Denmark*

Global Issues in Language, Education and Development

Perspectives from Postcolonial Countries

Naz Rassool

With case studies by
Maggie Canvin, Kathleen Heugh and Naz Rassool
with Sabiha Mansoor

MULTILINGUAL MATTERS LTD
Clevedon • Buffalo • Toronto

Library of Congress Cataloging in Publication Data
Rassool, Naz
Global Issues in Language, Education and Development: Perspectives from Postcolonial Countries/Naz Rassool, with case studies by Maggie Canvin, Kathleen Heugh and Sabiha Mansoor.
Linguistic Diversity and Language Rights: 4
Includes bibliographical references and index.
1. Language and education–Developing countries. 2. Language policy–Developing countries. I. Canvin, Maggie. II. Heugh, Kathleen. III. Mansoor, Sabiha. IV. Title.
P40.85.D44R37 2007
306.44' 9091724–dc22 2006022900

British Library Cataloguing in Publication Data
A catalogue entry for this book is available from the British Library.

EAN-13: 978-1-85359-952-1 (hbk)
EAN-13: 978-1-85359-951-4 (pbk)

Multilingual Matters Ltd
UK: Frankfurt Lodge, Clevedon Hall, Victoria Road, Clevedon BS21 7HH.
USA: UTP, 2250 Military Road, Tonawanda, NY 14150, USA.
Canada: UTP, 5201 Dufferin Street, North York, Ontario M3H 5T8, Canada.

The policy of Multilingual Matters/Channel View Publications is to use papers that are natural, renewable and recyclable products, made from wood grown in sustainable forests. In the manufacturing process of our books, and to further support our policy, preference is given to printers that have FSC and PEFC Chain of Custody certification. The FSC and/or PEFC logos will appear on those books where full certification has been granted to the printer concerned.

Typeset by Techset Composition Ltd.
Printed and bound in Great Britain by the Cromwell Press Ltd.

For
Joe, Fatima, Faiz, Ismail and Shuaib

and in memory of
Gadija (Diya) Adikary and Achmed Omardien

My moeder en vader in herrinering

اپنے ماں باپ کے نام ـــــ

جنھوں نے بے شمار قربانیاں دیں

اور بے لوث محبت کی

Contents

Series Editor's Foreword

In February 2005, the National Assembly in France 'passed legislation requiring school courses to recognize the "positive role" played by French colonialism' (Ramonet, 2006: 1). Even if President Chirac called for this act to be rewritten, the justification was that it 'divides France' (Ramonet, 2006), rather than because Chirac recognized that the grounds for the claim might have been less than solid.

Gordon Brown, the British prime minister in waiting stated to the *Daily Mail* on his visit to Africa (15 January 2005): 'The days of Britain having to apologise for its colonial history are over. We should move forward. We should celebrate much of our past rather than apologise for it. And we should talk, and rightly so, about British values that are enduring, because they stand for some of the greatest ideas in history: tolerance, liberty, civic duty, that grew in Britain and influenced the rest of the world. Our strong traditions of fair play, of openness, of internationalism, these are great British values' (see http://www.dailymail.co.uk/pages/live/articles/news/news.html?in_article_id=334208&in_page_id=1770).

In the USA, several websites, some backed by large right-wing organizations, are trying to silence critical voices at universities. They are targeting and listing professors who are critical of some aspects of US policies and reveal (government) misinformation and lies (see, e.g. www.discoverthenetworks.org, www.uclaprofs.com, http://www.susanohanian.org/show_atrocities.html?id=5806, and links in them; see also Younge, 2006).

Also in the USA, Michael Specter (2006) writes:

> The Bush Administration has worked tirelessly to control the speech and movements of American scientists. In 2004, the Department of Health and Human Services issued a policy forbidding researchers to lend their expertise to the World Health Organization (or to travel to international scientific conferences) without the department's permission. William R. Steiger, a special assistant to the Secretary,

> told government scientists that if they wanted to act as consultants in meetings of the World Health Organization they would first have to agree to advocate U.S. policy. The practical implications were both chilling and farcical. That year, the department, saying that it needed to reduce the number of scientists attending international meetings, prevented more than a hundred and fifty government researchers from travelling to the International AIDS Conference, which was held in Bangkok. Department officials said they wanted to save money; their decision came after the organizer of the conference refused a request by the U.S. to invite the evangelist Franklin Graham to give a speech promoting faith-based solutions to the AIDS epidemic. In January, James Hansen, one of the government's most highly respected climate experts, said that the Bush Administration has made several efforts to prevent him from speaking publicly since a recent lecture in which he called for the immediate reduction of greenhouse gases. 'This Administration has tried to restrict the very elements of scientific success: free and open inquiry', said Margaret A. Hamburg, who was a commissioner of health in New York City under both David Dinkins and Rudolph Giuliani and worked in the Clinton Administration as a senior health-policy adviser. 'You can't do science without understanding that theories are public and views often clash. You resolve differences by experiments and research, not by toeing the line.'

In times like this, the critical analysis in Naz Rassool's book is a cause for celebration. Naz is certainly not 'toeing the line' and offers powerful tools to others who do not want to do so. The book is not only a necessary and courageous counterweight to myths and outright lies about colonialism and its present-day continuation by other means. It is a warmly welcome addition to multidisciplinary analyses of the economic and political forces behind increasing poverty and gaps between haves and never-to-haves and at the same time behind the disappearance of the world's linguistic (and cultural) diversity. Few researchers appreciate the complexity of the web of the continuities in various types of globalisation and the impact this has on ordinary people's lives. Few who see the central role of language in upholding unequal power structures have described and analysed the processes involved in ways that can match Naz Rassool's insightful book. She synthesizes and integrates brilliantly the necessary multidisciplinary knowledge about language in globalisation. The case studies provide solid, up-to-date and interesting descriptive data, while successfully and consistently applying and testing the theoretical insights. Even if the contents of the book are demanding, the inspiration and new understandings make reading it a delightful – and sad – experience. This hopefully leads to action too.

Tove Skutnabb-Kangas

References

Ramonet, I. (2006) Liberty, equality, security. *Le Monde Diplomatique*, English edition, April 2006, 1.

Specter, M. (2006) The Bush Administration's war on the laboratory. *The New Yorker*, 13 March 2006, *Political Science*, 58–69. On WWW at http://www.wesjones.com/specter2.htm.

Younge, G. (2006) Silence in class. *Guardian Weekly*, 14–20 April 2006, 17–18.

Acknowledgements

Writing a book is a journey in which one meets many interesting people, encounters fascinating new concepts and ideas, works through issues and, above all, is humbled by the amount that one does not know. Whilst writing is very much a solitary affair, it is not a one-person effort. On this journey I have benefited from a community of warm and generous people.

I am immensely grateful to Tove Skutnabb-Kangas for her inspiration over the years and sisterly friendship, her sharp insight, her generosity and understanding – Kiitoksia oikein paljon, Tack så mycket, Mange tak. I am deeply indebted to Marjukka Grover for her patience and understanding throughout this project. I am grateful to Robert Phillipson for his interest, valuable comments on Chapter 1, and his generous sharing of information throughout the writing of this book. I want to express my appreciation to Maggie, Kathleen and Sabiha for their excellent contributions despite very busy schedules, and particularly for bearing with me in difficult times. I especially want to thank my colleague, Paul Croll, for undertaking my administrative responsibilities during Summer Term 2005, giving me much-needed time to write. I appreciate the collegial support and friendship of Viv Edwards. I would like to thank Carole Bloch at the University of Cape Town, for providing me with much needed information on the intellectualization of African languages. I also wish to thank Rosemary Jones, secretary, par excellence, Joan Mathews in the technical support services, and the inter-library loan team on the Bulmershe Court Campus, University of Reading.

Our families sustain us. During this period my postmodern family brought much to smile about. Dylan is a budding artist and also learned to write beautiful poems, Lewis can now write his name and is a champion swimmer; in California, Leo became an ace reader, Alex won a school science prize and is a footballer of skill, Sam collected merit certificates and Joseph became a budding actor. I'm impressed, guys! Thanks to Zarina, Reza, Ruth, Feyruz and Steve for familial love and much laughter and conversation around our perpetual dinner table. I am grateful to my nephews Basheer, Armin, Yushree and Zaid for keeping me in touch with my family in South Africa, for continuing to write me long and interesting letters despite many late replies. I wish to thank my god-daughter Yasmine, who during this period finally found her niche as a feature writer, for her loving phone calls and thoughtful ways. To Joe, my husband and best friend, I am ever-grateful for his enduring love, his enthusiasm and support in everything that I do.

Maggie, Kathleen and Sabiha express their thanks and appreciation to Tony, Anthony, and Mansoor, and their families.

I would like to thank the following people and organizations for kindly allowing me to use their data in this book: Professor Frederic Docquier, Global Languages.com, the UNHCR and Grant Makers Concerned with Immigrants and Refugees (GCIR).

Introduction

This book is not about language *per se*; neither is it explicitly about language rights discourses. Focusing on countries in the Sub-Saharan and South Asian regions, it examines the role that language-in-education policy, historically, has played in shaping development possibilities within these contexts. This discussion is juxtaposed with changes taking place in the global labour market, and the ways in which these are linked with language, education and development. Within this framework, the book examines the ways in which language-in-education policy interacts with history, politics, culture and economics – and how this ultimately impacts on societal development possibilities. In this discussion, it aims to examine the long-term impact of colonialism on the socio-political, economic and cultural base of colonized polities – and to highlight the influence of this on contemporary language and development issues within postcolonial societies. In the process, it seeks to highlight some of the ways in which colonialism disrupted the inner dynamic of colonized societies, eroding not only the existing socio-political base, displacing peoples and their languages, but also altering social relations, and the 'social character'. The concept of the 'social character' refers to the collective values and beliefs that gave coherence to their lives; the ways that societies historically have made and remade themselves (Williams, 1961). This reorientation of the collective and individual beliefs, values, expectations, aspirations, dreams and desires of colonized societies here are seen as representing the 'colonial habitus'. The concept of *habitus* derives from Bourdieu (1991) and, in a simplified sense, refers to the dispositions developed through experiences in society, culture and family. In this regard, the book examines the complex ways in which colonialism shaped the linguistic *habitus* of societies, cultures and individuals and how this has influenced post-colonial language-state relations. This includes the linguistic choices mediated by colonial policy, their establishment over time as societal 'norms' and, ultimately, their incorporation into the commonsense 'hegemonic' consciousness of colonized peoples. Oppressed groups, for a variety of reasons, often make linguistic choices that reinforce existing social, political and economic inequalities; and, in doing so, they collude in their own collective disempowerment and/or dispossession. In this regard, the book seeks to highlight intertextual links between colonial and postcolonial language policy choices. It further seeks to highlight the ways that postcolonial language choices have impacted on society and culture and, moreover, undermined long-term possibilities for development within these contexts.

Looking for historical origins, the book uses as its starting point two historical moments during the late 19th century, which transformed the socio-cultural, economic and political bases of countries in Sub-Saharan Africa and South Asia. This refers, first, to the creation of cross-border ethnolinguistic enclaves in India (and, *de facto*, Pakistan) at Partition in 1947 and, second, those that emerged in the carving up of Africa at the Berlin Conference in 1884–1885. The creation of these new political entities, it is argued, has contributed to the complex language terrain within these regions. The discussion examines the ways in which ethnolinguistic landscapes were altered as a result of competing colonial interests in Africa during the late 19th century and, moreover, the problems that arose in India during the process of decolonization. These historical forms of social displacement, it is argued, have given rise to conflict between different ethnolinguistic groups, contributing thus to social and political instability which, in turn, impacts on development possibilities.

Postcolonial Language and Development Concerns

Many postcolonial developing countries throughout the South Asia and Sub-Sahran Africa regions share common socio-political problems. These include sustained economic and social underdevelopment, fragile polities, systemic corruption, entrenched autocratic regimes, unstable national governments, underdeveloped social infrastructure, and under-educated populations – some (notably women and rural populations) with very basic levels of education and functional literacy. Many of these societies are riven with vast economic and political divides, with much of the power held by relatively small political elites. In most instances, the latter also represent language elites; in this regard, language and literacy inequalities reflect social disparities. This is a recurring theme throughout the book.

The significance of examining these issues now, lies in the fact that almost five decades after decolonization, and despite numerous

UNESCO funded mass literacy campaigns and major policy initiatives such as Universal Primary Education (UPE), and Education For All (EFA), there still is a significant knowledge and economic divide between high income industrialized and low income 'developing'[1] countries. These problems have been exacerbated by technological development and geo-political, cultural and economic changes taking place within the global terrain. In particular, the redefined workplace has created labour demands for high levels of technological skills and knowledge as well as sophisticated levels of linguistic and communicative competence (Rassool, 1999). The central role that language and communication play in the interactive global arena, underscores the need to examine historically unresolved language problems in postcolonial societies, and how these are related to low societal levels of literacy which, in turn, impact on adequately skilled labour supply. Intense competition within the global labour market has made it imperative for countries to develop their human resource base. This refers to the levels of skills and knowledge amongst the potential workforce to meet the evolving needs of both the national and international labour markets. The highly competitive global labour market has created the need for national governments to adopt coherent educational policy strategies in order to develop the skills and knowledge potential within postcolonial societies.

Elsewhere, in industrialized societies, this has been taking place on a sustained basis during the past two decades. Already during the 1980s the Organization for Economic Co-operation and Development (OECD) advised member countries to make policy adjustments to enable education to respond more effectively to rapid shifts in skills and qualification requirements within the labour market (OECD, 1989). Since then, most OECD countries have put into place resources to strengthen their educational infrastructure, and to support human resource development geared towards meeting the high skills and knowledge demands of the global labour market. In the UK, for example, a National Curriculum was introduced in the Education Reform Act of 1988, aimed at catering for the knowledge and skills needs of the 21st century. Similarly, the US concentrated on capacity building in relation to enhancing the national information infrastructure (NII) by building interactive networks in institutions across the country (Rassool, 1999).

In contrast, long-term underinvestment in education in many postcolonial societies in Sub-Saharan Africa, and South Asia, has contributed to the under-development of human resources (labour skills supply) as well as under-developed educational and linguistic infrastructures.

These factors represent major constraining factors to social and economic development within these contexts, limiting their ability to participate effectively in the global cultural economy.

Analytical Framework

The book has a discursive orientation. It aims to link macro-perspectives with local policies and practice, whilst taking account also of the dialogical relationship between past and present language and development issues in postcolonial societies. The main argument underpinning the book is that it is only by examining the complex economic, socio-political and cultural relations of colonialism, and the legacy of postcolonial statehood that we can begin to understand contemporary language and development problems in these societies, and aim to work towards alternative, more empowering, solutions/approaches. Put simply, the book represents a search towards a better understanding of language, education and development issues in postcolonial societies. In order to clarify the book's frame and terms of reference further, the next section discusses key concepts used in the rest of the discussion.

What is Postcolonialism?

'Postcolonialism' here features as a contested concept. First, it is understood as marking the 'period of nation building that followed decolonization during the 1960s and 1970s'. Second, 'it also incorporates wider sociocultural changes that have taken place within the global terrain since that time'. In this regard, it represents a dynamic process of change taking place within both the postcolonial state, and the postcolonial mother country following decolonization. Young (2001: 57) summarizes it thus:

> The postcolonial is a dialectical concept that marks the broad historical facts of decolonisation and the determined achievement of sovereignty – but also the realities of nations and peoples emerging into a new imperialistic context of economic and sometimes political domination. (...) The postcolonial also specifies a transformed historical situation, and the cultural formations that have arisen in response to changed political circumstances, in the former colonial power.

Third, the 'postcolonial' is interpreted as representing a 'theoretical framework' within which complexities around identity formation, marginalization, exclusion, displacement, difference or 'otherness', and hybridity grounded in the colonial experience are articulated. In this sense, it can be seen as representing a counter-hegemonic discourse interrogating the grand narratives of colonialism; a form of 'talking back' (hooks, 1989) against the dominant discourses of colonialism that, historically, have positioned the colonized as docile subjects. At the same time, it also highlights the complexities, ambiguities, contradictions and tensions in which colonial hegemony existed – as well as the ambivalence and dilemmas that often marked the cultural and linguistic choices of the colonized. In a general sense, it constitutes, simultaneously, a meta-narrative theorizing the political transition from colonialism to postcolonialism; and a counter-hegemonic discourse that engages critically with the historical 'effects' of colonialism.

Fourth, it also refers to 'postcolonial language relations', especially, the predominance in postcolonial countries of erstwhile colonial languages such as English, French and Portuguese, as official languages. Following decolonization, it refers also to the strengthening of languages of wider communication such as, for example, Kiswahili, Hausa, and Bambara, as national language.

Fifth, within the global arena, national states are part of an interdependent world system underpinned by interactive, dynamic economic, cultural and political inter-relationships and inter-dependencies. Postcolonialism therefore has to be seen also in relation to the 'evolution of new social relations' within the global terrain defined by interactive information, cultural and capital flows. Yet it also has to be seen in relation to the emergence of intensive forms of regional power blocing, and local struggles. Arguments foregrounding 'world languages', that is, ex-colonial languages and particularly English, as prerequisites for participation in the global cultural economy are in ascendancy (Dow Templeton Associates, 1997; cited in Skutnabb-Kangas, 2000). Clearly, there is a need to examine the linguistic base of the post-colonial national state, the official languages for teaching and learning, and educational provision as well as to concretize the role of language and education in the development process.

Transmigration

The past two decades have also been marked by unprecedented levels of mass transmigration across regions, countries and continents as consequences of civil wars, natural disasters, increased poverty and political instability within nation states. Of significance is the fact that developing countries throughout Sub-Saharan Africa and South Asia have carried the burden of large numbers of refugees. These constant flows of people have altered not only the ethnolinguistic landscapes of individual countries but also have placed added burdens on national states already politically insecure and/or under economic pressure. Issues related to the long-term impact of transmigration on the sociocultural, economic and political base of receiving countries are discussed in Chapters 3 and 4.

What is 'Development'?

Societal 'development' also is a contested concept. The notion of societal development is grounded historically in the European idea of the nation-state based on the principles of internal coherence, integration, political legitimacy. Within this framework, the concept of development has traditionally referred to a strengthening of the material base, mainly through industrialization. This Eurocentric view of development has been influential in shaping policy discourse in relation to postcolonial development throughout South Asia and Sub-Saharan Africa. In a more general sense, it is assumed that societal development involves structural transformation which implies cultural, political, social and economic changes leading to a more complex institutional and societal base. Moreover, the linking of the idea of economic growth with social progress suggests that development is continuous, organic, directional, cumulative, irreversible and purposive.

However, this represents a one-dimensional view of development. It does not take account of complexities, historical discontinuities and the fact that societal development can totally be reversed, or that it can be interrupted or undermined. For example, particular forms of development could, potentially, be imposed on societies from outside (as was the case with colonialism, and currently, the impact of international agencies such as the World Bank/IMF/WTO), and that these forms of development might conflict with, and undermine indigenous forms of development. In the long-term, this could contribute to un- or underdevelopment by eroding existing infrastructures as well as indigenous ways of life. Development policies can also be undermined from within, by various power interest groups including religious/cultural/ethnic groups, and competing political parties. Other factors contributing to underdevelopment include, for example, wars, political instability, and corruption, natural disasters such as drought (as was the case in different regions of Sub-Saharan Africa in recent years), flooding (as was the case with the recent tsunami in South East Asia, and annually in Bangladesh), and earthquakes (as recently occurred in Kashmir). As can be seen later in the book, sometimes all these factors are concentrated within one country resulting in intense or prolonged periods of underdevelopment.

Of further significance, is the fact that the model of development adopted within society, also represents a particular worldview; a particular view of people and their role and place within society. These, in turn, are integrally tied in with particular economic, political and hegemonic projects of the state, on the one hand, and those of international agencies, on the other. Neoliberalism represents the dominant model of development and is grounded in a free-market ideology. Societal development then, is not a linear process; neither is it a neutral process.

The concept of development here is viewed as a reflexive, self-defining process; it is a dynamic and discursive process. In other words, whilst economic growth indicators are key elements in the measurement of societal development, there are also important non-economic indicators to consider. The latter include, for example,

- overall gains in societal literacy rates;
- improvement in schooling provision, attendance and results;
- the ability to provide schooling in a child-safe environment nationally;
- improvement in health conditions and services;
- provision of adequate housing;
- a coherent and cohesive social organization, that is, the degree of national integration and sense of national unity;
- the extent of mass communication, and levels of access;
- the level of effectiveness of the country's financial institutions;
- sustained political stability;
- the availability of a coherent social, economic and political infrastructure;
- a balanced economy comprised of different sectors e.g. manufacturing, and service industries, finance capital, commodities, and agriculture;
- an adequately skilled labour supply to meet evolving national and international labour market needs.

Development, therefore, is seen as involving structural transformation in response to ongoing cultural, economic, political and social changes taking place within society. The 'economic dimension' of development involves the growth of the country's Gross National Product (GNP) and an increase in goods and services; within the competitive international labour market, development relies to a significant extent on adequate levels of human resource development. The central role that language plays in this is discussed in the case studies, and in the concluding chapters. The 'sociopolitical-cultural dimension' includes democratic sharing of power – a literate, knowledgeable and active citizenship, participation in decision making, cooperation, social integration and justice; the sociocultural dimension involves not only the satisfaction of basic needs such as food, shelter and clothing, but also non-material goods such as freedom of access to information, education as well as social justice for, and inclusiveness of all citizens, and political stability sustained by common goals.

What is Human Resource Development?

The increasingly technologically driven, interactive, and competitive global cultural economy of the 21st century has created labour demands for high levels of technological capability, communicative competence, and continuous upgrading of skills. The integration of these knowledge and skills areas into the labour market means that they represent key elements of 'human resource development' (HRD). This organic relationship between HRD, society, and the economy means that skills and knowledge development has important implications for education and training policy. In most industrialized countries educational policy has incorporated the notion of HRD into the ideal of the 'learning society'. This idea of HRD is based on an economic model grounded in a continuous accumulation of transferable skills and knowledge as important 'human capital' to be exchanged within a constantly changing labour market. Within this discourse workers represent units of production. This contrasts with a humanistic view of workers which focuses not only on the economic potential of workers but also on the cultural and political development of people, and as active citizens within society. However, in order to build my argument progressively, the dominant economistic construction of HRD features in the discussion in the next few chapters. A redefined view of HRD in relation to linguistic and communicative competence and 'cultural capital' (Bourdieu, 1991) is implicit in the critiques throughout the rest of the book.

The Aims of the Book

The argument that the issue of language in education and development is, fundamentally, political is a recurring theme. The book has four interrelated aims:

(1) It aims to examine the relationship between language and social development within the context of the social, technological, cultural

and economic changes taking place within the global cultural economy. Emphasis is placed on the relationship between language and national identity, linguistic and knowledge competence and human resource development within the broader framework of the global labour market as well as issues related to language and cultural power.

(2) The book argues that the dynamic developments taking place globally need to be viewed also in relation to the economic, knowledge and technological divides that exist between the metropolitan world, and developing countries. Thus it aims to explore the historical relationship between language relations within the colonial state, and contemporary language problems in developing countries as well as the relationship between postcolonial language policies and national literacy levels and, ultimately, their impact on human resource development.

(3) Using three national case studies, the book aims to provide insight into the rich tapestry of languages that prevail in developing countries in the Sub-Saharan and South Asian regions, and to identify some of the dilemmas and constraints faced by these societies with regard to language choice in relation to education and social development. And, at the same time, to identify and discuss some of the strategies adopted by governments to address these problems.

(4) Drawing on key motifs identified throughout the discussion, the book aims to identify commonalities and differences between language and social development possibilities as well as constraints within the societies discussed in the book. Issues for policy and practice are identified.

How the Book is Organized

The book is divided into three inter-related parts.

Part 1: Language diversity in development discourse

This section of the book explores the relationship between colonial and postcolonial social policies, and unresolved language problems that prevail in developing countries in sub-Saharan Africa and South Asia.

Chapter 1

Language and the Colonial State looks for some of the origins of contemporary language and social development problems in postcolonial societies. It discusses issues related to national language policy within the colonial state including the imposition of colonial 'mother tongues', and the role that this played in the marginalization of local languages in educational policy and practice. Language and literacy inequalities are identified, and discussed in relation to social development.

Chapter 2

Postcolonial Development, Language and Nationhood provides a brief discussion of the theoretical origins of the concepts of 'nation' and state' within the liberal democratic framework of the 19th century. These are then discussed in relation to colonialism. It addresses the issues of national identity and state power within societies in Sub-Saharan Africa and South Asia emerging from colonial rule during the 1960s and 1970s. Particular emphasis is placed on the relationship between national language policies, nation-building and modernization theory, which underpinned postcolonial development discourse during this period. Labour market needs at the time are highlighted, and discussed in relation to human capital theory. Problems related to the educational entitlements of linguistic minority groups, literacy inequalities, and the failure of postcolonial development policies, are discussed within an analytical framework that takes account of the legacy of colonialism, issues of governance and international policy imperatives.

Chapter 3

The Global Cultural Economy: Issues of Language, Culture and Politics defines the concept of the global cultural economy that prevails in contemporary development discourse. This includes a discussion of language and education issues related to the changing labour market, paranational power blocs such as the World Bank/IMF and UNESCO, as well as transmigration and their impact on developing countries.

Chapter 4

Language in the Global Cultural Economy: Implications for Postcolonial Societies, discusses the political economy of language in the contemporary world. It highlights the central role that language plays in the global cultural economy, and examines the negative impact of unresolved language problems in developing countries, on development possibilities. This is discussed further in relation to the sophisticated skills and knowledges that form the basis of human resource development within the global cultural economy. This includes a discussion of the changes that have taken place within the technologically driven international labour market. Key issues in the debate about 'world' versus local languages are discussed in relation to social and economic development imperatives in developing countries. Problematizing these issues, the chapter discusses the dilemmas faced by individuals, and societies, with regard to language choices within the global cultural economy. These are discussed in relation to knowledge exchange, national language choices and 'world' languages such as English. Implications for language policy and language planning in postcolonial societies, in Sub-Saharan Africa and South Asia, are discussed.

Part 2: Case studies

This section of the book comprises case studies, presenting the main language and literacy issues in policy and practice in three developing countries. These chapters provide a focus on, for example:

(1) a sociolinguistic profile of the country;
(2) literacy levels;
(3) historical and contemporary language policy frameworks and their debates;
(4) historical and prevailing cultural, economic and political factors and their impact on language policy and provision;
(5) language attitudes, language choices;
(6) key human resource development issues;
(7) curriculum issues, teaching materials including textbooks and multimedia resources;
(8) teacher supply, teaching quality including issues of pedagogy, assessment and classroom organization;
(9) problems and dilemmas;
(10) future developments.

Chapter 5

Language and Education Issues in Policy and Practice in Mali, West Africa by Maggie Canvin.

Chapter 6

Language and Literacy Issues in South Africa: Policy and Practice by Kathleen Heugh.

Chapter 7

Contemporary Issues in Language, Education and Development in Pakistan by Naz Rassool and Sabiha Mansoor.

The significance of these case studies lies in the fact that they provide the perspectives of scholars living and working within postcolonial developing countries. The case studies allow an in-depth focus on individual countries. They also enable issues raised in the discussion throughout the book, to be addressed in further detail, highlighting commonalities as well as differences within and between countries.

Part 3: Globalization and linguistic diversity

Part 3 draws on key motifs identified in the previous two sections, and discusses language as an important aspect of cultural capital within the interactive global cultural economy. Language as cultural capital here is viewed in terms of its relationship with identity, knowledge and cultural power, and their dialogical relationship with social and economic development.

Chapter 8 *Postcolonial Perspectives: Major Issues in Language and Development in the Global Cultural Economy* summarizes key issues raised throughout the book. It re-examines the concept of human resource development in relation to the linguistic skills and knowledge demands of workers within the global cultural economy, the language rights, literacy and knowledge entitlements of national and global citizens as well as individual linguistic, cultural and worker identities within the broader framework of reflexive self definition.

Note

1. The concept of a 'developing country' is contested. Here it simply refers to a country that has a low income average, a relatively undeveloped infrastructure and a lower Human Development Index rating when compared to the global norm (http://www.wikipedia.com).

Part 1

Language Diversity in Development Discourse

Chapter 1

Language and the Colonial State

The language medium through which knowledge is mediated, generally does not present a problem in Western industrialized societies. Within these contexts, education normally takes place through languages, which are seen as representing 'the national culture or cultural heritage of the country' (Skutnabb-Kangas, 2000: 306). Highlighting the significance of using languages grounded in their cultures and societies in the learning process, Prah argues that:

> ... in free societies knowledge transfer takes place in the language or languages of the masses; the languages in which the masses are most creative and innovative; languages which speak to them in their hearts and minds most primordially. (Prah, 2002a: 2)

The concept of an inherently 'free' society raised here by Prah, is clearly problematic but, unfortunately, cannot be discussed further here; it lies beyond the scope of this book. Moreover, as is discussed in Chapter 3, the notion of an intrinsically culturally homogeneous (or alternatively, pluralist), linguistically stable metropolitan nation state, implicit in Prah's argument, is contested. What I want to highlight here, is the fact that the importance of using languages that people know, and can relate to in the learning process *is* significant, not only in relation to skills and knowledge acquisition, but also with regard to language maintenance and cultural reproduction.

In contrast, many developing countries, especially those in Sub-Saharan Africa (SSA), are faced with unresolved questions regarding the choice of language(s) that would best support economic and social development. As is indicated earlier, the significance of language in development lies in the fact that it provides the medium through which skills and knowledge are acquired, and is therefore central to the concept of human resource development. In consequence, the linguistic dilemmas faced by developing countries regarding the choice of language(s) of teaching and learning, have implications for their relative ability to sustain adequate levels of HRD – and, *de facto*, to accumulate enough 'cultural capital' to be exchanged within an increasingly knowledge-based, highly competitive, international labour market. Moreover, the language medium of teaching and learning is also important in relation to cultural transmission. Language and literature provide the means through which society's historical narrative, and its 'social character' is produced (Williams, 1961). As is argued earlier, this refers to its collective disposition or habitus, beliefs, values and expectations. These, in turn, are produced and reproduced within, and through, the knowledge frameworks, and the philosophical principles that underpin curricula.

Many developing countries have histories embedded in colonialism. Whereas the nation-builders of Europe could build intertextually, and progressively, on the 'cultural, linguistic and patriotic unity' of past empires:

> African states are building nations of new identities defined by the boundaries of their colonial past ... Africa's colonial past (...) has left a legacy of multiple identities and a crisis of legitimacy for post-colonial governments ... the relics of colonialism lie deep in African societies. (Paku, 1996: 172)

As can be seen in Chapter 2, this argument can, to a significant extent, also be applied to India and Pakistan. One of the most endurable legacies of colonialism has been its negative influence on the self-concept of colonized societies. Whilst, in most instances, colonialism was imposed through coercion, it was maintained through more subtle hegemonic processes. That is to say, by winning the hearts and minds of colonized peoples through the legitimation in language and literary practices, of the cultural traditions, social norms, values, and beliefs of the 'Mother Country' – indigenous ways of speaking, ways of knowing, and ways of doing in colonized societies across the world, were eroded. This is best described as the shaping of the 'colonial habitus'. Fanon underlines the significance that language played in maintaining colonial cultural hegemony, and the subtle means by which this penetrated the consciousness of colonized peoples:

> Every colonised people – every people in whose soul an inferiority complex has been created by the death and burial of its local cultural originality, finds itself face to face with the language of the civilised nation, that is, with the culture of the mother country. The colonized is elevated above his jungle status in proportion to his adoption of the mother country's cultural standards. (Fanon, 1967: 18)

In this construction, the colonial mother tongue became the benchmark against which the relative cultural standards of the colonized were measured – and, in the process, it shaped their aspirations, dreams and desires. As can be seen in the discussion below, and again in Chapter 2, these hegemonic meanings impacted on the ways in which many colonized societies, historically, imagined themselves as a 'nation', and how they have redefined themselves as postcolonial nation-states. Language and discourse played a significant role in securing colonial hegemony; it represented a potent expression of colonial power. Exploring these issues further, the next section discusses some of the ways in which colonized peoples were constructed in social discourse, giving rise to the stereotypes that served as powerful rationale for domination and subjectification.

Colonial Discourse and the Shaping of Colonial Hegemony

Discourse is constituted in dual meanings. It 'not only facilitates our understanding of the world, it also limits our perception and understanding of the phenomena around us, including social processes, social institutions and cultural forms' (Kemshall, 2002: 13). It not only provides a particular way of looking at the world, but also frames, or influences, what can, and should be said as well as who is allowed to speak (Pecheux, 1982). Colonial discourse presented a particular view of 'reality' from the perspective of the colonizers. Colonial discourse operated at societal and global level articulated in key defining sites, and was mediated within and through cultural practices such as the mass media, education and other 'discursive processes'.[1] Thus colonial discourse represented a powerful means through which cultural and racial 'truths' about colonized peoples, their languages and cultures were legitimated. The interpretation, and representation of the cultural beliefs, values, experiences, expectations, aspirations, and mores of the colonized, within dominant theoretical frameworks, served to integrate the discursive lives of geographically dispersed peoples having different histories, and social experiences, into a unified and linear narrative centred predominantly on their cultural 'otherness' and racial 'inferiority'. Thus it constructed a homogenized and homogenizing 'truth' discourse (Foucault, 1980), universal in scope.

As can be seen below, this was certainly the case with Orientalist discourse, which constituted ' "the Orient" as a unified racial, geographical, political and cultural zone of the world' (Bhabha, 1994: 71). Similarly, the rich and diverse cultural tapestry throughout Africa, became reduced to homogenizing racially descriptive categories such as the 'natives', 'Negroes', 'Bantu', 'blacks'; the derogatory 'Kaffirs' and 'hotnots', 'boesmans', 'non-Europeans' and 'non-whites' in South Africa.

Colonial discourse also provided the means by which 'truths' about the inherent cultural, social and military supremacy of the 'mother country', were systematically constructed, regulated, and circulated within, and through, sociocultural practices and processes (Foucault, 1980). In French, and British, colonial discourse this was epitomized in jingoistic notions of '*la grandeur de la France*' and 'the glory of the British Empire'. For the British, 'the right to rule' was embodied in Rhodes' belief that 'we happen to be the best people in the world, with the highest ideals of decency and justice and liberty and peace, and the more of the world we inhabit, the better it is for humanity' (cited in Morris, 1968: 124). For the French, a self-defined superior 'race', the colonial project represented a *mission civilisatrice*. Prime Minister Jules Ferry expressed it in this way:

> Gentlemen, we must speak more loudly and more honestly! We must say openly that indeed the higher races have a right over the lower races . . . I repeat, that the superior races have a right because they have a duty. They have the duty to civilize the inferior races . . . (Jules Ferry, 1884: 199; cited in the *Internet Modern History Sourcebook*, http://www.fordham.edu/halsall/mod/1884ferry.html)

Grounded in power institutions, articulated from particular ideological positions, and obtaining legitimacy from the social position occupied by the definer, colonial discourse represented a configuration of 'power/knowledge' (Foucault, 1980) *par excellence*. It constructed a narrative of 'truths' grounded in self-evident, recognizable cultural and 'racial' stereotypes in everyday discourse, producing 'the colonized as a social reality which is at once an "other" and yet entirely knowable and visible' (Bhabha, 1994: 70–71). The power of the stereotype lies in this ambivalence; it describes what is already known and understood and, at the same time, it has to be constantly restated, repeated and renewed. Thus 'Orientals' became 'an object of study, stamped with an (essentialist and exotic) otherness' (Chaterjee, 1986: 36) (information in brackets added). Orientalist scholarship provided the cultural stereotype around which 'scientific truths' about the languages, religions, and cultural ways of life, values and beliefs of the colonized peoples of the East were constructed in social discourse. This was also the case with 'Africanist' scholarship during the 19th century.

Classical racism[2] pervasive during this period, formed an unquestioned, taken-for-granted part of scholarly discourse centred on the intrinsic superiority of the Europeans throughout history (Blaut, 1993). Accordingly, within the knowledge frameworks of 19th century scholarship, the 'miracle' of European development grounded in colonial empire was ascribed to the 'innate' racial and, therefore, cultural and linguistic superiority of the European 'race'. It is no surprise therefore that 'the vocabulary of classic nineteenth-century imperial culture is replete with such words as "inferior" or "subject races", "subordinate peoples", "dependency", "expansion", and "authority" ' (Said, 1993: 8). Certainly, the image of uncivilized, lazy, and ignorant indigenous peoples within the colonies was a potent one. In his book *The History of British India*, James Mill (1820), repudiating stories telling of the existence of ancient Indian and Chinese civilizations, expressed the view that:

> Both nations are to nearly an equal degree tainted with the vices of insincerity; dissembling, treacherous, mendacious, to an excess which surpasses even the usual measure of uncultivated society. Both are disposed to excessive exaggeration with regard to everything relating to themselves. Both are cowardly and unfeeling. Both are in the highest degree conceited of themselves, and full of affected contempt for others. Both are, in the physical sense, disgustingly unclean in their persons and houses. (James Mill, 1820; cited in Larrain, 1989: 25)

The pivotal position that the stereotype occupied in colonial discourse, ultimately, provided legitimacy to 'the discursive and political practices of racial and cultural hierachization' (Bhabha, 1994: 67). The views of liberal intellectuals, represented here by Mill, served to legitimate not only discourse meanings but, ultimately, also colonial processes and practices of domination and subordination. At the heart of colonial discourse was the need to construct the 'subject-nation', 'to construe the colonized as a population of degenerate types on the basis of racial origin, in order to justify conquest and to establish systems of administration and instruction' (Bhabha, 1994: 70). Driven as it was by a predatory colonial state, the good that came from colonialism can only be seen as having taken place 'by default, by the iron law of unintended consequences' (Mazrui, 1980: 41). Colonialism was not neutral, either as an ideology, or as a political or economic project, nor was it altruistic in its governance of the colonies.

Discourse also does not operate in a linear way; rather, it represents a multidimensional and dynamic social practice having discursive effects. For example, since these beliefs of cultural and 'racial' superiority pervaded societal hegemonic cultural consciousness throughout Western Europe, they were evident also in the thinking of major intellectuals such as Karl Marx who referred to the 'hereditary stupidity of the Chinese', and Engels who supported the US invasion of Mexico, and 'the snatching of California from the lazy Mexicans, who did not know what to do with it' (cited in Larrain, 1989: 57). Hegel argued that:

> It is characteristic of the blacks that their consciousness has not yet arrived at the intuition of any objectivity, as for example, of God or the law, in which humanity relates to the world and intuits its essence ... He (the black person) is a human being in the rough. (Hegel, 1975: 138)

Similarly, Weber referred to the 'hereditary hysteria of the Indian' and the genetic incapability of Africans to do factory work, as against the rational thinking and decision-making capability of the European (cited in Blaut, 1993).

At the same time, it is important to recognize that discourse is also constituted in discontinuities, inconsistencies, contradictions, ambiguities and ambivalences. Bhabha provides an example of the ambiguity in the representation of black people in colonial discourse:

> ... the black is both savage (cannibal) and yet the most obedient and dignified of servants (the bearer of food); he (*sic*) is the embodiment of rampant sexuality and yet innocent as a child; he is mystical, primitive, simple-minded and yet the most worldly and accomplished liar, and manipulator of social forces. (Bhabha, 1994: 82)

These ambiguities presented no problem within the grand narrative constructed around the colonized, the main purpose was the social construction of racial 'otherness', of inferiority, and therefore deserving of either being 'saved' or 'colonized/subjugated'. In this discourse the colonized is objectified.

Discourse meanings are also not static or uncontested; they exist in tension. Anglicists and Orientalists, policy makers in India, and Africanist scholars as well as missionaries in Africa during the 19th century, for example, argued from competing positions regarding the relative value of local cultures and languages. Despite these differences, they did have a shared understanding of, and belief in, the intrinsic superiority of British culture, and the importance of English language and literature to the civilizing mission of the colonial government.

In order to examine some of these issues further, the rest of the chapter focuses on Macaulay's Education Minute (1835), and the 'Scramble for

Africa' consolidated at the Congress of Berlin (1884–1885), as two distinct historical moments in which the self-concept of colonized nations was formed, and some of the complex issues that surround language relations in many postcolonial countries, have their origins. The next section examines the political project of British colonialism in India, the dynamics that it generated within Indian society, and the policy strategies adopted with regard to language in education during different periods of colonial rule.

Language-in-Education Policy Discourse in British Colonial India

Faced with a well-established aristocratic elite British colonialism in 17th-century India concentrated, largely, on establishing its own domain of power. This was achieved, on the one hand, by exerting coercive modes of control. On the other hand, the colonial government sought to win over the local elites and to incorporate them into the colonial project. To this end, Orientalism embodied in the study, learning, and teaching of Indian vernacular languages, religions and culture, was actively pursued by the British India Company as a political strategy, to engender hegemonic support for the burgeoning British Raj. Orientalism emphasized respect and admiration for indigenous languages and culture and, therefore, was seen as representing attempts at reinvigorating, rather than replacing Indian civilization (Evans, 2002). During this period, the Calcutta Madrassa and the Sanskrit College at Benares were established under the tutelage of Governor-General Warren Hastings (1773–1785). The political approach of accommodation and conciliation pursued by Governor-General Hastings, aimed as it was at winning consent amongst the Indian intellectual elite, had potent hegemonic value. In a letter to the chairman of the Court of Directors, Governor-General Hastings wrote:

> Every accumulation of knowledge, especially such as obtained by social communication with people over whom we exercise dominion founded on the right of conquest, is useful to the state. (Cited in Roy, 1994: 86)

This approach, therefore, also served the pragmatic purpose of gaining local knowledge important to the establishment of a governing bureaucracy, which required insight into intricate property laws and 'quasi-feudal rights and obligations that were determined by local traditions' (Roy, 1994: 86). This was reinforced by an active policy of incorporation amongst the local aspiring middle classes, with the intention of creating a new Anglicized landed gentry, who had a vested interest in the colonial project, and could act as a buffer class between the rulers and the aristocratic elite. It was, for example, amongst the upwardly mobile *dadani* merchants as well as other British East India Company workers, whose job prospects within the bureaucracy would be enhanced (Roy, 1994), that the clamour for English had started during the 17th and 18th centuries. For this group of people, English language fluency facilitated trade, and also represented significant cultural capital to be exchanged within the labour market. Roy argues that:

> It was also this class of Indians who had established (the) Hindu (later Presidency) College in 1817 in Calcutta, and (the) English School in Benares in 1818, and the Elphinstone Institution in Bombay a decade later to educate the sons of upper-caste Hindus in English. (Roy, 1994: 96)

During this period, there was a gradual shift in policy, away from support for indigenous languages and culture in education, to 'a belief that Indians should become acquainted with Western knowledge, and the English language, in order to assimilate themselves to their rulers' (Evans, 2002: 263). Writing his treatise *Observations on the State of Society among the Asiatic Subjects of Great Britain* in 1792, Charles Grant, of the British India Company, argued that:

> The true cure of darkness is the introduction of light. The Hindoos err, because they are ignorant; and their errors have never fairly been laid before them. The communication of our light and knowledge to them would prove to be the best remedy for their disorders. (Cited in Zastoupil & Moir, 1999: 83)

Grant advocated the establishment of free schools, providing English language instruction, and the introduction of English as the language of government (Evans, 2002).

Twenty-five years later, John Mill writing his *History of British India* (1817), in addition to English language, also supported the teaching of utilitarian European knowledge through texts translated from English into Indian vernacular languages. By 1833, Charles Trevelyan, upon his appointment to the General Committee of Public Instruction (GCPI), started his campaign in support of the Anglicist cause in the press, publicizing his 'controversial scheme to romanise the Indian vernaculars, and in private correspondence with Bentinck (...) he advocated the establishment of "our language, our learning, and ultimately our religion in India" ' (Evans, 2002: 267). By that time, the situation in England had changed considerably, with Haileybury College producing young men wishing to pursue a career in the British Administration in India. As a result, resources previously provided for the printing of indigenous language texts, were significantly reduced as 'there seemed little reason to promote Oriental learning' (Roy, 1994: 88). Seemingly then, advocacy of English at the time was grounded in a variety of discourses revolving around issues of governance, productivity, and the transmission of European cultural values and beliefs.

As stated earlier, the pursuit of English, as language medium for teaching and learning, was already prevalent amongst the Indian populace, especially those who would benefit within the labour market. Moreover, the Permanent Settlement Act of 1793 had 'created a new rentier class, divorced from the productive forces, which settled in Calcutta and formed alliances with British capitalists' (Arnove & Arnove, 1997: 92). Amongst this group 'the effect of anglicization took firm hold, socially and culturally' (Roy, 1994: 96). Arnove & Arnove (1997: 92) argue further that '(i)n addition to this rentier class of absentee landlords and money lenders, there emerged an English speaking class of professional and tertiary workers such as lawyers, teachers, doctors, administrators, and clerks who were indispensable auxiliaries of the empire'. By the 19th century, the Indian entrepreneur/social advocate Raja Ram Mohan Roy, having benefited from an English education, campaigned for the teaching of European knowledge grounded in the principles of the Enlightenment as opposed to the learning of Sanskrit and Arabic, which he regarded as retrogressive. Pursuing such a policy, he argued, would facilitate modernization in India. On 11 December 1823, Mohan Roy wrote to the British Indian Government, decrying the employment of Hindu pundits to teach in the Sanskrit School of Calcutta, rather than:

> European Gentlemen of talents and education to instruct the natives of India in mathematics, Natural Philosophy, Chemistry, Anatomy and other useful Sciences, which the Nations of Europe have carried to a degree of perfection that has raised them above the inhabitants of other parts of the world. (Cited in Thirumalai, 2003: 3)

This gives an indication of the extent to which the colonized in India were incorporated into the dominant cultural paradigm.

These developments support the argument that Macaulay's Education Minute of 2 February 1835, did not arise within an ideological vacuum; it consolidated already existing discourse meanings and practices (Roy, 1994). Macaulay's Minute, nevertheless, had potent hegemonic value. It decried the inherent cultural and linguistic inferiority of India, advocated English as the medium for teaching and learning, and called for the abolishment of the Sanskrit and Madrassa colleges. Macaulay argued for an English education aimed at creating 'a class of persons, Indian in blood and colour, but English in taste, in opinion, in morals and in intellect' (cited in Anderson, 1991: 91). Formalizing the Minute in the Education Act (March, 1835), Governor-General Bentinck wrote that '... the great object of the British Government ought to be the promotion of European literature and science among the natives of India; and that all the funds appropriated for the purpose of education would be best employed on English education alone' (cited in Thirumalai, 2003: 2). This was a strategic policy initiative. Previously, Governor Bentinck had inserted a clause into the 1833 Charter Act 'opening up all government posts to qualified persons 'irrespective of religion, birth, descent or colour' (cited in Evans, 2002: 267). Evans argues further that:

> Bentinck's scheme to make greater use of Indians in the public sector was inextricably linked to his policy to adopt English as the official language in place of Persian. The gradual introduction of English in government during the 1830s, and (particularly) the company's announcement in 1844 that English-educated Indians would receive preferential treatment in public-sector appointments, fuelled the already existing demand for English in the centres of British administration in India. (Evans, 2002: 268)

Thus, in addition to its instrumentalist labour market orientation, Bentinck's strategy also had potent hegemonic value. Instituting English as the official medium of teaching and learning in government-funded schools, effectively, legitimized the Western knowledge paradigm aimed at instilling secular European values and beliefs as the basis for modernization. In the process it would, potentially, engender a common worldview including shared aspirations of economic gain and upward social mobility which, in turn, would facilitate both economic development, and colonial governance. Subliminally, the incorporation of English, and the European knowledge model, into colonial educational policy in India, also served to legitimate meanings of cultural and linguistic difference and inferiority in relation to indigenous Indian cultures.

The adoption of English in education was reinforced by subsequent social policies. In 1837 English replaced Persian as the official language of the law courts (Phillipson, 1992). By 1844, 'it was decreed that when Indians were recruited to posts under the government, preference would be given to those who had received an English education' (Phillipson, 1992: 110–11). The adoption of English as the language of preference in all formal domains meant that it, *de facto*, became the lingua franca throughout the Indian sub-continent (Phillipson, 1992; Roy, 1994) and, therefore, it became the language of power.

Yet there were ambiguities since this did not necessarily mean that teaching did not also take place through local languages. By the 1840s teaching and learning took place through 'the medium of English books' as well as 'good and careful translations from English into the vernacular dialects' (Bureau of Education, 1922: 105, cited in Pennycook, 1998: 73). The key issue here though, is that since government educational funding was channelled primarily to the teaching of English, this mixed language economy did not prevail at all levels of education. In practice, education through the medium of vernacular languages was largely a piecemeal, disparate and peripheral phenomenon restricted mainly to elementary education. The Charter Act of 1813 had made it:

> 'obligatory but not lawful' for the (British East India) Company to set aside funds for the 'revival and improvement of literature and the encouragement of the learned natives of India . . . and for the promotion of a knowledge of the sciences among the inhabitants of the British territories in India' . . . to promote interests and happiness of the Indian people and that educational measures ought to be adopted 'as may tend to the introduction among them of useful knowledge, and of religious and moral improvements'. (Roy, 1994: 87, information in brackets added)

To this end, the Charter Act of 1813, specifically set out a *lac (Lakh)* (100,000) of rupees to be spent on education, but only 'out of any surplus which may remain of the rents, revenues, and profits . . . after defraying the expenses of the military, civil, and commercial establishment, and paying the rest of the debt' (Roy, 1994: 87). This resulted in a chronically under-funded state education system in British colonial India. Although the Charter Act of 1813 made provision for the education of the Indian population, the issue of language in education was not resolved officially until 1835. And, as can be seen below, even then it was subject to further changes.

For example, Sir Charles Wood's Educational Despatch of 1854 introduced a modernizing education system centred on the diffusion of arts, science, philosophy and literature through the medium of English at secondary and tertiary levels, and vernacular languages at elementary level. In the rural areas, however, vernacular languages received less government attention and funding, and education, *per se*, also less support from the rural Indian populace (Whitehead, 1992; Evans, 2002). Furthermore, in a general sense, the emphasis on an academic curriculum based on schools in England was inappropriate, linguistically, and culturally as well as in relation to meeting the career needs of the students effectively. Lack of adequate provision for language teaching and learning was to have deleterious effects on the development of fluency in English, creating what was referred to as the 'Babu' class of English speaking Indian.

Although the influential Report of the Indian Commission of 1882 supported English language as the medium of instruction during the later years, preceded by the vernacular in the early years, it stated its purpose as follows:

> ... primary education (is to) be regarded as the instruction of the masses through the vernacular in such subjects as will best fit them for their position in life. (Report of the Indian Education Commission of 1882, quoted in Pennycook, 1998: 71, information in brackets added)

Vernacular languages, limited thus to primary school education, were motivated not by altruistic pedagogical principles, but colonial expediency. This transitional model of bilingual education, therefore, can be seen as having served as a means of curtailing opportunities of the colonized within society as well as in the labour market. As can be seen later, this remained a potent ideological motif in policy discourse within different colonial and neo-colonial situations across time and space.

Lord Curzon's subsequent review of education resulted in the formulation of a government resolution in 1904, which highlighted some of the problems encountered in education, and stated that:

> As a general rule a child should not be allowed to learn English as a language until he (sic) has made some progress in the primary stages of instruction and has received a thorough grounding in his mother-tongue .... Much of the practice, too prevalent in Indian schools, of committing to memory ill-understood phrases and extracts from text-books or notes, may be traced to the scholars' having received instruction through the medium of English before their knowledge of the language was sufficient to enable them to understand what they were taught. (Cited in Evans, 2002: 278)

This is a significant point. Some of these residual teaching approaches also derived from existing cultural mores centred on rote learning of religious texts, in the Madrassas and Sanskrit schools.

Policy effects

Language-in-education policy in British Colonial India had concrete and long-lasting effects on the country's population. First, it engendered socio-economic differences between the various population groups. Although English was associated with power, status, privilege and the means to upward mobility amongst all sections of Indian society, in practice, 'only the upper castes and subcastes who, traditionally, were the educated class' (Roy, 1994: 90), benefited from a full English education. They were incorporated into the labour market as clerks, interpreters, secretaries/scribes, debt collectors, those who could negotiate with Mughal courtiers, and managers of households (Roy, 1994). Since most of these people lived in the major cities, the language-in-education policy largely supported human resource development in favour of the urban labour supply, leaving rural areas, largely, outside formal education. Thus it created a skills and knowledge divide closely linked with access to English. In other words, those who had access to English would have favourable employment possibilities within the labour market. Those, who were limited to vernacular languages, would have fewer employment possibilities within the formal labour market. English, therefore, obtained powerful exchange value within the colonial labour market.

Second, unequal access to English also created a linguistic, social and power divide between the elites, and non-elite groups, and 'education for the masses remained a fantasy' (Roy, 1994: 101). The urban intelligentsia were detached from the masses educationally, linguistically, and culturally. The British, from the 1850s onwards, pursued a differential education policy:

> While the highest ranks of the colonial civil service were to be filled by Indians schooled in English in government schools, the remainder serving the colonial enterprise (still a small minority of the population) were to be provided a core vocational education. This stratified education system was to intensify existing caste, religious and social class divisions in the society as it was usually the Brahmins who received the most prestigious education in English or classical languages, while some of the lower castes were educated in the missionary schools in the vernacular. A wedge was also driven between Hindus and Muslims, for the latter were more resistant to British education and were increasingly displaced by Hindus in the British courts and colonial administration. (Arnove & Arnove, 1997: 91)

Universities based on the London examining model established in Calcutta, Bombay and Madras, provided access to the whole Indian population irrespective of caste, class and religion. In order to facilitate access, third level entry standards were lowered. Although this strategy increased numbers, it also resulted in Indian university education being viewed as inferior against the high status of an England-based education. These factors, subliminally, helped to shape the self-concept of Indian society in relation to the relative value of their education system – always gazing towards European universities, which they regarded as embodying superior knowledge models, and ways of knowing.

Summary

Although Macaulay's Minute had less concrete impact on educational practice than is generally asserted in some polemical arguments, the view that the significance of the Minute is often over-stated since a more relativistic language economy prevailed (Pennycook, 1998), nevertheless, is problematic. In practice, vernacular languages in education remained under-funded, despite the rhetoric regarding their intrinsic value. Moreover, having obtained exchange value in the labour market, English remained the language of choice amongst the Indian population throughout the colonial period. In this sense, the valorization of English, secured in the 'glorification' of colonial culture and, *de facto*, the 'stigmatization' of local cultures as inferior and, subsequently, the rationalization of English in education (Skutnabb-Kangas, 2000: 196) played a significant role in shaping colonial cultural hegemony.

The main significance of the Minute lies in the fact that it lent legitimacy to the racially inscribed concept of the 'subject-nation'. In order to justify the subjugation of a people, it is necessary first to construct them as different and inferior, by ordering and classifying them, and thus to stigmatise them as 'other'. In this regard, the Minute had potent symbolic power. Roy highlights the organic relationship between language and power in British Colonial India:

> The desire to absorb India more thoroughly and effectively in(to) the nexus of trade and exploitation expressed itself directly in educational policies. More than anything, the administration of the Company's territories in India required uniformity and centralization, and these were achieved, in part, through the introduction of English as the common currency of commercial, administrative, legal, and intellectual intercourse. (Roy, 1994: 89)

Ultimately, the significance of the emphasis on the maintenance of vernacular languages, and their acquisition amongst officers of the British Raj based in different regions of the country, lay in their central role in facilitating governance. In this regard, the proceedings of the

Government in the Home Department (Punjab), No 134, under date Fort William, the 15 January 1873 passed the resolution that 'the great importance to the administration of a knowledge on the part of Public officers of the languages by the people with whom they have to deal has lately been prominent brought to the notice of the Government of India.' It explained that:

> there is reason to fear that, especially in the wilder districts peopled by aboriginal tribes, sufficient attention has not been paid to the subject, although it is admitted that constant and easy intercourse between Government officials and the people is essentially necessary to the good government of half-civilized races. (Cited in Rangila *et al.*, 2001)

Language-in-education policy in India subsequently influenced policy developments in British colonies elsewhere. Having learned the lessons of India, a pro-vernacular policy endorsed by the Imperial Education Conference, was formally agreed in the Advisory Committee's Report, *The Place of the Vernacular in Native Education*, in 1927 (Whitehead, 1991). Examining this policy in education in colonial Africa, the next section discusses the 'Scramble for Africa' in relation to cultural and linguistic shifts generated by the partitioning of Africa in 1885.

The Scramble for Africa

The 'Scramble for Africa' provided the catalyst to global expansion of colonial territory during the late 19th century, pre-empting the New Imperialism that evolved during this period. The New Imperialism represents a social, economic and cultural dynamic; arising out of capitalist expansion it refers to 'the emergence of monopoly capitalism at the national level, the dominance of finance capital, the export of capital and capitalist relations of production, and the division of the world between a small group of metropolitan powers' (Dixon & Heffernan, 1991: 2). During this period, Britain conquered Burma, France consolidated its Indo-Chinese empire including Vietnam and Laos, and Queen Victoria became Empress of India.

Colonial expansion: Economic imperatives

What has become known as the 'Scramble for Africa' represents the cumulative outcome of a discursive range of socio-political, economic and cultural factors that prevailed in Europe during the late 19th century, culminating in the redrawing of the map of Africa at the Berlin Conference 1884–1885. As is stated above, during the 19th century, new capital accumulation regimes evolved in consequence to conditions prevailing in Europe at the time, for example:

(1) The Long Depression, which lasted from 1873 to 1896, had created the need for a restructured economic base that was less reliant on industrial capital.
(2) New technologies such as the steamship had facilitated international travel, with major implications for trade.
(3) The discovery of gold and diamonds in different regions of the world, increased competition amongst European nations including France, Germany, Italy and Belgium.
(4) In response to the annexation of the Congo Free State by King Leopold II of Belgium (see below), the rest of the colonial powers in Europe sought to expand their colonial base in order to secure their 'spheres of influence'.
(5) In Britain, during this period, economic policy emphasis shifted away from industrial capital towards finance capital, government protection of overseas investments, and the development of the services sector.

Factors that accelerated the pace of the Scramble include:

- French colonial expansionism including its treaty with Britain for dual control over Egypt in 1879;
- the ratification of the treaties made by Count de Brazza in the Congo;
- the revival of the French colonial enterprise in Tunisia and Madagascar;
- Germany's annexation of South West Africa, Togoland, the Cameroons and German East Africa (Uzoigwe, 1985).

These political factors, and King Leopold II of Belgium's annexation of the Congo Basin rich in ivory, copper, oil, uranium and diamonds underscored the drive amongst various colonial powers to consolidate their claim to 'free trade' within the region. Although what has become known as the 'Scramble for Africa', in practice, took place over a number of years, the Berlin Conference (1884–1885) provided the arena within which the division of land was formalized, and the principles of competition were ratified. The Conference served to regulate the competition for colonies amongst European nations by consolidating their 'spheres of influence' acquired 'through settlement, exploration, establishment of commercial posts, missionary settlements and occupation of strategic areas, and by making treaties with African rulers'

(Adu Boahen, 1985a: 31), and setting new rules for trade and exploitation. The Treaty of Berlin (1885), therefore, is generally viewed as having inaugurated the New Imperialism grounded, largely, in the commercial exploitation and appropriation of the new colonies.

Fierce competition amongst the colonial occupiers resulted in the establishment of chartered companies such as the German and British East African Companies, the South Africa Chartered Company set up by Cecil John Rhodes to develop the Zambesi Valley (1888), the Italian Benadir Company to develop Somaliland (1892), and the Royal Niger Company (1896) (Berlin Conference Background: http://library.thinkquest.org). Each colonial power annexed regions, established new states and protectorates, and exploited their raw materials for the benefit of the 'mother country'. In order to grasp the impact of the Scramble, and the subsequent partitioning and occupation of the whole continent of Africa, on the socio-cultural, political and economic base of African societies caught up in this upheaval, it is useful to look at the ideology that underpinned colonialism during the late 19th century, and the discourse in which this phase of partitioning was rationalized. In parallel, it is equally useful to gain some insight into the conditions that prevailed generally in Africa, during the period that preceded the Conference of Berlin. The next section discusses the meanings attached to the concept of *terra nullius* in relation to colonial occupation.

'No Man's Land': The Discourse of Occupation

Historically, the notion of *terra nullius* has provided justification for the appropriation of land by colonial states across space and time; it constituted a defining factor in the mass annexation and division of African land at the Berlin Conference. The legal concept of *terra nullius* has its origins in Roman property law referring to territories lying outside Rome, as automatically being subject to Roman law, and thus Roman occupation. Literally, it refers to land that is not inhabited; a territory on which no state exercises sovereignty, and which can therefore be occupied by any state. In other words, it is therefore deemed to lie outside the jurisdiction of international law. Different political interpretations of this notion, historically, have provided the rationale for colonization. During the 16th century, for example, the Conquistadors had rationalized Spanish colonialism in South America, using the argument that the Inca territory, although it had a superior civilization, represented *terra nullius* because it was not inhabited by *Christians* (Beyene, 1998). In general, to the European colonizers of the 19th century, Africa represented an undifferentiated mass of savage life in need of civilization. Thus by the time of the Berlin Conference in 1884–1885, the concept had altered to define land that was not inhabited by *civilized peoples*. Politically then, the concept of *terra nullius* referred to a territory that did not possess a territorial organization based on the European model of governance.

The Social Darwinist idea of black barbarism with Africans existing at the bottom of the evolutionary ladder, and who, therefore, had to be rescued and civilized, formed part of the hegemonic consciousness of European society. That is to say, it represented a common worldview at the time, including also, amongst German socialists belonging to the Labour Movement during this period. Reporting from the Commission on Colonial Policy at the Stuttgart International Congress in 1905, the prominent socialist reformist, and social democrat, Eduard Bernstein expressed the view that:

> ... the colonies are here to stay: we have to come to terms with that. Civilised peoples have to exercise a certain guardianship over uncivilised peoples – even socialists have to recognise this ... much of our economic life rests upon products from the colonies which the natives were not able to utilise. On all these grounds we must accept the resolution of the majority. (Bernstein, cited in Kautsky, 1907: 5)

The view amongst German socialists, at that time, was that if the colonial powers were to relinquish their colonies, the colonized would fall back into barbarism (Kautsky, 1907).

Pre-Colonial Socio-Political Structures and Processes

In actual fact, the African continent constituted a complex cultural, linguistic, economic and political tapestry incorporating different levels of socio-political organization. The notion of an entirely illiterate, and 'savage' African continent, is contested by the fact that there were:

> ... some areas of Africa where written languages had histories predating the arrival of missionaries. In the Horn of Africa, particularly in Ethiopia, Geez and its allied forms and also Amharic far predate the impact of western missionaries. Indeed, Christianity here predates much of the Western European experience. In West Africa, amongst the Vai, and a few ethnicities all the way down to Cameroon, symbolic expressions, ideographics and some concepts were developed long before the arrival of missionaries. In the Sahel, various types of *Ajami*, that is African languages written in Arabic script, were developed

> centuries before missionaries came into the picture. In all these forms religious literature was the most predominant product of literary endeavours. (Prah, 2002b: http://www.casas.co.za)

According to Mazrui and Mazrui (1998: 74), '(t)here are records of Amharic written verse in honour of Ethiopian kings that can be traced back as far as the fourteenth century'. Moreover, by the 14th century, Kiswahili was used not only as a language for trade and commerce, but also in poetry, written in orthography based on Arabic amongst groups such as the Waswahili and Mijikenda (Mazrui and Mazrui, 1998). Momolu Duwalu Bukele invented the Vai script in 1830 transforming 'a preexisting system of ideograms or pictograms into a syllabic system' (Mazrui and Mazrui, 1998: 72).

Different levels of political organization also prevailed. According to Gann and Guignan (1977: 11):

> African polities included all kinds – from stateless societies held together by age-set or neighbourhood arrangements to city-states and extensive kingdoms, the latter including both limited and absolute monarchies. (Gann & Guignan, 1977: 11)

Language played an important role in the self-identification of ethnic groups and the formation of political entities; 'each language, in effect, constituted a binding force that linked families (nuclear and extended), lineages, clans, and the entire ethnic group together' (Obeng & Adegbija, 1999: 354). Islamic political systems, in existence by the 15th century, included cosmopolitan Swahili city-states such as Mogadishu, Barawa, Mombassa, Gedi, Pate, Malindi and Zanzibar. Although these were finally undermined by Portuguese colonialism during the 16th century, by the 19th century, the continent still comprised a mature, pluralist set of social, economic and political institutions. Political trends, at the time, included increased centralization in, for example, the Sokoto caliphate as well as the Massina, al-Hadjdj and Samori Ture empires, and the evolution of the Nguni states in Southern Africa following the Mfecane (Ade Ajayi, 2003). Economic trends during this period revolved around the abolition of the slave trade and the shift to agricultural exports. It is suggested that this form of economic progress was limited:

> . . . because the change to agriculture was not accompanied by a technological change in the means of production, nor in the industrial processing of the products before exportation, Africa remained a feeder to the capitalist and industrialized economy of Europe. (Adu Boahen, 2003: 25)

Nevertheless, commercial trade did result in the development of economic links throughout the continent. This includes trade routes linking:

> East, Central and North Africa together through the instrumentality of Arab, Swahili, Yao, Kamba, and Nyamwezi traders in East Africa; Tio, Ovimbundu, and Chokwe traders in Central Africa; Arab traders in Egypt, and Arab and Sudanese traders across the Sahara. (Adu Boahen, 2003: 25)

The establishment of these routes boosted trade, and facilitated the commercial unification of Africa whilst, at the same time, opening up the interior to European and Swahili influence (Adu Boahen, 2003). Previously unknown African scripts were discovered, and many African languages began to be written in European scripts. Moreover, 'some Europeans and their African agents took an interest in the historical traditions of various communities and began recording them' (Ade Ajayi, 2003: 1). Contact with the Europeans also brought societal modernization, in the form of railways, telegraphs, the printing press (in Egypt in 1822, and Portuguese Luanda in 1841), technical education and finance capital. In practice though, much of this social infrastructure was developed to benefit colonial trade, not to improve the lives of the colonized *per se*.

In pre-Scramble Africa, in some regions, there were also moves towards political modernization. The influence of the burgeoning Westernized African elite who had benefited from a missionary education (see below), and the influence of the Muslim Ulamaa in some areas, resulted in pressures for changes in the constitutional field (Adu Boahen, 2003). In West Africa:

> ... especially the West Coast, the demand for power by the new elite was pursued by constitutional procedures. An example was the constitution of the Fante Confederacy of the Gold Coast in 1874. The spirit of the Fante Constitution was to promote cooperation among the several Fante groups that made up the Confederacy. (Adu Boahen, 2003: 24)

In practice then, Africa did not constitute *terra nullius* politically, socio-culturally, or economically. The developments discussed here, challenge common arguments providing a rationale for colonization at the time, namely that, 'there was no real history among African peoples, only a generalized ethnographic past of customs and settlement patterns' (Parsons, 1999). Within the political discourse frameworks of the 19th century, the concept of *terra nullius* therefore represented a powerful hegemonic construct; it provided the *raison de'être* for the partitioning of

Africa. In other words, since Africa existed outside the framework of European, and therefore, international law, it could be occupied by the colonial nation-states. Adu Boahen argues that it is important to note that whilst in Africa:

> ... Europeans dealt with individual African rulers and states, and concluded several treaties with them. In Europe they decided to exclude African states from recognition in international law. Thus, they took steps to partition Africa, without the participation of African rulers, and as if Africa was no-man's land. (Adu Boahen, 2003: 322)

The carving up of the African continent, by European colonial powers, was further enabled by the series of internal wars such as the Mfecane[3] as well as the Yoruba and Maasai wars during the early 19th century. Although these conflicts had strengthened political institutions, and state power, through the rise of centralized kingdoms 'served by new bureaucracies and military organizations' (Ngcongco, 1989: 91), they also eroded traditional solidarities amongst ethnic groups. Combined with the social and economic effects of the slave trade during the preceding half-century, these conflicts created a general state of instability within the Central and Southern Africa regions, weakening existing polities, and thus making them more vulnerable to external manipulation. The Mfecane, in particular, contributed significantly to the depopulation of a large part of the Southern Africa region, enabling the Boers to settle in what they called 'no man's land', that is, *terra nullius*. Describing the extent of the conflict situation in Africa at the time, Uzoigwe argues that:

> Africa was marked by inter-state and intra-state conflict and rivalry – the Mandingo against the Tukolor, the Asante against the Fante, the Baganda against the Banyoro, The Batoro against the Banyoro, the Mashona against the Ndebele, etc. (Uzoigwe, 1985: 39)

The lack of unity amongst African states was evident in the extent of the support and co-operation that some of them gave to the invading Europeans and which, ironically, allowed them to become incorporated into the colonial project.

Fractured identities and political fragmentation

Existing political and cultural boundaries were fractured in the carving up of Africa at the Berlin Conference, and replaced by colonial divisions grounded in economic expediency. Britain emerged with the greatest gains, taking nearly 30% of Africa's population under its control.

During the period 1885–1914 'Nigeria alone contributed 15 million subjects, more than in the whole of French West Africa or the entire German colonial empire', 15% went to France, 9% to Germany, 7% to Belgium and 1% to Italy (http://en.wikipedia.org/w/wiki/Scramble for Africa.html).

Maps drawn, often following river basins such as the Nile, and Congo, resulted in the evolution of a number of land-locked countries throughout sub-Saharan Africa. Examples of land-locked countries include Mali, Upper Volta, Botswana, Burkino Faso, Niger, Uganda, Chad, Lesotho, Malawi, Swaziland, Zambia and Zimbabwe. This, obviously, impacted on trade possibilities as well as political relations amongst neighbouring countries, and has had a long-term impact.

The partitioning of Africa achieved at the Berlin Conference was consolidated by military conquest, annexing land, breaking up existing African empires, and establishing new geopolitical entities, at least until the beginning of the First World War in 1914:

> The Sokoto caliphate and the Borno Empire lost large tracts of territory by the time the boundaries of the Colony and Protectorate of Nigeria emerged. In the case of the 'peripatetic empires' of Samori Turé and Rabi ibn Fadlallah, these were simply parcelled out between adjoining colonies. The secondary empires of Msiri and Tippu Tib in Central Africa were similarly shared out among the Belgians, the Portuguese and the British. (Caldwell, 1985: 493)

The partitioning of Africa into colonized 'nation-states' having arbitrary national borders, displaced millions of people, and created minority ethnic enclaves within border regions in some parts of sub-Saharan Africa. A situation previously defined by shifting and imprecise frontiers, was now transformed into a few colonies with fixed and marked boundaries (Caldwell, 1985).

> Attempts were made in international boundary conventions and treaties to take into account the pre-existing political and economic zones. However, such other considerations as the claims of rival powers, the lure of natural frontiers (hills, rivers etc.) and of lines of longitude and latitude tended to carry more weight than African claims. As a result, closely related and sometimes previously politically united peoples at times found themselves on opposite sides of agreed boundary lines. (Caldwell, 1985: 493)

The European colonial divide of Africa put the same ethnic groups on two, or more, sides of national boundaries, thus undermining ethnic group unity and the necessary sense of national belonging (Kromah, 2002). Ethnic clusters around border regions, in many instances, also reflected a shared linguistic heritage. For example, ethnic groups such as the Hausa and Fulani were fragmented and displaced, partitioned as they were among the colonies of Nigeria, the Cameroons, the Gambia, Niger and Chad. The Mandara people were split between northern Nigeria and the Cameroons. The Mandingo people were dispersed in the colonies of Senegal, Guinea, Mali, Ivory Coast, Gambia and Sierra Leone, whilst the Mende were divided amongst Liberia and Sierra Leone (Adib Rashad: http://www.afrikanz.com).

Commenting on the spurious unity, and ethnolinguistic homogeneity, of the nation-states created during the 19th century, Prah argues that:

> Masai in Kenya and Tanzania share culturally greater commonality than they do with a great number of the other ethnicities in the two countries. Borana in Kenya have culturally much more in common with Oromo in Ethiopia than with Kalengin or Kikuyu in Kenya. Ewes in Ghana have more in common culturally with Ewes in Togo and other Gbe language speakers like the Fon in Benin, Mina in Benin, Gun in Benin, or Mina in Togo, than they have with the Ashanti or Gur speakers in Northern Ghana. The Yoruba in Nigeria cannot culturally be separated from the Yoruba in Benin. (Prah, 2002a)

In many of these cases, ethnolinguistic groups, dispersed amongst different colonial nation states, were now also subject to different colonial administration systems. The Bakongo, for example, were divided by 'the boundaries of Angola, Belgian Congo, French Congo and Gabon', the Somali were dispersed amongst Ethiopia, Kenya, Somalia and Djibouti; the Senufo were divided by the boundaries of Mali, Ivory Coast and Upper Volta (Adu Boahen, 1985b: 786). Similarly, political allegiances also became divided amongst the different new 'states'. For example, the Ewe in Ghana 'were torn between allegiance to Ghana and to Ewes in the neighbouring state of Togo. So also the Nzema and the Brong (Akan groups) in Ghana were torn between Ghana and other Nzema and Brong (Abron) in Cote d'Ivoire' (Obeng & Adegbija, 1999: 356). These artificial divisions created political problems that have remained unresolved across the centuries.

Political effects

The partitioning that took place at the Berlin Conference, and subsequent colonial policy, also had broader political and sociocultural consequences. The imposition of the bureaucratic colonial state on

African societies undermined previously existing, diverse indigenous forms of government. African peoples were conceived of in terms of neatly bounded homogeneous 'tribes' and 'nations' as opposed to the more fluid, and flexible socio-political entities centred on kinship groups, or multilingual and multicultural communities integrated into larger states that existed before the partition (Berman, 1998). Already during the 15th century, a complex state formation was in process and what is now Angola:

> ... was not one homogenous state but a large number of distinct ethno-linguistic groups varying in size, level of economic development, and degree of political organisation. Some were 'tribes', others constituted larger nations. The kingdom of Kongo, for example, dominated the political landscape in the region. Ruled by a monarch, the kingdom was divided into six provinces, five of which had their own subordinate rulers ... The 'scramble for Africa' split this kingdom into three modern-day African states: the Republic of Congo (Brazzaville), the Democratic Republic of Congo (DRCongo), and Angola. (Malaquias, 2000: 100)

The key issue here is that despite its diverse ethno-linguistic composition, the pre-Scramble region constituted relatively cohesive political entities, progressing towards state building. As is evident in the examples discussed above, the partitioning of Africa at the Berlin Conference interrupted this process and forced 'different ethno-linguistic groups with different histories and political aspirations' into the reconstituted colonized 'state' (Malaquias, 2000: 102). Moreover,

> ... by forcibly binding different ethnic groups into one centrally administered territory, colonial rule inevitably led to the politicisation of ethnicity as different ethnic groups retreated into primordial constructs for cultural, if not political, self-preservation. (Malaquias, 2000: 95)

Colonial rulers exploited ethnic differences within many regions throughout Africa, allocating power, resources and access to education differentially. In the case of Rwanda/Burundi, despite the fact that they shared the same cultural heritage, including language, the Tutsis were regarded as 'ethnically' superior, and were educated and incorporated into the colonial administration. The Hutus and Twas were excluded. In Uganda also, ethnic divisions were created. The people of the South who, as was the case with the Tutsis in Rwanda/Burundi, were educated and subsequently incorporated into the administration where they became instrumental in the system of indirect rule[4] instituted by the

British. The people from the North, on the other hand, were regarded as having great physical strength, and were recruited into the military and Police Force, and also supplied labour and services to the South. Under indirect rule, each administrative area, comprised a homogeneous linguistic and cultural 'tribe' 'in which people continued to live within the indigenous institutions and were subject to 'tribal discipline through local structures of authority' (Berman, 1998: 315). Bakwesegha argues that:

> Some ethnic groups were seen as more intelligent and more civilized than the others; and the development process followed ethnic considerations in general throughout the country with various ethnic groups being governed by different colonial policies. This, in turn, resulted in destructive regional disparities and in ethnic divisions and hate. (Bakwesegha, 2000: 10)

Thus ethnic elites were created. The long-term impact of these divide-and-rule colonial policies is evident in the ethnic conflicts that abound in contemporary Africa. The boundary changes effected, during the period of the Scramble for Africa, also generated language inequalities that have had long-lasting effects on the sociocultural, economic and political base of different countries throughout sub-Saharan Africa. Some of these issues are discussed below, and again in Chapter 2.

Language as political strategy in colonial Africa

Social Darwinist theory played a significant role in constructing a correlation between language, and racial 'otherness' during this period. Writing in 1884 Comte de Gobineau argued that 'the hierarchy of language corresponds rigorously to the hierarchy of races' (cited in Curtin, 1965: 395). In this discourse, the evolution of language followed the same course as cultural evolution; African languages, therefore, were positioned at the lower end of the evolutionary scale. Against this, colonial languages were seen as representing important cultural resources through which primitive African peoples could be 'civilized' into cultured people (Bebel, cited in Kautsky, 1907). However, the language issue existed in tension. As can be seen below, in practice, knowledge of African languages and culture assumed a position of major importance to missionaries, and later to some colonial administrations.

The missionaries

The impetus for missionaries to learn African languages lay in the need for them to establish trust and goodwill and, moreover, to understand and communicate with potential converts. The missionaries emphasized a catechism-based curriculum. The need for converts to be able to read the Bible focused attention on literacy. The Church Missionary Society in 1816, highlighted 'the advantage, and indeed the necessity of teaching the children to read their own language in order to their being useful to their parents and other countrymen, by reading the Scriptures and religious Tracts' (cited in Spencer, 1974: 163). This underpinned the drive to develop books in African languages as well as the development of dictionaries, and teaching materials, in local vernaculars. The importance to the missionary project, of the ability to communicate in African languages, is highlighted in the fact that, 'from 1909 the policy of the ABM (American Board Mission), for all its missions worldwide, was that every new missionary, "wives included" should not be allowed voting rights in the decisions of their mission until they had passed a detailed examination in the local vernacular' (Jeater, 2001: 455, information in brackets added). When it expanded its work in Portuguese East Africa in 1913, the ABM advocated that:

> For at least one year the attention of the missionaries in Beira should be devoted to the acquisition of the Portuguese and native languages and no evangelistic, school or other work should be undertaken which would interfere with the mastery of these languages. (Cited in Jeater, 2001: 455)

Increased reliance on translation and interpreting in the law courts, underscored the significance of studying local languages as well as the compilation of grammars. Translation provided further opportunity for gaining insight into ways in which indigenous ideas might be mapped onto Christian theology. In 1893, Reverend A.M. Hartmann argued that:

> . . . the more we can enter into the habit of thought of natives, the more perfectly we shall speak their language . . . The more exactly, then, we can represent to ourselves the ideas of the natives, the greater will be the precision with which we shall express our thoughts in their language. (Cited in Jeater, 2001: 456)

Thus they were engaged not only in:

> . . . recreating the languages in textual form, making decisions about phonetics, orthography and word-division based on the European language traditions. They were also bending the vernaculars to their will and making them do new things; through their language project they were able to appropriate African languages, and to reinvent them within the Christian tradition. (Jeater, 2001: 456)

In addition, the quest for translations of the Bible, led to the use of different orthographies and spellings, depending on the translator. Missionaries, Prah (2002a: 31) suggests, translated languages idiosyncratically '... as they found them in the areas in which they found themselves without due cognisance of the phonological, phonetic, syntactic and grammatical continuities of the speech forms on the ground'. This, he argues, contributed to the evolution of different spelling systems for 'languages that are, practically, in terms of their mutual intelligibility, more or less the same' (Prah, 2002a: 2). As a result, there now exist rival forms of, for example, Sesotho, Nguni, Akan, Bambara, Pulaar, Yoruba and many other languages (Prah, 2002a). Missionaries also tended to compile 'grammars and dictionaries from one among a diversity of local dialects, usually spoken around the mission station', which they then transformed 'into the authoritative version of the language of a whole "tribe" and propagated it through their schools' (Berman, 1998: 322). In this way, new 'languages' were created, giving rise to contemporary arguments that Africa constitutes a veritable 'tower of Babel with small groups of people speaking obscure and unrelated languages' (Prah, 2000: 8). In actual fact:

> over 75% of Africans speak no more than twelve core languages these being Nguni, Sotho-Tswana, Swahili, Amharic, Fulfil, Bambara, Igbo, Hausa, Luo, Eastern Inter-lacustrine and Western Inter-lacustrine (Kitara). Other core languages include the Oromo/Somali/Rendille/Borana cluster, the Akan cluster and the Gur group. (Prah, 2002b: 2)

The standardization and classification of African languages, created 'approved' versions of the vernaculars. These were legitimized in dictionaries and grammars. The significance of this, lies in the fact that that words and phrases crystalized in dictionary definitions, circumscribe the range of possible meanings, and thus the possibilities for literally, and symbolically, naming the world (Skutnabb-Kangas, 2000). Missionary and colonial linguistics, therefore, can be seen as representing power/knowledge discourses (Foucault, 1980). That is to say, the study of African languages at the time, and the academic discourse in which it was embedded, played an instrumental role in constructing selective versions of African cultural life, including the invention of languages, as universal 'truths'. Since these activities took place within missionary and colonial institutions, Africans were excluded from having a formal input into the shaping of their languages, and the recording of their cultures.

As was the case with Orientalism, African languages and cultures also had their European defenders who were engaged in recording the history, and documenting African ways of life. Like their Indian counterparts, Africans also were constituted as objects of study, and their languages and cultural experiences, became reified in the arbitrary classificatory knowledge frameworks of 19th century missionary scholarship. Fostering literacy in vernacular languages, facilitated the missionaries' religious and moral quest to win souls and, in the process, to civilize the 'barbarian' populations of Africa. In practice, the induction of these populations into colonial mores, and expectations, also facilitated their integration into the labour market. They were workers, not citizens. Using vernacular languages as primary mediums of communication, therefore, served in the interest of both a moral and political economy. The ways in which the colonized resisted, and challenged dominant discourses and practices, are discussed later.

In some areas, missionaries also made use of languages of wider communication such as Swahili. In order to help integrate different 'tribal' groups into a common Christian community, missionaries throughout Central Africa adopted Swahili as the language of the Church. By the 1890s, the use of Swahili extended to the publication of religious books and newspapers as well as a Swahili-English dictionary (Abdulaziz, 1971). The use of Swahili, throughout the region, also facilitated 'the transfer of teachers and missionaries to different mother-tongue areas' as well as reducing 'the heavy load and the cost of translating the Bible into all the vernacular languages' (Abdulaziz, 1971: 164). As such, investing in Swahili as lingua franca was cost-effective.

The school became an important institution in the evangelist endeavour of the missionaries. Afigbo (1985: 491) argues that 'education and evangelization were so closely linked that for many parts of Africa the pitching of the missionary tent was synonymous with the establishment of a school. Among the Nguni the opening of a school is said to have preceded the opening of a church at all times'. Whilst in some regions, such as, East and Central Africa, the missionaries met with little interest amongst the local people for their schools:

> In some cases, for instance in Bechuanaland, the missionaries were actually invited to establish schools by the native rulers. But this had little to do with an interest in Christianity. Rather the missionaries were known to procure and repair guns, weapons which had assumed an important role in hunting and warfare. (Ball, 1984: 119)

The approach to language-in-education policy also differed amongst the missionaries. In the French colonies, teaching and learning took place in French only. Whereas the British had a mixed language economy, teaching in both African languages and in English, the Germans and Belgians generally used only African languages in education, and vehemently opposed the teaching of colonial languages. As can be seen below, colonial education built on the foundations and model put in place by the missionaries.

Colonial Language-in-Education Policy in Africa

The 'language question' presented a two-edged sword to the colonial powers. On the one hand, as was the case in India, there was a need for an elite group educated to a level where they would be useful as intermediaries/functionaries within the colonial administration. Colonial administrations in Africa, similarly, hoped that education would yield the 'low-grade personnel they needed for staffing the bottom echelons, social and moral – as would enable Europe to exploit as fully as possible what were regarded as the hitherto untapped resources of Africa' (Caldwell, 1985: 491). On the other hand, there was general concern, mainly amongst the Germans, that educating the natives in European languages also had the potential for the emergence of an 'educated proletariat ... which is presumptuous and also easily rebellious' (Council of German Protestant Missionary Societies, 1897, cited in Kwah, 2000: 30). In 1904 the Council argued that education of the native populations through the medium of German could:

> ... become a threat to the colony ... as in this manner one rears a conceited, presumptuous and easily dissatisfied breed; for the natives learn from the Europeans much that is damaging and are tempted, when they speak the language of the Europeans, to place themselves on an equal footing. (Cited in Prah, 2000: 30)

Given the unsettled political situation in Europe at the time, the views expressed here by the German missionaries, to all intents and purposes, echoed those held generally, and highlight the tension that traversed the colonial education policy terrain. Whilst education was seen, on the one hand, as representing an evil bearing 'the danger of creating an awareness of exploitation and oppression, at the same time the colonial system could not operate without a tutored cadre of locals' (Prah, 2002a: 31). There are also other ambiguities. For example, Africans were sometimes also used as interpreters in the law courts, whilst others became evangelists and established their own churches – thus they were incorporated into the hegemonic project of colonialism. Yet, somewhat ironically, their ability to absorb and appropriate elements of European culture, including 'labour skills, Christianity and language – and using them in autonomous, unsanctioned ways' (Jeater, 2001: 468) challenged white domination of labour and production markets. In consequence, by the early 20th century 'native policy' changed towards governing them within 'existing institutions rather than attempting to move their social systems towards industrial proletarianization' (Jeater, 2001: 459).

As was the case amongst missionaries, language-in-education policies differed also amongst the colonial powers. Policy approaches were embedded in the ideology subscribed to by the colonizing powers. Colonial administrative policies were divided into two ideological camps, namely, the 'associationists' like the British 'who wished to preserve the connection between European and African societies, but without the culture of the one permeating the other' (Manning, 1988: 93). That is to say, they regarded African cultures as self-sustaining systems that should not be disrupted by European civilization. The indirect rule model of governance adopted by the British, promoting a limited form of indigenous relative autonomy required an educated local elite, who were fluent in English, and also had an understanding of British cultural practices (Prah, 2000). English thus became the language of choice in education in the later years, preceded by local vernaculars during the primary school phase. There were exceptions though in British West Africa, where selected African languages including Yoruba, Hausa, Igbo, Efik, Ga and Ewe were taught up to secondary level (Obanya, 1998). This was the case also in Kenya until the 1940s and 1950s, when the rise of the Land and Freedom Movement ('Mau Mau') posed a threat to British colonial hegemony. As a result, 'community-established "independent schools", were closed, teaching in the vernacular was eliminated, and English was mandated as the language of instruction' (Arnove & Arnove, 1997: 95).

Whilst the Belgians supported the teaching of African languages in primary schools, their overall education policy was oriented towards vocational training centred on, for example, producing carpenters, bricklayers and medical auxiliaries (Prah, 2000). Except for German South West Africa, which was a settler colony, the Germans supported the teaching of African languages, but not the colonial language. The official German view was that 'reading and writing is ... in the interests of his master ... not desired. This knowledge only nourishes the vanity of the coloured man and tempt him to abuse it' (cited in Prah, 2000: 30). These views replicated those expressed by the German missionaries discussed earlier. Throughout the period of German colonialism, African languages flourished, and resulted in the invention of a writing system for the Bamun language in 1896 by Sultan Njoya of Bamun. This language was subsequently adopted as language medium for teaching and learning in schools (Echu, 1999).

'Assimilationists', like the French, regarded African cultures as inherently inferior and, therefore, unsustainable; thus they sought to assimilate Africans into European culture. Underlying this was the belief that African elites would first adopt French language and European culture, and that Africans, generally, 'would more gradually learn to fit into French society' (Manning, 1988: 93). It was through education in the colonial language then, that the European (French) elite manufactured an African elite to do the bidding of the 'mother country', by incorporating them into the colonial culture (Sartre, 1977). Alongside these hegemonic strategies, the French system of 'direct rule' sought to bring the colonized under the control of the 'mother country' through coercion, and '(s)ubjugation by military force became an ironic but ever-present aspect of assimilation. The establishment of unified political dominion, rather than equality, was the key objective in the assimilationist view' (Manning, 1988: 61). French and Portuguese colonies fostered their own metropolitan languages throughout all phases in education.

Policy Effects

The cultural politics of French, and Portuguese, colonialism resulted in overt forms of linguistic and cultural imperialism. In other words, whilst validating their own languages and cultures, they silenced African languages, and subjugated indigenous cultures, supplanting them with European 'knowledges' and cultural ways of knowing, imbuing them thus with the colonial worldview. This policy approach insidiously eroded the indigenous cultural base, ultimately contributing to mental and cultural alienation amongst the colonized.

Although using the vernacular language as medium of teaching and learning made sound pedagogical sense, and, therefore, represented a positive unintended outcome of colonial education policy it, nevertheless, had minimal effect on the long-term cultural development of the majority of African pupils. By the time that they went to secondary school, pupils had to make the transition to English language. The colonial model of education did not tap into the indigenous cultural base of African society, especially existing literacy practices which formed part of the cultural heritage of many countries in Central Africa; thus leaving many indigenous languages under-developed. Furthermore, the percentage of children attending school and becoming literate remained small, many receiving less than four years of schooling (Phillipson, 1992).

There were also broader sociocultural effects:

(1) Since the use of African languages in education was limited largely to elementary education and they were not incorporated into social institutions, it did not provide opportunity for the development of these languages to incorporate social change, and in this way, allowing them to evolve into literary and subject languages functional to modernity.
(2) The mixed language economy adopted by the British, did not detract from the fact that indirect rule provided status to selected languages of indigenous elite groups, chosen to serve the political and economic interests of the colonial project in Africa. Through this, it created inequalities amongst different African languages and, *ipso facto*, peoples and their cultures. Despite policy shifts from English to the vernacular during different periods 'local languages were never accorded high status in any colonial society' (Phillipson, 1992: 112).
(3) Since English became a prerequisite within the labour market it, ultimately, became legitimized as the language of power.

Collectively, these factors underscore the argument made throughout this chapter, that development of the ethnolinguistic and cultural base of African society was not part of the colonial project. The latter, ultimately, had its basis in economic exploitation and political domination. By the end of the colonial period, Africa's peoples had experienced cultural change on a grand scale, including the status, and use, of their languages for economic, cultural, social and political purposes as well as their religions. The geopolitics of colonialism displaced peoples, languages and identities, and contributed to the erosion of cultural ways of life as well as the disintegration of historically derived cohesive socio-political entities. They had been 'civilized', 'pacified' (subjugated), became colonial 'subjects', and were turned into exotic objects of study, as a species apart. Most had suffered the removal of their collective and individual human rights, including maintenance of their linguistic, cultural and religious heritage. For the elites and aspirant/proto-elites, cultural self-abnegation had become a way of life; they colluded in the marginalization of their own peoples, languages and cultures. These different forms of 'symbolic violence' (Bourdieu, 1991) exercised on colonized peoples, represent a sharp contrast with dominant notions of the 'civilizing' project of colonialism, and, in the case of the French colonial state, the democratic principles of the modern liberal nation state enshrined in the third republic.

Conclusion

This chapter examined the political exigencies that underscored the expansion of the colonial project into new territories in Africa, and the Indian Sub-Continent, during the late 19th century, and the impact that this potentially had on shaping language relations within these contexts. It discussed the important role that language in education policies played in mediating colonial hegemony during the 19th century. Although there were clearly many differences between the colonialism of post-Scramble Africa, and India during the period of Macaulay's Education Minute, there were also commonalities in policy approaches and outcomes. Certainly, the lessons learned in India informed educational policy in British colonial Africa. A common thread is the important social engineering role that language and culture played in shaping the consciousness of colonized peoples. The missionary scholar J.N. Farquhar, summarizing the success of British colonial education policy in India, highlighted the significant role that English language and culture played in securing colonial hegemony in his argument that:

> The new educational policy of the Government created during these years the modern educated class of India. These are men who think and speak in English habitually, who are proud of their citizenship in the British Empire, who are devoted to English literature, and whose intellectual life has been almost entirely formed by the thought of the West, large numbers of them enter government services, while the rest practice law, medicine or teaching, or take to journalism or business. (J.N. Farquhar, cited in Colonial Rule in India – British education, racism, eurocentricism, indology: http://members.tripod.com/INDIA_Resource/britishedu.htm)

Language-in-education policies giving pre-eminence to colonial languages facilitated the transmission of Western knowledge, and ways of knowing to culturally 'inferior' societies. Colonial languages and literature were suffused with Euro-superiority, and Euro-centricism, and played a significant role in engendering Westernised 'natives'. This view is summarized thus by Ngũgĩ:

> In Kenya, English became more than a language: it was *the* language, and others had to bow before it in deference (...) language and

> literature were taking us further and further from ourselves to other selves, from our world to other worlds. (Ngũgĩ, 1993: 438–39)

Implicit in Ngũgĩ's argument is the view that the choice of language in which the education of the nation takes place is important in relation to its role in shaping people's awareness as citizens, and in maintaining national unity. Ngũgĩ's argument also suggests that the substitution of local knowledge, and cultural ways of knowing with the knowledge paradigms of European colonialism, to a significant extent, undermined local cultural heritages, contributing thus to the alienation of colonized peoples from their cultural base. Some of the ways in which this was achieved are reflected in Hall's argument that:

> The ways in which black people, black experiences were positioned and subjected in the dominant regimes of representation were the effects of a critical exercise of cultural power and normalisation. Not only, in Said's 'Orientalist' sense, were we constructed as different and other within the categories of knowledge of the West by those regimes. They had the power to make us see and experience *ourselves* as 'Other' (original emphasis). (Hall, 1993: 394)

In this regard, colonial language-in-education policy can be seen as representing a potent form of 'symbolic domination'; the maintenance of a system of power by means of the transmission of culture (Bourdieu, 1991). Thus it played an instrumental role in shaping colonial subjectivities. Similar motifs prevailed in the representation of the colonial state. Berman argues that:

> ... colonial states were obsessed with depicting themselves as omnipotent and omniscient – the constant British concern with maintaining their 'prestige' before their African subjects or the menacing Belgian metaphor of 'bula matari' (crusher of rocks) in the Congo – and projecting an image of unchallengeable power over a far more ambiguous and contested reality. (Berman, 1998: 314)

Other commonalities include the paternalism of the British colonial state in which indirect rule was seen as representing a form of trusteeship ultimately leading to self-governance. This is a paradox. In practice, all colonial administrations constituted bureaucratic despotisms. Although they may have evolved pragmatically within the processes and exigencies of everyday life, as is often claimed with regard to British colonialism, colonial administrations were not benign or altruistic; they were deeply imbued with the ideology of colonial occupation, principally serving the 'just' interests of the colonial 'mother country'.

Compared with almost 500 years in India, colonialism in post-Scramble Africa officially lasted only 50 years; yet it wreaked immeasurable destruction economically, socioculturally and politically. In particular, the under-education of colonized peoples, a curriculum based on the metropolitan elite education model, chronic under-funding of education, the educational divide between rural and urban education provision, the heritage of colonial languages in education, and the lack of educational infrastructure to sustain adequate levels of human resource development, generated long-term development problems in these societies. The status accorded historically to colonial 'mother tongues', has left an enduring dilemma with regard to language planning and language policy in developing countries. These issues will be discussed further in Chapter 2.

Notes

1. Discursive processes refer to 'institutional practices, ideological position, power relations and social position, which influence how words change their meanings within, and between, discourses' (Rassool, 1999: 101).
2. Classical racism refers to the belief that different human 'races' have different, biologically determined, endowments.
3. The *Mfecane* literally means 'crushing' or 'hammering' in Bantu languages. As a political phenomenon it refers to a series of wars conducted mainly by the Zulus under the leadership of Chaka, which attacked, overthrew and replaced old states and dynasties. This resulted in the destruction of established economies and large numbers of people being displaced or enslaved. 'The Mfecane led to the depopulation of a large portion of Southern Africa thus facilitating the taking over of African land by white migrant settler communities called Boers. These Boers did not only appropriate the best part of African land for themselves, they also enslaved Africans and plundered that remained of their lands (Ngcongo, 2003: 39).
4. 'Indirect rule' refers to colonial practice during the late 19th–early 20th century in which colonized 'Native chiefs' were given well-defined duties 'with the British Resident acting primarily in an advisory, not executive capacity, and with the African 'chief' continuing in a traditional role ... (they were left) with their old responsibilities, functions, perquisites of office so that they would continue to appear in the eyes of the local populations as the legitimate rulers' (Betts, 1985: 318).

Chapter 2

Postcolonial Development, Language and Nationhood

Chapter 1 gave an account of the colonial origins of many of the unresolved language problems that currently exist in developing countries. This chapter continues that 'past-present' dialogue. It focuses on the intertextual links between colonialism and national language policy choices in postcolonial states, and their collective impact on social and economic development. Given the historical context within which the idea, and ideal, of the modern liberal democratic 'nation' state evolved in Europe – and its relationship, in many instances, with colonialism – its influence on shaping the postcolonial national state is significant. In this chapter, therefore, issues surrounding language and development in postcolonial societies in Sub-Saharan Africa and South Asia are situated within the hegemonic, political, and economic projects of colonialism. This discussion focuses attention specifically on:

- the formal politics of state and nation, grounded in the ideological principles of universalism (as opposed to particularism), as this emerged in Western Europe at a specific historical moment in its development;
- colonial expansionism and the emergence of the colonial state;
- the social relations engendered by colonial rule; and
- the impact of these on the sociopolitical, cultural and economic base of postcolonial societies.

The emphasis throughout, is on the central role that language played in the colonial project, and its dialogical relationship with postcolonial realities. This includes a consideration of colonial state power and its influence on shaping language relations within colonized countries, the cultural, political and economic purposes thus served – and their collective impact on social, economic and political development possibilities within colonial – and, subsequently, postcolonial states. Some of the main political and cultural legacies of colonialism are summarized, and discussed further with regard to their relative impact on language, literacy and development in postcolonial states.

In order to clarify key issues and concepts in the chapter, the next section seeks to clarify the concept of the liberal democratic state in relation to the social construction of the 'nation', the ideology of 'nationalism' and definitions of the 'state'. It further examines the ways in which the liberal democratic 'nation' state, historically, articulates with the cultural, political and economic projects of colonialism.

The Liberal Democratic Nation-State, Language and Modernity

Historically, the emergence of the liberal democratic 'nation' state has been associated with the project of modernity in Western Europe, during the 19th century. The concept of modernity here refers to the universalist cultural ideals of the Enlightenment. This includes the development of modes of thought based on reason, the accumulation of scientific knowledge which signified a break with myth and tradition, and their collective contribution to the development of 'rational' forms of social organization, embodied in the emergence of a secular, sovereign, state and the development of civil society. Modernity also refers to the development of industrial capitalism and the fundamental economic, sociocultural and political changes that this generated throughout Western Europe. Thus modernity signifies the transition from the absolutist state, to the modern capitalist liberal democratic 'nation' state. However, it is important to recognize that the latter represents not only a form of governance embodied in systems, practices and processes, but also a powerful hegemonic construct. In order to further examine the principles that underpin the idea of the liberal democratic 'nation' state, the following sections engage with the concepts of 'state', 'nation' and 'nationalism' separately before proceeding to look at the construction of the modern (metropolitan) 'nation' state. This will be followed later by a critique of common usages of these terms as well as a critical analysis of the construction of postcolonial national states.

Matters of state

Although the modern liberal democratic state is a Western European concept, as a form of social and political organization, different forms of the state have existed, historically, in various polities. Generally, the idea of the state is seen as constituting a system of administration and governance of a sociocultural community, having a shared set of aims, beliefs, rules and values, existing within common boundaries. Thus it is regarded as having political sovereignty within a defined territory. The state derives its legitimacy from a set of regulatory rules embodied in the law, and through this, plays a central role in maintaining order in the way that society lives and works. The modern state, embedded as it is, in a complex bureaucracy, represents the institutionalization of political, cultural and economic power. Coercive power implicit in its apparatuses, such as, the military and police force, is intrinsic to the way in which the state operates, *per se*. The liberal democratic state, however, depends also on more consensual forms of power, centred on the cooperation of its citizenry, to realize its political aims on an everyday basis. Together, these meanings are reflected in Gramsci's (1971: 408) broad definition of the state as constituting 'the entire complex of practical and theoretical activities with which the ruling class not only justifies and maintains its dominance, but manages to win the active consent of those over whom it rules'. The process of winning consent takes place through subtle forms of hegemonic control within, and through, educational institutions, the mass media, courts, and the Church, 'where the intellectuals of the state are active in promoting certain views of the world and certain ideologies through which civil society is organized and brought into conformity with aspirations of the dominant class' (Green, 1990: 93). State power penetrates civil society through these, more subtle, processes of control.

Central to the liberal democratic state, is the idea of ruling by consent rooted in a universal system of representation through which the 'sovereign will of the people' is given expression in the principle of 'one-person-one vote'. Together these practices are embodied in civil society, and citizenship centred on collective and individual rights and responsibilities to the state, and of the accountability of the state to its citizenry. The idea of civil society refers to the social, public domain constituted by private individuals (Seligman, 1995; see below for further discussion). Historically, this derives from the fact that 'as states came to depend on their citizens for support and resources, their structures and policies became subject (...) to political negotiation and compromise' (Held, 1992: 116). In this regard, the democratic will of the people, represents an important organizing principle of the modern state. As is suggested earlier, the democratic will of the people, at least theoretically, represents a means of securing the accountability of political power, to the public interest. Politically, civil society represents an arena within which people can 'exercise pressure and restraint on the state and thereby strengthen the assumptions and practices of democratic self-government' (Leftwich, 1995: 435).

Whilst the state arises from society and is 'powerfully shaped and constrained by the social relations which surround it' (Hall, 1990: 22), it is not '*wholly* determined in form and function by society'; ultimately, the state is invested with the power and authority to govern society (Hall, 1990: 23). And, in this sense, it can be seen as managing, monitoring and controlling society – in other words, to keep order. For example, although the state is always in the process of balancing the needs and wants of society, it also frequently overrides the will of the people, acting instead in its own interest, for example, to maintain power and legitimacy in the face of external or internal threats such as powerful interest groups within the state or in society – and as can be seen in Chapter 3, increasingly also within the global terrain. The emergence of the modern state, during the 19th century, focuses attention also on the ideology of nationalism and the social construction of 'nation'.

Conceptualizing the 'nation'

There are various, and often competing definitions of what constitutes the nation. Arguing within a *sociopolitical* perspective Gellner (1988) maintains that the nation can be defined only in relation to the age of nationalism in Europe, grounded in the universalizing principles of the Enlightenment, during the 19th century. The nation comes into being:

> ... when general social conditions make for standardized, homogeneous, centrally sustained high cultures, pervading entire populations and not just elite minorities, a situation arises in which well-defined educationally sanctioned and unified cultures constitute very nearly the only kind of unit with which men (*sic*) willingly and often ardently identify. (Gellner, 1988: 55)

In other words, specific sociocultural conditions, and historical forces within Europe during the 19th century, notably, the ascendancy of industrial capitalism, gave rise to a particular form of socio-political identification within which the nation represented:

> (t)he establishment of an anonymous, impersonal society, with mutually substitutable atomized individuals, held together above all by a shared culture of this kind, in place of a previous complex structure of local groups, sustained by folk cultures reproduced locally and idiosyncratically by the micro-groups themselves. (Gellner, 1988: 57)

This sociocultural transformation, translated kinship into a universal *political* identity lived through individual citizenship, given coherence by a mass sociocultural identity. In this sense, the nation is seen as forming an intrinsic element in the societal modernization process.

A *sociocultural* perspective grounded in the notion of a homogenized nation rich in symbolism, centres on the idea of an intrinsically cohesive nationhood grounded in a common history, language, and religion as well as a set of common values and beliefs (Kellas, 1991). Such a view of the nation has potent hegemonic power and, historically, has provided the cultural motifs around which nationalist discourse has been constructed. In practice though, Kellas' view of a culturally homogeneous and inherently stable 'nation' is, of course, highly problematic. Different nations *can* exist within a singular state as is the case, for example, with diasporic Jewish communities historically, who, although ethnically, socially and linguistically diverse, nevertheless, are integrated as a cohesive religious-cultural and politically self-defined 'people'; or what is referred to as 'sub-state' nations, such as the 'Quebecois, and Cree in Canada, the Tamils in Sri Lanka, Basques and Catalans in Spain as well as the Irish, Scottish and Welsh in Great Britain' (James, 1996: 15). Various 'sub-state' nationalisms (Guibernau, 2000) then, exist within the confines of sovereign nation states having a cultural/linguistic pluralist base. In addition, many nation states in Europe represent a coalescence of diverse local or regional polities, often comprising distinctive population groups speaking various languages, and often also having different cultural traditions. Tilly (1990: 2) refers to these societies as 'national' states, which he describes as 'states governing multiple contiguous regions and their cities by means of centralized, differentiated, and autonomous structures', rather than as culturally homogeneous and autonomous 'nation' states. Politically, there is some merit in this perspective and I return to it again later.

Mass transmigration and the idea of 'nation'

The *political* concept of 'nation' also includes the diversity, and fluidity engendered by mass transmigration embodied in the rich tapestries of cultures, languages, and discursive socio-political experiences that define the lives of many peoples in the world. It also includes consideration of the discontinuity in popular histories that have shaped ethnically complex, multilingual and culturally plural nation states such as the US, Canada, Chile, Argentina, South Africa and Australia having their origins in an earlier phase of colonial expansion. Comprised of various layers of transmigratory groups these countries are defined, to a significant extent, by diasporic group identities that have evolved discursively across time, space and place. These transmigratory groups, historically, have engaged in a process of reflexive self-definition involving a degree of social integration or assimilation whilst, at the same time, also contesting the boundaries of the nation state by infusing society with a plurality of voices and languages. That is to say, although they may have adopted a new national identity, many of these groups have, for several generations, continued to exist as cohesive ethnic/religious enclaves within the broader context of the adopted country. In the US 'hyphenated identities' such as Italian-Americans, African-American, and many other combinations of hybridized cultural identities, are commonplace self-identifications. These 'New World' nation states are complex both culturally, and politically. They exist in conflict and tension in the day-to-day negotiations taking place amongst various religious and ethno-linguistic fractions living within their national boundaries. National language policy and the educational process, play a major role in integrating these disparate fractions into the aims, expectations, aspirations, dreams, desires, values and belief system – the ideology – of the (in effect, multi-national) homogenized nation state.

However, if we take account of their evolution within the context of the colonial, and neo-colonial, projects of the late 19th century, the concept of the 'nation' within these societies becomes more problematic. These nation states of the 'New World' have a deeper, less democratic history. During the colonial period, each of these culturally plural 'nation' states of the 'New World' represented white dominions providing 'outlets for emigration, (...), securing strategic routes and outposts like the Cape of Good Hope, attaining or maintaining status and power equivalence in the European inter-state system' (Smith, 1983: 23). These colonial, and later, neo-colonial, *settler* states had their origins in the genocide and mass displacement of indigenous peoples – and as a result, the erosion of previously cohesive kinship groups, inherited sociopolitical and cultural landscapes, including their languages, ways of knowing, and ways of seeing the world. These 'New World' nations, therefore, can be seen as ideological constructs fundamentally constituted in historical discontinuities. Moreover, they exist on the basis of exclusions and the denial of the cultural, linguistic and socio-political rights of indigenous peoples. Their narratives generally are marked by gaps and silences on indigenous kinship or clan myths, symbols, totems, traditions and shared cultural memories. Their socially constructed national identity therefore is grounded in a renarrativization or, rather, the invention and reproduction, of a fictitious past.

The *political* construction of a homogeneous national identity, historically, has placed the dominant ethnic group at the centre of the nation, in effect, positioning minority and subordinated ethnic and other social groups, their cultures and histories, at the periphery. In this regard, the hierarchy of languages within many nation states reflect economic, cultural, and political hierarchies within society (see Case Studies in Chapters 5, 6 and 7). Historically, nationalist discourse has provided the meta-narrative, in which many of these inequalities have been rationalized, and reworked into alternative themes, constructing a unique and distinctive nationhood into which previously displaced ethnolinguistic groups, or dispersed cultural nations, ironically, have to be re-integrated.

Political perspectives: Nation and nationalism

Nationalism symbolizes the universalist ideology that underpins the taken-for-granted, social construct of the 'nation'. In this regard, 'one-nation' nationalism represents a meta-narrative that builds, selectively, on the existing cultural base of given societies, often transforming them radically by reviving dead languages, reinventing traditions, restoring, as could be seen above, 'quite fictitious pristine purities' and 'the cultures it claims to defend and revive are often its own inventions, or are modified out of all recognition' (Gellner, 1988: 56). Implicit in this narrative framework is the legitimation of selective forms of cultural identification. This means that the construction of national identity then, is predicated on a collective forgetfulness 'that is to say, what is selected to be remembered is partially determined by what is chosen to be forgotten, that which is to be dismissed as being "inappropriate" ' (Allan & Thompson, 1999: 42). In this construction, the idea of 'nation' is given coherence by a narrative often reinventing the past, to lend legitimacy to preferred constructions of national identity; as such, it is an 'imagined political community' (Anderson, 1991). Nationalism therefore plays a major role in securing the political legitimacy of the politically defined nation state. This, of course, represents a macro-socio perspective of nation.

Ultimately, the political concept of 'the nation' derives its meaning, largely, from the specific political and hegemonic projects pursued by the state. This includes building a cohesive nation grounded in a 'shared national' culture that transcends cohesive minority group cultures or 'sub-state' nations existing within the boundaries of the state. As could be seen above in relation to, *inter alia*, the Quebecois in Canada, the Catalans in Spain as well as the Welsh, Scots, Cornish and Irish, these 'sub-state' nations represent inner tensions within the dominant version of the politically created 'nation-state'. The point to be made then is that the hegemonic construction of the political concept of nation, despite its emphasis on unity and cohesion is, in practice, fundamentally constituted in difference. It is suffused not only by different cultures, tongues, and histories, but also disparate group aspirations, expectations, beliefs, values, voices, dreams and desires, some of which might conflict with those of the politically unified nation-state. This particular narrative of nationalism is grounded in the hegemony of otherness; it excludes those who cannot be integrated into the nation. In other words, '"us" (those who belong to the nation as a community) is defined in relation to a (hierarchical) projection of "otherness", that is, those who do not "belong", who are "outside of our history"' (Allan & Thompson, 1999: 41). There are extreme forms, historically, of this projection of national identity. For example, grounded in a discourse of racial superiority, nationalism in Italy and Germany during the 20th century, gave rise to the ideologies and practices of Fascism and Nazism respectively. Similarly, the collective nationalist dream of the – essentially hybridized – settler group, the Afrikaner 'Volk' in South Africa expressed in the notion of 'white supremacy', ultimately, became a key organizing principle of the politically defined Apartheid 'nation state'.

In practice, the Afrikaner 'nation' comprised a hybridized community incorporating all the other ethnic, religious, linguistic and social class fractions amongst the diverse white population groups in society (see Chapters 6 and 8). Significantly, it excluded the majority black population group – itself marked by ethnic, linguistic, and social group differences. National identity, referring to the dominant Afrikaner 'nation', represented a cultural system in which language (Afrikaans) was regarded 'as central to the essence or character (Volksgeist) of the nation; language (Afrikaans) became the *most* important distinguishing characteristic of (Afrikaner/'Boere') nationhood – indeed, its very soul' (May, 2001: 57, information in brackets added). Afrikaner nationalism was articulated around the slogan of 'Een Vlag, Een Taal, Een Volk' (One Flag, One Language, One People); the Afrikaner 'Volk'. In practice, it comprised an amalgam of Dutch, German and French Huguenot immigrant groups. Afrikaans essentially constitutes a Creole, or hybridized language, incorporating not only European but also African, Khoisan and Malay linguistic influences. It is, therefore, rather ironic that Afrikaans represented a central principle of the 'eiesoortigheid' (racial purity) ideology that underscored the Apartheid doctrine. As such, it became a potent symbol of white domination. 'Non-white' peoples were excluded from this construction of nationhood. The Apartheid state protected the interests of the universalized, political construct of the 'white' nation. Cultural groups who had inter-married across the cultural divides, were classified pejoratively as 'coloureds'; the other 'ethnic nations' included the 'blacks'/Africans, and the 'Indians'. Initially, these groups were integrated under the category of 'non-Europeans'; following independence (from colonial Britain) in 1960 they were reclassified as 'non-whites'. These politically constructed sub-state cultural 'nations' were hierarchically organized in society, and subjected to a differential distribution of power, land, wealth, rights, jobs, housing and other social goods. Each of these 'ethnic' sub-state nations, therefore, were fractured internally along a vertical axis of 'racial (and class) differences', and a horizontal axis of religious/ethno-cultural and linguistic differences. Ultimately then, the preservation of Afrikanerdom was predicated on the maintenance of the 'Boere nasie' (Boer-nation) through the policy of cultural/'racial' separateness (Apartheid) insulating different ethnic groups within their own communities geographically, politically and culturally.

Apartheid South Africa highlights the contradictions and dangers that inhere in a strategically constructed ethno-cultural 'nationhood'. In this instance, the idea of nation represents a means by which a selective, economically and politically powerful, group of people could identify themselves as a culturally cohesive political community. And, in doing so, it consciously disidentified with the rest of the population who, in turn, were constructed as *untermenschen;* 'pariah' peoples. As such, the idea of a cohesive Afrikaner nationhood represented an invention *par excellence*; a powerful hegemonic construct sustained by its ideology of *exclusion*.

Summary

Seemingly then, *cultural 'nations'* or 'ethnies' representing cohesive, historically derived communities, defining themselves in relation to a common set of beliefs, language and customs (as is the case, for example, with the Catalans in Spain and the Cree in Canada) have cultural validity. In the modern world, they often exist as sub-state nations within the framework of the politically constructed 'nation-state'.

In contrast, the 19th century *political* construction of the nation as an integrated, trans-cultural homogenized population and, significantly, its colonial derivatives, in practice, represents a powerful hegemonic construct. As such it represents:

> a fictional unity (...) because the 'us' on the inside is itself always differentiated (...) what is produced is not an identity or a single consciousness – nor necessarily a representation at all – but hierarchically organized values, dispositions, and differences. (Donald, 1993: 167)

Since they comprise different sociocultural, and politically unequal, fractions nation-states are highly differentiated. Moreover, as could be seen in the discussion above, they are constituted not only in difference, but also in unequal power relations; thus they exist in tension. The socio-historical specificity of the politically constructed concept of the modern 'nation-state' is addressed in the next section.

What then, is the modern nation-state?

As stated earlier, by the 19th century, in Western Europe the democratic rights of the people had replaced the divine right of the monarchy, and the nation integrated into the state formed a new political community. The modern nation state evolved within the context of territorial wars in Europe, and the Industrial Revolution. As such, it represents an historical construct grounded in the ideological principles of the Enlightenment, and the economic, cultural and political projects of the evolving industrial capitalist state. In other words, it was integral to the political, cultural and economic modernization of Western European societies. This period marks the growth of the political infrastructure, the locus of the power of the state within a sovereign geographical context, putting into place systemic mechanisms, technologies and techniques to facilitate governmentality – and through this – to enable state power to be exercised within all aspects of social life, to maintain stability to support economic growth, and to protect it from external military threats. In this regard, 'the nation state came to prevail because it proved most successful in meeting the economic and military demands of a changing world economy and international order' (Beetham, 1990: 210), dominated by Western European power interests grounded, to a significant extent, in colonialist expansion.

Theorizing the nation state

From a sociological perspective, the nation state exists only in relation to an assemblage of other nation states; it represents 'a set of institutional forms of government maintaining an administrative monopoly over a territory with demarcated boundaries (borders), its rule being sanctioned by law and direct control of the means of internal and external violence' (Giddens, 2002: 121). However, Giddens' emphasis on structural aspects, the institutional apparatuses of the nation-state, does not clarify the concept of the nation in relation to the state. It lacks consideration of the people-nation, and their dialogical relationship with culture, economy and society. Guibernau integrates structural meanings with the cultural aspects of developing a national identity. The nation state thus has the capacity to exercise:

> legitimate use of force within a demarcated territory and seeks to unite the people subjected to its rule by means of homogenisation, creating a common culture, symbols, values, reviving traditions and myths of origin, and sometimes inventing them. (Guibernau, 1996: 47)

In this view, nation and state coincide. In other words, the nation state is seen as representing a form of political organization incorporating the administrative and coercive power of the state. This, in turn, articulates with the sociocultural, economic and political goals, aspirations, needs and desires of the peoples living within its boundaries. Thus it consolidates a national identity, the idea of a nation working towards common national goals. Comprising, in practice, a hierarchy of structured differences placing the dominant ethnic group at the top, the state pursues political projects centred variously on integration, segregation, exclusion, assimilation and/or incorporation to secure control over its citizenry. In the process, it often engenders struggles for self-determination, or competition for control over power and resources amongst different ethnolinguistic, religious and other cultural fractions and power interests within the nation. Together these factors fracture the theory of the 'nation' state built on the idea of cultural exclusivity/homogeneity. Constituted in unequal social relations, asymmetries of power and resource distribution, the political construction of the nation state, fundamentally, exists in tension and contradictions.

Other issues internal to the nation state revolve around citizenship and democratic rights, national self-determination and political legitimacy, the need to maintain social cohesion as well as creating optimum conditions for sustained economic development. Nation states therefore are political, economic and cultural power configurations *par excellence*.

Summary

To conclude this discussion, it could be argued that although each nation state that evolved within Western Europe had their own development trajectory, they were all historical products arising out of the struggles of nationalist movements of the nineteenth century. Ultimately, they formed part of the process of social, economic and political modernization. That is to say, they evolved within the context of the changing social relations induced by technological development and industrial capitalism, creating new policy imperatives regarding the protection of national boundaries, cross-border economic exchanges. It also included socio-political changes revolving around different ways of organizing social life as a result of urbanization, the redefinition of work, and the emergence of new, organized, labour relations. These developments also engendered sociocultural changes, notably, the normalization of everyday life according to national standards, the sanctioning of official languages by the nation state, state sponsored literacy (in standardized languages) and mass schooling, the introduction of the popular vote and, *ipso facto*, the development of civil society. The notion of civil society, in a general sense, here refers to the community of citizens that forms the basis of the democratic nation state, and their involvement in institutions such as the church, education, cultural organizations, trade unions, social movements and political parties. In this regard, the knowledge, skills and interactive social and political networks embedded in civil society, constitute a major part of a nation's cultural and social capital.

In an overall sense, these social transformations generated more centralized forms of administrative and coercive state control to regulate different areas of everyday life. This historical shift from an absolutist state to the nation state formed part of a fundamental social, economic, political and cultural transition from the traditional society to modernity. The Western European nation state therefore can be seen as having evolved out of a particular cultural system at a specific historical juncture, driven by a burgeoning industrial capitalist economy, and underpinned ideologically by the universalist principles of the Enlightenment.

Colonial and Postcolonial Realities

In contrast, postcolonial societies are products of a different set of historical circumstances. Historically constituted in unequal power relations, they were subordinated polities. Here we have social experiences defined by enforced breaks in the historical narratives of cohesive socio-cultural groups, and the polities in which they were embedded. Colonial domination – the imposition of alien customs, beliefs, institutions, economic and political systems, and sociocultural practices – had displaced the cultural heritage of previously relatively cohesive sociopolitical entities. In other words, it had interrupted the development of precolonial polities, the reflexive forging of sociocultural, political, and economic possibilities as part of the process of societal self-definition.

Because of their colonial history, postcolonial societies are defined by discursive collective memories, and the habitus of subjectification. This means that they, at least in part, had developed a colonial hegemonic consciousness; they had assimilated aspects of the dominant colonial culture, including the expectations and aspirations of a subject people. As could be seen in Chapter 1, in most instances, they also have a legacy of artificially created complex language relations, and cultural landscapes marked by conflictual identities and cultural identifications. With regard to their political systems they, on the whole, inherited the bureaucracies of the colonial state and also, as we shall see later, underdeveloped social infrastructure unable to cater for the complex needs of the whole society. Issues related to sovereignty and boundaries linked to colonialism, feature strongly in the construction of the postcolonial 'nation' state.

Boundaries, sovereignty and self-determination

As is discussed in Chapter 1, the arbitrary boundaries that resulted from the 1885 Congress of Berlin effectively reconstructed polities in sub-Saharan Africa in line with the ambitions of colonial states. The power of the colonizing state to dominate and control, to redefine and restructure, is implicit in the fact that '(t)he colonial authorities named the new states, drew their borders, built up their capital cities, and established a central administration and political institutions to suit their economic needs and prestige' (Guibernau, 1996: 116). Again, as is discussed in Chapter 1, this redrawing of the territorial map, and the accompanying restructuring of the sociocultural base, disrupted traditional societies and, ultimately, reshaped the political and cultural geography of the region. Classificatory discourse frameworks, in many ways reflecting the ascendancy of the natural sciences, and cartography, during this period, legitimized the pseudo-scientific categorization of peoples positioned within externally reconfigured political entities, generating maps of often artificially created 'tribes' and territories.

The new states constructed in this way – the colonies, or protectorates – comprised 'a collection of peoples and old states, or fragments of these, brought together within the same boundaries' (Akintoye, 1976: 3); they were inherently culturally and linguistically fragmented. Again, as could be seen in Chapter 1, many postcolonial societies in sub-Saharan Africa, comprise population groups extending 'beyond the boundaries of the existing state, as is the case of the Somali where a third of their population lives in neighbouring Ethiopia, Kenya and Djibouti' (James, 1996: 14). Similarly, the Ewe people were split between Ghana and Togo; the Nzema and the Brong were split between Ghana and Cote d'Ivoire. In the Bunyoro Kingdom the Toro, who had historically been seen as forming part of the Nyoro cultural grouping, became classified as a distinct administrative and cultural entity, and 'the regional variant of the Bunyoro language was treated as a distinct speech code' (Young, 1994: 227). In addition, boundary changes took place sporadically as was the case, for example, with the territory now known as Mali which, in 1890, became an administrative entity known as French Sudan – was disbanded again in 1899 – and part of it distributed amongst border territories (Touval, 1999) (see also case-study of Mali in Chapter 5). This pattern of reconstituting boundaries and, therefore, altering the territorial base of individual states, was repeated throughout the sub-Saharan region. For example:

> In 1902 a new colony under the name of Senegambia and Niger was created. In 1904 the western parts of the colony were detached, and its name was changed to Upper Senegal and Niger. The eastern part of the colony was detached in 1919 and included in the new colony of Upper Volta. Consequently, the reduced territory of Upper Senegal and Niger was renamed French Sudan. In 1932 Upper Volta was abolished, and two of its *cercles* (a French administrative division) comprising some 50,000 square kilometers and containing approximately 700,000 inhabitants were attached to Sudan . . . (and) in 1947 were detached from Sudan and returned to Upper Volta, which was reconstituted as a separate territory. (Touval, 1999: 12, information in brackets added)

Many of the displaced groups living in the ethnolinguistic diasporas constructed by the continuously shifting colonial territorial map, ended up having divided loyalties with regard to political as well as ethnic and linguistic group allegiances. These were often politically exploited; the policy of 'divide and rule' adopted by colonial regimes 'set the patterns of future hostilities' (Akintoye, 1976: 4) between different ethnic groups.

Divide-and-rule policies

In the case of India, whereas previous colonial empires such as the Asoka and Mughal Empires had integrated peoples divided by religion, language and caste into a cohesive social group, the British Empire used 'racial otherness' to underscore differences between the colonized and colonizers, thus creating a hegemonic power divide between rulers and ruled. As colonial subjects, the culturally diverse Indian peoples (as was the case with diverse African populations) were socially constructed as culturally homogenized ignorant 'Natives' steeped in idolatory and superstition (Chatterjee, 1993), laziness, and dishonesty as against the intrinsic cultural, political and economic superiority of the colonial culture. Chapter 1 charted important aspects of the discourse of 'racial otherness' shaped around the colonial experience in India. Ethnic and religious differences were exploited on several levels to achieve the aims of territorial conquest, already since the period dominated by the British East India Company. Nederveen (1990) highlights the *imperial chain* that underscored conquest involving the recruitment of already conquered groups in further conquest. He argues that:

> Hindus from the northern provinces were recruited by the British against the Muslim Muhghal empire; Muslims were deployed against the Marathas; Hindus and Muslims of the plains were used against the Gurkhas of the Hills of Nepal; Gurkhas reinforced the ranks who defeated the Sikhs in the Punjab; while Gurkhas and Sikhs were mobilized to subdue the Indian Mutiny of Hindus and Muslims on the plains of Delhi, and later, against the Pathans and Baluchis in the Afghan wars. (Nederveen, 1990: 119)

Different population groups were thus incorporated into the politics of conquest (divide-and-conquer). British rule relied, to a great extent, also on existing local power groups including landlords (*zamindars*) in the provinces, and maharajahs in the princely states, who were richly rewarded for their collaboration. In this way, existing elite and economic proto-elite groups (i.e. those created by the colonial powers) were systematically incorporated into the colonial project and, subsequently, collaborated in the politics of dominion (divide-and-rule). Of significance, was the fact that during the military and political clampdown that followed the Mutiny of 1857, some of these elite groups working within the administration, refrained from intervening on behalf of their peoples. Similar alliances were forged in colonial territories elsewhere between colonial authorities and 'chiefs, landlords and other traditional authority figures' (Potter, 1997: 213), leading Nederveen to conclude that:

> Divide-and-rule on the one hand and collaboration on the other together make up the logic of empire: a symbiotic logic in which the conquered become instruments of the conquerors, while the conquerors serve the interests of (some of) the conquered, a process by which conquest is transmuted into dominion. (Nederveen, 1990: 121)

Viewed as such, these strategies can be seen as representing a potent form of symbolic violence (Bourdieu, 1991); the process by which oppressed groups tacitly collude in their own dispossession and/or disempowerment through the economic, cultural, and political choices that they make. Underlying the strategies of divide-and-rule, and divide-and-conquer, was the promotion of sectarianism with its hegemony of mutual mistrust and exclusion, and the counter-hegemonies and struggles that they subsequently have generated in postcolonial societies.

In order to manage and control potential internal and external threats, and to maintain social equilibrium, the colonial state relied on 'the powerful bureaucratic-military apparatus and mechanisms of government which enable(d) them to subordinate the native social classes' (Saul, 1986: 457), and in the case of sub-Saharan Africa, discrete ethno-linguistic fragments living within its boundaries. Politically then, the colonial state derived its legitimacy largely from coercive forms of power. As stated earlier, colonized polities, on the whole, were dominated by a state defined by strong centralized forms of control grounded in the idea of a sovereign administrator (the governor) who was appointed by the metropolitan political authorities, and who had been vested with supreme power (Smith, 1983). This model of governance did not subscribe to the ideas and principles of modernity; rather, they reflected the autocratic forms of government of premodern Europe. The notion of sovereignty so central to the idea of the modern nation state therefore cannot, realistically, be seen to have applied in the colonial situation. Instead, the state, in the colonies, represented a 'subspecies of state ... a dependent appendage of an externally located sovereign entity, alien to its core. Its inner logic was shaped by the vocation of domination'. (Young, 1988: 7).

Yet, at the same time, boundaries defining a new political space, *were* established which, in turn, were framed by a central government having its own institutions (e.g. legal and administrative) as well as a new common (colonial) language. Together these bureaucratic systems facilitated administration, and maintained social cohesion; they also aided capital accumulation processes. Although, technically, some of the criteria of statehood were met, colonial occupation precluded the right to self-determination and self-governance of colonized peoples. Subjected to domination and control by the colonial state they were relegated to the outer-periphery of colonial society. Colonized peoples were excluded from participating in the democratic process. The existence of a subject-people undermined the idea of a sovereign 'people-nation'. Clearly then, the authoritarianism of the colonial state prevented the development of a sustainable sociopolitical infrastructure to support the development of civil society inclusive of local peoples. Whilst new, and modern, economic and political systems in many instances equivalent, or based on those in Europe, had been put into place within colonized territories, the majority of the population, the local peoples, were excluded systematically from participating in the political process. They were not citizens within their own countries. Together, these factors highlight the fact that the policy and practice of colonial statehood existed in contradictions, ambiguities and tension.

Furthermore, whilst education was extended to local peoples, this was done on a limited basis, with only a small elite benefiting from a full formal education. This had implications for the long-term development of human resources/labour power suited to a modern economy. As is discussed in Chapter 1, educating traditional elite groups to occupy a range of low ranking posts, within the colonial administration, generated an under-educated workforce in the long-term. Traditional elite groups, such as local aristocracies, over generations managed to obtain the requisite cultural capital to participate in the modern capitalist economy established within the colonies. In addition, educated elite groups (or the proto-elite) include those who would have completed their formal school education as well as tertiary education, through the medium of the colonial language, which represented the language of power. Imbued thus with appropriate cultural capital they, ultimately, became the intellectual, linguistic, economic and power elites occupying key positions within the colonial bureaucracy and, subsequently, nationalist movements – and later, in postcolonial administrations. In other words, they were best placed in accessing the educational market and, as a result, ultimately also the labour market.

Language played a key role in the shaping of these elite groups. Commenting on the proto-elite in postcolonial Nigeria, Agheyisi argues that:

> It is now possible to talk of a special social 'class' of Nigerians, comprising members of various ethnic and linguistic groups, for whom the 'public', and indeed prominent use of English exists as one of their salient status symbols . . . This educated elite of the urban communities, like its counterpart in other developing countries, constitutes a highly influential social group, whose values and patterns of social behaviour serve as models for the aspiring masses. (Agheyisi, 1977: 99)

Although policy support for the teaching of colonial languages differed amongst the various colonial powers, and during different epochs, their association with trade, commerce and high status culture, influenced aspirations amongst colonized populations to be educated in colonial languages. Colonialism impacted on almost every aspect of social, economic and social life throughout these regions. Of significance to the discussion here are the long-term effects of the sociocultural, political, and economic practices and processes set in train by colonialism, and their collective impact on language and development in postcolonial societies. Examining this further, the next section focuses on issues of governance, model of development, education and human resource development, and language-state relations. Residual influences within the sociocultural, economic and political terrain are discussed in relation to infrastructural constraints, and the 'colonial' habitus continuing to inhibit postcolonial development. Some of the major effects of colonialism on language, educational and civic possibilities in postcolonial societies, are highlighted.

Cultural and economic legacies of colonialism

Governance

As could be seen in Chapter 1, there were variations in the policies pursued by the colonial powers. British colonies, in particular, extended more cultural freedoms to their subjects than was the case with Belgium, France and Portugal. This included support for local languages in primary education. In addition, the state bureaucracy, particularly, at the lower levels, were staffed to a major extent by local people who had been educated by the colonial regime. Underlying this, was the need for human resources to maintain the bureaucracy, and thus to facilitate governance. Therefore, although as Brutt-Griffler (2004: 42) suggests 'the need for a small proportion of English-speaking subjects necessarily arose without any separate language policy goals' the pursuit of English, in effect, underscored a political economy grounded in control, containment and economic benefit. As such, it constituted informal policy, especially since authoritarianism masked as a benign paternalism represented the overriding model of governance. Colonial authorities wielded absolute power deciding 'how the people should be governed, how their society would be ordered, and their economic resources disposed of' (Akintoye, 1976: 2). Moreover, colonial government was founded on conquest, not on consent; it positioned the colonized as subject-peoples existing outside civil society. That is to say, in contrast to the centrality of citizenship to the burgeoning Western European nation-state at the time, colonized peoples were not citizens. They did not inform policy-making decisions; neither were they enfranchised voters able to participate in the democratic process.

Economic management

Throughout the colonial world, the state acted in the interest of the colonial economy, using networks, agencies and structures (including physical infrastructure such as ports, roads, and rail for transport) established for that specific purpose. This, *ipso facto*, undermined the development of production, trade networks and markets in the interest of the local economy. In Africa, this extended to the 'establishment of state monopoly control over the purchase and export of agricultural goods through various marketing agencies or boards', resulting in colonial state control over the principal cash income in the economy (Potter, 1997: 213). Collectively, these factors contributed to the under-development of the national economic base generally and, therefore, uneven development throughout different regions.

Education

It is true to say that a positive effect of colonialism was the establishment of formal education systems in the colonies. At the same time, however, colonial education also eradicated traditional school systems such as the 'bush schools' embedded in local cultures. Bush schools were incorporated into the missionary framework where they became catechetical schools, and later under colonial rule, they became the first village elementary schools (Fafunwa, 1982). Missionary education, especially during the early years, was largely disparate with each mission rooted in its own particular ideology and practice. Although missionaries provided much of the educational infrastructure within the colonies, and fostered local languages, missionary education lacked coherence and co-ordination on a macro-scale. The school curriculum, with a predominance of religious education, had a narrow focus on essential skills and functional knowledges.

Under the colonial system most schools, including primary schools, were fee-paying; and the limited number of schools meant that students had long distances to walk to school. We shall see later, the extent to which these influences have endured during the postcolonial period. Much of the emphasis, particularly in the British system, was on an academic curriculum, with little policy consideration for vocational and professional education. These factors, combined with 'the neglect of technical education; lack of provision for commercial and agricultural specialization; unsatisfactory methods of teaching; inadequate facilities for training teachers; undue importance attached to examinations and degrees' (Basu, 1974: 236) inherited from colonial rule, constituted major impediments to postcolonial social development. Moreover, colonial schooling was marked by religious and racialized segregation that, in turn, contributed to 'a lack of uniformity in standards and facilities amongst the African schools' (Fafunwa, 1982: 24). In Tanzania and Kenya, separate schooling was provided for different ethno-cultural groups, for example, Europeans, Asians, Arabs and Africans (Fafunwa, 1982). Similarly, in Nigeria Quranic schools flourished in the Muslim north and Christian schools in the south. Ideologically, these schools served to reinforce ethnic, cultural and religious differences. Schooling within the colonial system was also marked by differential access to education for different groups. For example, in Tanganjika education for Africans was restricted to Standard 6 until 1937, with limited extension to Standard 7 after 1937, whilst Europeans and Asians could advance beyond Standard 8.

Human resource development

Within the colonies the development of the local human resource base was undermined by the fact that the majority of the population had been denied opportunity to acquire the skills and knowledge necessary to access higher level skilled jobs within different sectors of the economy. The highly regulated colonial labour market allowed only a small local elite group access to higher levels of employment within the colonial administration (see also Chapter 1). State regulation of the indigenous labour force extended into broader areas of the economy. In India, for example, the colonial government's economic policy prevented 'new scholars from entering business or industry in any capacity other than as clerks' (Basu, 1974: 191). This resulted in many aiming to enter the civil service, or the professions. Since it provided the best means of accessing the skilled labour market, credentialism became an integral part of self-defined human resource development. African students' entrance into the labour market was carefully controlled by British colonial administrations, to prevent their advance within the administration. In Tanganjika it was argued that '... the ideal for a system of African education would be based on an employment census and a careful forecast of economic development; educational activities, other than village schools having a definite agricultural bias, should be rigidly limited in output to the estimated capacity of the country's power of absorption' (Annual Report of the Ministry of Education, 1926, cited in Roy-Campbell, 2001: 43). The emphasis was, therefore, on elementary education only for African populations. These state control strategies had long-term effects; they failed to develop a human resource base capable of sustaining an independent local economy, and serving the employment needs of the whole society.

Although education expanded considerably in the aftermath of the Second World War, under-education of the majority population remained a long-term legacy of colonial educational policy.

Language relations

Colonial language policy was informed fundamentally by the ideological, political and economic drives of the metropolitan state. Colonial languages were therefore adopted in the colonial administration, education, business and industry. This strategy had multi-levelled impacts. In addition to the subjugation of local languages, and the underdevelopment of literacies in local languages and cultures, the centrality of the colonial language to the formal education process, secured the hegemonic consciousness of colonized peoples through the curriculum content, knowledges, ways of knowing, and ways of seeing the world that it legitimated. The emphasis placed on the link between language and the shaping of a colonial worldview is evident in the following statement by a senior inspector with responsibility for overseas education in Francophone Africa in 1910. He argued for the need '... to attach them (the colonized) to the Metropole by a very solid psychological bond, against the day when their progressive emancipation ends in a form of federation, as is probable ... that they be, and they remain, French in language, thought, and spirit' (cited in Phillipson, 1993: 114, information in brackets added). The effectiveness of this strategy in the British colonies is evident in the following statement made by Dr Abdurahman, a disenfranchised community leader in South Africa, in the aftermath of the defeat of the Boers in 1902. He argued that,

> (t)he question naturally arises, which is to be the national language. Shall it be the degraded forms of a literary language, a vulgar patois; or shall it be that language which Macaulay says is 'In force, in richness, in aptitude for all the highest purposes of the poet, the philosopher, and the orator inferior to the tongue of Greece alone?' Shall it be the language of the 'Kombuis' [kitchen] or the language of Tennyson? That is, shall it be the Taal [Afrikaans] or English? (African Peoples Organization (APO), 13/8/1910 cited in Adhikari, 1996: 8)

Dr Abdurahman encouraged his people to 'endeavour to perfect themselves in English – the language which inspires the noblest thoughts of freedom and liberty, the language that has the finest literature on earth and is the most universally useful of all languages' (Abdurahman, APO, 13/8/1902, cited in Adhikari, 1996: 8). A similar view is expressed by Cliff (1985: 12–13) who describes the success of British colonial discourse in making 'you believe absolutely in the hegemony of the King's English and the form in which it is meant to be expressed. Or else your writing is not literature; it is folklore and never can be art'. These statements capture the potency of the cultural hegemony obtained by

English language and literature, under colonial rule. They also reflect the success that full immersion into colonial language and culture in the courts, radio (at least since 1932), church, schools, and industry as well as everyday road signs, books, newspapers and magazines had on shaping the hegemonic consciousness of colonized peoples. The social and economic value attached, generally, to the acquisition of colonial languages amongst colonized peoples in different societies, resulted in their becoming a prerequisite for upward social mobility (see Chapters 1, 5, 6, 7 and 8). The incorporation of colonial languages into economic, political and sociocultural institutions contributed to these languages becoming a potent form of hegemonic cultural capital, representing that which everyone had to have, in order to function effectively within society (Rassool, 1999). Together these factors provide some indication of the ways in which colonialism altered ethno-linguistic and cultural relations within occupied countries, orienting the expectations, aspirations, dreams and desires of the colonized away from native cultures, and towards the norms of the dominant (colonial) culture. Generating thus a conflict of interest between displaced or subjugated indigenous languages, and the economically and socially powerful language of the 'mother country', colonialism set in train a linguistic and cultural ambiguity within the psyche of the colonized that has endured across time and space. In the case of Sub-Saharan Africa, 'under colonial sponsorship, the "man of two worlds" was created. A cultural schizophrenic, the westernized African inverted the truths of African culture and history' (Prah, 1999: 550). The impact of this on postcolonial language relations, and their impact on societal development, will be discussed further in the case studies in Chapters 5, 6 and 7. Colonial language relations also influenced the language-in-education infrastructure put into place within the colonies, which, in turn, impacted on postcolonial educational development possibilities.

Infrastructure

Colonialism dislocated the sociocultural, economic and political infrastructure of precolonial polities and replaced them with structures, practices and processes imported from the colonizing metropolitan nation state. Constructed mainly to support the needs and demands of the colonial state, these infrastructures were under-developed with regard to their ability to cater effectively for the diverse needs of the majority population. The education systems put into place, on the whole, represented a mirror image of the metropolitan education system in character, structure, content, language medium, textbooks, literature, curriculum content, examinations and pedagogy. Although the African Education Commission (1921–1922) supported by the Phelps-Stokes Fund, advocated the use of vernacular languages in education they, nevertheless, recommended the use of English as medium for teaching and learning at secondary level where the infrastructure existed to support this. Ultimately then, educational policy served to support the development of colonial languages and, in the process, engendered acculturation[1] and assimilation. In practice, secondary school systems were under-developed and, moreover, many teachers were under-qualified. Moreover, because they were not fluent in English, they used the local indigenous language as a vehicle through which to acquire literacy in English. This, in turn, often resulted in the under-development of literacy in either language. As can be seen later in the case-studies in Chapters 5, 6 and 7, this remains an unresolved issue in many postcolonial societies.

Social cohesion

Mass displacement of ethnolinguistic groups in sub-Saharan Africa, and the seeds of potential ethnic and religious conflict sowed in the divide-and-rule policies of colonialism, contributed to historical discontinuities in the development process. It also contributed to the lack of a cohesive societal/national identity on which to build postcolonial nationhood. Although ethnolinguistic groups divided by arbitrary boundaries in sub-Saharan Africa in 1885, had evolved into new political entities marked by a rich tapestry of languages and cultures, inadequate educational infrastructure inhibited their further development as cultural, political and economic resources. Colonial education supported schooling in local languages, mainly at primary school level. Whilst an economic elite educated through the medium of a colonial language, and schooled in Western mores, later emerged as leaders of anticolonial nationalist movements, the uneven distribution of educational opportunities created a knowledge, skills, economic and social divide between them, and the rest of the population. Imbued thus with cultural capital, they also became a political elite at the center of the decolonization process. In India this gave rise to rivalries amongst different linguistic groups. According to Basu (1974: 232), the three most educationally advanced groups 'the Bengali *bhadralok*, the Chitapavans of Maharashtra and the Tamilian Brahmins had assumed political leadership in their respective geographic regions'. The infiltration of Western ideas and thought into the languages and cultures of these provinces resulted in Bengali, Marathi and Tamil asserting their superiority over other languages in the Presidencies (Basu, 1974). Consequently, dominant language groups often monopolized political leadership. Colonized societies, invariably, were polarized economically, socially and politically. As can be seen below, and again in Chapter 3, these factors have had implications for postcolonial social, political and economic development.

Colonial model of development

Colonialism represented a particular model of development. In essence, it underpinned the social, political and economic modernization of Western European nation states during the late 19th century. Colonial economies had played an important role in supporting the development of the political and administrative infrastructure of the metropolitan nation state, including the growth of bureaucracies, the military and corporate commercial organizations. In this way, colonialism facilitated the political transition to secularist nation states in Western Europe as well as the economic transition, from largely agrarian accumulation regimes, to industrial capitalist economies, and the concomitant sociocultural changes. The key issue here is that the logic of the colonial model of development was grounded in the sociocultural, political, and economic *under-development* of the colonized territories.

To summarize the discussion so far, I argued first that colonial government was authoritarian and excluded local peoples from civil society; thus they did not take part in the democratic process. Second, educational and linguistic infrastructures were under-developed where these related to colonized peoples. Third, a mixed language economy existed amongst the different colonial rulers. Amongst these, British colonialism used local languages in education in the primary school sector, and the transition to English-based education occurred at secondary school level. Assimilationist ideology lay at the heart of colonial cultural relations, in which language played a key role. Colonized peoples though, were not fully absorbed into colonial society. Rather, they remained a subordinate group – which, itself, was internally segregated along ethnic/linguistic, class, and religious/cultural lines. This contributed significantly to the development of a divided ethnic consciousness, and often competing aspirations amongst subjugated groups. Fourth, colonialism engendered small economic elites, who were also language elites. Fluency in colonial languages facilitated (partial) absorption into the skilled labour market, particularly, in the lower echelons of the state bureaucracy. Representing thus a potent symbol of higher aspirations and upward social mobility, it became the language of choice in education amongst the colonized peoples. Colonial languages and their literary canons, cultural thought and behaviours, to a significant extent, became hegemonized in individual consciousness. Fifth, colonialism eroded existing cultural, economic and political infrastructures, and supplanted these with an administrative system that was alien to the local social base. Sixth, differential access to education for different social groups, emphasis on an academic curriculum, and an under-developed educational infrastructure contributed to an under-developed human resource base. As can be seen below, these factors had long-term impacts on development possibilities in the aftermath of decolonization, and the emergence of independent postcolonial states engaged in nation-building as well as economic and social modernization.

Postcolonial Development

As is suggested earlier, 'postcolonialism' is a contested and multifaceted concept (see Introduction). Here it is seen as representing a sociopolitical process characterized by 'the shift in global relations which marks the (necessarily uneven) transition from the age of Empires to the post-independence or post-decolonisation moment' (Hall, 1996: 246). Postcolonialism therefore also refers to an historical epoch marked by the emergence of independent states in the aftermath of post-Second World War decolonization. However, rather than constituting a definitive break with the past, decolonization represents a complex process of disengagement from the colonial encounter, involving not only socio-political change, but also cultural, economic and ideological shifts and readjustments. As could be seen in Chapter 1, colonialism constituted not only an economic and political strategy, it inscribed itself into the cultural fabric of both colonial and colonized societies, altering both from within. Emerging postcolonial societies therefore are 'decolonized' not only through settlement agreements, they also have to engage in a reflexive process of self-definition and self-identification to disentangle themselves from the discursive sets of controls that had underpinned colonial policy and practice.

Colonialism ended with fractured cultural landscapes, and fragmented ethnolinguistic populations in many countries, as a result of boundary changes during the colonial period and, in some instances, the creation of new political entities. India, as a cohesive political entity, itself was a colonial construction arising as it did from different kingdoms integrated under the British Empire. Here colonialism ended in Partition, the political division of the country creating the new Muslim dominated state of Pakistan which, in turn, was divided by the Indian land mass into two sections, West Pakistan and East Pakistan. Following a civil war in 1971, the latter became Bangladesh, which represents an autonomous language (Bengali) community. Unresolved boundary issues between Pakistan and India have contributed to intermittent warfare and tension between the two countries. Furthermore, the provinces of Jammu and Kashmir, which were ceded to India in 1947, have remained a source of ongoing conflict between the two countries. The postcolonial language situation in Pakistan is discussed in one of the case studies in Chapter 7.

Throughout the sub-Saharan region, decolonization did not undermine the integrity of the territories constructed under colonial occupation. The newly emerged postcolonial states largely adhered to the governmental framework and, to a large extent, also the boundaries left by colonial partition. Neither did they seek to revert to tribal government, or to reinstate indigenous monarchies; they built on existing structures, practices and processes. Nevertheless, the emerging political entities encountered major challenges related to 'statehood', 'nationhood' and governance revolving around:

(1) centralization of political *authority*, often referred to as the process of state-building;
(2) creating *unity* among heterogeneous groups in their polity, often referred to as *nation-building;*
(3) providing avenues for political *participation;* and
(4) distributing scarce but allocatable resources.

(Elaigwu & Mazrui, 2003: 446)

That is to say, the first task of the new political dispensation was to put into place, the necessary political structures for governance, and civic engagement in the democratic process, and creating possibilities for the political integration of discrete social groups, thus to engage in building a cohesive nation. This represented the ideals as well as the immediate development goals of the emerging postcolonial states. However, as can be seen below, they encountered many problems, some of which were directly related to colonial policy and practice.

Postcolonial state and nation building

The legacy of artificial boundaries, and the resultant lack of social cohesion, presented major problems to emerging postcolonial states with regard to maintaining social equilibrium. Although the All Africa Peoples Conference (AAPC) held in Accra in 1958 'denounced artificial frontiers drawn by imperialist powers to divide the peoples of Africa, particularly those which cut across ethnic groups and divide people of the same stock' (cited in Touval, 1999: 56), and resolved to have these abolished or adjusted, they were not. Politically, emerging postcolonial states in Africa encountered the ever-present threat of disputes over national borders as well as the potential for cross-border ethnic, religious and linguistic conflict. In the case of Somalia, for example, 'the entire length of its boundaries cut across grazing grounds and divided the people' (Touval, 1999: 84). Boundary and territorial issues were also raised elsewhere in Congo, Cameroon, and West New Guinea. Emerging postcolonial states also faced struggles for self-determination amongst secessionist ethnic 'states' as was the case with the Somalis in the Ogaden, the Ibos in Biafra (Guibernau, 1996), the Ewe in Ghana, the Tuareg in Mali, and the people of Southern Sudan and Katanga province in Congo. New territorial unity, sovereignty, and legitimacy had to be created. Nation-building was therefore integral to the formation of the postcolonial state. As can be seen below, this applies to a major extent also to India and Pakistan.

Nation-building within the postcolonial context contrasts with Western Europe where the nation, generally, is seen as having arisen out of long-term nationalist struggles, and thus as having preceded the emergence of the modern state. Nation-building within that milieu represented a process that, over time, developed collective attitudes, beliefs, and values, ultimately constituting a political culture comprised of 'a congruity of cultural and political identities' (Elaigwu & Mazrui, 2003: 438) underscored by the universal principles of the Enlightenment. In Africa, the process of nation building took place over a short period of time and, in effect, was forged in the drive for securing the territorial integrity and legitimacy of the postcolonial state. In many instances in Africa, the state preceded the nation; frequent boundary changes during the colonial period had resulted in the fact that:

> (m)any groups of peoples were arbitrarily sandwiched into a territorial unit, which then formed a geopolitical entity called the state. To many peoples of these states, there was no identification with the state as a symbol of the people, a political community. (Elaigwu & Mazrui, 2003: 439)

Nation-building within this context became a task for the emerging post-colonial state, whose responsibility it was to secure social cohesion. The aim therefore was to develop a national identity that transcended ethnic, religious, linguistic and social class differences, by integrating different ethnolinguistic, cultural and religious groups into a cohesive national consciousness. In an ideal sense, this centred on a 'recognition of the rights of other members to a share of common history, resources, values and other aspects of the state – buttressed by a sense of belonging to one political community' (Elaigwu & Mazrui, 2003: 438). What emerged is referred to as 'state-nations' (Guibernau, 1996) in which the state provided the central politically integrative force in society, rather than 'nation-states' in which it was the responsibility of the state to execute the will of the people-nation, as was the case in Western Europe.

Nonetheless, following the Western European model of development, decolonization emphasized the creation of modern 'nation' states as the political basis of postcolonial development. In practice, though, the differences in the historical development process, especially, the discursive forms of domination and subjugation experienced by colonized countries over sustained periods of time, make the application of the Western European idea and ideal of the nation state problematic in the postcolonial context. The postcolonial 'nation' state developed in distinctive ways in different countries, depending on their colonial history and cultural traditions; each encountered complex sets of problems unique to their situation. Whilst in India a pluralist administration under a secular government was put in place, in many countries in Sub-Saharan Africa, the state apparatus that emerged at the end of colonialism tended to reproduce the authoritarian model of the colonial state despite nominal claims of supporting democratic political practices. In many instances, this comprised a one-party political regime dominated by either the military, or charismatic chiefs, or in some instances, political leaders who had been democratically elected. As stated earlier, many of them had received a Western education in metropolitan countries and, therefore, were imbued with the cultural hegemony of Europe grounded in the idea of a classical education through the medium of the colonial language. These colonial sensibilities amongst the political leaderships had an impact on the educational systems and curriculum models put in place in many postcolonial societies. Linguistic, cultural and economic elites who also became the political elites, often created political parties that were essentially mono-ethnic in composition, thus engendering the potential for ongoing conflict amongst the different ethnic groups. As a result, many postcolonial states continued to be beset by the challenges of political polarization, and through this, perpetuating the social relations of colonialism as well as generating the potential for social unrest. Civil wars lasting many years became the reality of several Sub-Saharan postcolonial states.

Most countries had further complexities in their development histories. As is discussed above, in Kenya, South Africa, South West Africa (Namibia) Northern and Southern Rhodesia (Zambia and Zimbabwe), white settler communities had established themselves as new states and pursued neo-colonial policies. Of these, South Africa represented the extreme form of neo-colonialism. Here the dominance of the authoritarian white Afrikaner 'nation' state, underpinned by the racist ideology of Apartheid, secured a different development trajectory to the rest of post-colonial Sub-Saharan Africa in the aftermath of the Second World War. As stated earlier, language and a racialized nationhood grounded in the ideology of *herrenvolkism* (racial superiority of the white 'Volk'), played a significant role in securing the policy of separate development (Apartheid). Politically, the English-speaking settlers were incorporated into the Apartheid state, and formed an integral part of the 'white' privileged 'nation'. This reinforced already existing economic, social and political inequalities engendered by colonialism, and a fragmented, racially stratified, ethnic consciousness amongst the majority population. The postcolonial language situation in South Africa is discussed in one of the case studies in Chapter 6.

As countries achieved independence, language and identity became central variables in nation-building and the self-definition of the postcolonial 'nation'-state. In Sub-Saharan Africa this coincided with a period of ethnic revivalism, the claiming back of identity as a form of 'disidentification' (Pecheux, 1982), that is, engaging in a process of working against the ideological constructions of colonialism. This involved, *inter alia*, changing the names of individuals and countries from their European forms to African names, for example, Gold Coast became Ghana, and Upper Volta became Burkina Faso (Obeng and Adegbija, 1999). A similar revivalism of African languages occurred in the mass media, for example, Twi, Fante (Akan languages), Ewe, Ga, Nzema and Dagbani used in radio broadcasts in Ghana, Nigerian languages used in television and radio as well as the publication of newspapers in local languages (Obeng and Adegbija, 1999). Nevertheless, viewed at macro-policy level, the choice of languages for nationhood and national development, presented major challenges to the emerging postcolonial states. This relates, first, to the cultural, economic and political influences of colonialism on shaping the hegemonic consciousness of society. That is to say, their self-concept as individuals, and as a people, including their aspirations, expectations, hopes, dreams and desires (see the discussion of the legacies of colonialism above for examples of this). Second, it also relates to the fact that upon decolonization, the new states became part of the international system of national states, which already were integrated into the competitive global capitalist economy. Postcolonial states, therefore, not only had to become independent states and integrated nations internally, they also had to have the ability to interrelate politically, and compete economically, with other, already existing states – including the former colonial states. This relationship was from the beginning of their political existence, fundamentally, an unequal one. The colonial legacy of high levels of illiteracy, the complex language terrain, and unresolved boundary issues, the under-development of the human resource base as well as the need still to integrate diverse ethnic and religious groups into a cohesive political entity, presented major inhibiting factors to social and economic development.

Key policy issues revolved around language as:

(1) an important cultural resource involved in the transmission of culture;
(2) a political resource central to governance and the building of a cohesive nationhood; and
(3) an economic resource, that is, as a means of communication, and as a medium through which to acquire skills and knowledge, ultimately to be exchanged within the labour market.

These factors featured centrally in policy drives aimed at facilitating societal modernization. How successfully these could be incorporated into national educational policies and, moreover, how effectively they could be implemented, depended significantly on the educational infrastructures in place as well as the requisite teaching and learning resources made available in different educational sectors. We saw earlier, the emphasis placed during colonialism on academic knowledge and qualifications, to the detriment of vocational and professional education. In the section below, I examine the modernization of postcolonial states and the struggles that took place around language and the state.

Modernization: Issues of language and literacy

The discussion thus far, highlights the fact that the notion that colonialism brought rational order and development to colonized countries, is fractured by the reality of social displacement and dispossession, not only of material goods but, more importantly, of people and their political and cultural rights. It is also evident in the discussion thus far that policies of linguistic imperialism, which here refers to the hierarchization of languages resulting in some languages being preferred over other, subjugated, languages (Phillipson, 1992, 1997), have left a legacy of unresolved problems, and ambiguity around issues of language and identity in the lives of many different groups of people. Colonial languages represented the language of the colonial administration, and through the processes of

British indirect rule, had penetrated the everyday lives of large sections of the employable population working, largely, in the lower echelons of the state bureaucracy. Within this context, colonial languages represented cultural capital to be exchanged in the labour market and, consequently, many people aspired to acquire them. Yet this does not mean that these took place unproblematically; and that the colonized peoples were incorporated without challenge into the hegemonic project of colonialism. Despite the popularity of colonial languages as a means of improving employment possibilities within the colonial administration, the need to retain their languages and culture formed an integral part of the anticolonial struggle within several colonized societies, as was the case in South Africa (see Chapter 6).

India

In India, the struggle for the maintenance of local languages was central to Gandhi's political project. Arguing for the need to free the Indian nation from the hegemony of the English language, Gandhi emphasized the importance to the nation to retain the vernaculars as medium of teaching and learning, and maintained that the loss of their mother tongue was equivalent to 'national suicide' (Basu, 1974: 78). In 1938 Gandhi advocated that '(t)he medium of instruction should be altered at once and at any cost, the provincial languages being given their rightful place' ... and later stated that '(t)o get rid of the infatuation with English is one of the essentials of Swaraj (self-government)' (cited in Rama Rao, 2002: 4, information in brackets added). Gandhi regarded this process of self-definition as central to the emergence of India as a modern nation. He identified five requirements for any language to be accepted as the national language. Underpinning this were the following views:

(1) It should be easy to learn for government officials.
(2) It should be capable of serving as a medium of religious, economic, and political intercourse throughout India.
(3) It should be the speech of the majority of the inhabitants of India.
(4) It should be easy to learn for the whole of the country.
(5) In choosing this language, considerations of temporary or passing interests should not count.

(Das Gupta, 1970: 109)

In this regard, Gandhi was a keen advocate for the development of Hindustani, and argued that 'all underdeveloped and unwritten dialects should ... be sacrificed and merged in the great Hindustani stream. It would be a sacrifice ... not a suicide' (cited in King, 1999: 88). Gandhi's argument was integral to the principles of the Constructive Programme of the Satyagraha Movement (1940–1941). Gandhi saw this compromise between Hindi and Urdu as the best means of gaining support for a national language. The underlying intention was that the retention of the Perso-Arabic script would preserve the culture of the Muslims, and that this combined with the retention of the Devanagari script for the Hindus, would serve as a means of securing social cohesion.

At the time, the Indian Congress also guaranteed New and Basic Education and the mother tongue teaching medium for up to seven years of schooling (Thirumalai, 2005). In practice, this maintained continuity in the language-in-education policies pursued by the British. Language represented a major contested area during the period preceding Partition. Jawarharlal Nehru, the first postcolonial national leader, emphasized the importance not only of self-government and nation-building, but also the need for rapid economic development. Recognizing the value of language in this process, Nehru had the Constitution of India translated into all the provincial languages. Regional/provincial languages provided a source of unity and, therefore, could play an important role in supporting the development of a mass independence movement. The Indian Congress, as early as 1920, demarcated the provincial structures on a linguistic basis. Following Partition, state boundaries were constantly reconfigured over a sustained period of time. They were ultimately 'codified in the States Reorganization Act of 1956' resulting in state boundaries coinciding, relatively, with linguistic boundaries (Sonntag, 2002: 165–66).

India is divided into 24 states and eight Union Territories. These geographical divisions had their origins in the British colonial period during which they served as administrative entities, and territories were added as the British Empire expanded in India. This contributed to the fact that 'the borders of such provinces cut across ethnic, religious, social, and linguistic lines' (Mallikarjun, 2004: 2) contributing thus to high levels of multilingualism within most states. Moreover, there are at least 14 different scripts for Indian languages, of which, various scripts are used for particular languages. For example:

> Kannada script is used to write (in) Kannada, Kodagu, Tulu, Banjari, Konkani, Sanskrit . . . Sanskrit is written also using the Devangari, Telugu, Tamil, Malayalam script . . . Kashmiri is written using the Perso-Arabic, Sharada and Devanagari scripts . . . Sindhi in India is written in both Perso-Arabic and Devangari scripts. (Mallikarjun, 2004: 2)

In these instances, script does not necessarily represent a barrier between languages.

In 1947 India became a federal state within which the regional polities referred to above, were integrated into a cohesive nationhood. Hindi, written in the Devanagari script, with international numerals, became the official language of the Indian Union (Das Gupta, 1970). English obtained associate status, and was retained as the language of the judiciary, and legislature. India adopted a three-language policy in education including Hindi, English, and a major (effectively a regional) language provided for in Schedule VIII of the Constitution. Thus the country sought to maintain ethnolinguistic diversity and a cohesive nation whilst, at the same time, facilitating modernization by accommodating English as an international language. There are currently 22 official 'Scheduled' languages: Assamese, Bengali, Bodo, Dogri, Gujarati, Hindi, Kannada, Kashmiri, Konkani, Maithili, Malayalam, Marathi, Meitei/ Manipuri, Nepali, Oriya, Eastern Panjabi, Sanskrit, Santali, Sindhi, Tamil, Telugu and Urdu (Ethnologue, 2005). Representing national languages of India, they have played an important symbolic role in nation building. India then is defined by both macro- and state level multilingualism, with Kerala representing in all likelihood the most linguistically cohesive state. Increasing levels of internal migration related to job opportunities have led to people moving from one linguistic state to another, particularly, major industrialized cities such as Ahmadabad, Mumbai, Calcutta and Bangalore – effectively creating new linguistic minorities within these urban spaces (Mallikarjun, 2004). In a general sense, it can be argued that postcolonial India has managed to secure a cohesive, culturally plural, liberal democratic 'nation' state grounded in the principles of unity in diversity whilst, at the same time, securing for itself access to the world economy, and the international political process. In practice though, the picture is more complex. The 1961 Census documented 1652 languages which, in turn, are related to five different language families. In addition, 527 languages were considered unclassifiable at the time. According to Mallikarjun:

> The 1991 Census had 10,400 raw returns and they were rationalized into 1576 mother tongues. They (were) further rationalized into 216 mother tongues, and grouped under 114 languages: Austro-Asiatic (14 languages, with a total population of 1.13%), Dravidian (17 languages, with a total population of 22.53%), Indo-European (Indo-Aryan, 19 languages, with a total population of 75.28%, and Germanic, 1 language, with a total population of 0.02%), Semito-Harmitic (1 language, with a

population of 0.01%, and Tibeto-Burman (62 languages with a total population of 0.97%). (Mallikarjun, 2004: 1)

Many languages in India have a population of less than 10,000 and, therefore, many languages recorded in the Census could not be classified with regard to their origins and thus featured as Unclassified Languages (Mallikarjun, 2004). This means that language policy necessarily is multi-layered, and complex and it is also often fraught with ambiguity. As stated earlier, each state, in effect, is multilingual and has its own language policy, 'designating usually the most widely spoken language as its official language and sometimes conferring secondary official language status on significant minority language(s) within the state' (Sonntag, 2002: 166). The cohesiveness of the 'nation' state is also continually challenged by language-based nationalist struggles within some of the regions. The struggle for Kashmiri independence, for example, is articulated around the autonomy of the Kashmiri language. Moreover, Telugu speakers living in Madras resented the dominant position held by Tamil speakers in the cultural, political and administrative life of the state, and later, started the movement for a separate Andhra state (Basu, 1974). The unity of the Indian 'nation' state is also fractured by other minority cultural groups, for example, the 'low caste' Dalit population group in their quest, increasingly, for social justice and equity in the job market, and the Christians of Nagaland who are seeking self determination. Similarly, language conflicts remain between Urdu and Hindi, especially with the rise in Hindu fundamentalism, with Urdu seen as a major threat to Indian nationalism despite it having been included in Schedule VIII since 1956. Furthermore, although India is successful in maintaining 'the world's largest democracy', the vast economic and social divides between rich and poor as well as issues related to civil society including access to, and dissemination of information, and public debate informing policy remain key issues to be resolved (Ramesh, 2004). Communicative competence including literacy in local languages, within this context, would form a basic requirement of building an informed and knowledgeable civil society. Language issues related to the current phase of economic globalization will be discussed further in Chapter 4.

Pakistan

Pakistan comprises the provinces of Sindh, Punjab, Baluchistan, the North West Frontier Province (NWFP), and the Federally Administrated Tribal Areas (FATA) which are integrated into a federal nation state. As can be seen later in the case-study of Pakistan (see Chapter 7), in its quest to build a cohesive nation, Pakistan opted for a unitary approach to language using Urdu as the national language. As is the case with India, Pakistan (or the region that now is Pakistan) is, historically, a complex society socially and linguistically. Pakistan comprises a rich variety of languages and dialects as well as a diversity of cultural values, practices and beliefs amongst its diverse population groups. Linguistic and religious struggles within the provinces, have contributed to the fact that social cohesion here exists in tension.

When the provincial government of Sindh province passed a law in 1972 raising the status of Sindhi (the regional language) to the equivalent status of Urdu (the national language), riots broke out throughout the province (Ahmed, 1998). At the centre of this social unrest were the Urdu speakers, the *mohajirs* (migrants – see below) living in the province, who viewed this policy support for Sindhi as undermining the symbolic significance of Urdu as the national language of Pakistan. Underlying this struggle over language were deeper issues related to the distribution of political power, jobs and resources amongst the Urdu speakers, and Sindhi speakers who constituted the majority language group (Rahman, 2000).

The cultural/linguistic hegemony of the different regions is also contested from within provincial borders. Punjab province, for example, has been challenged historically by Siraiki nationalism, based on the claim that Siraiki is an autonomous language rather than a dialect of Punjabi. Thus Siraiki speakers have asserted their separate Siraiki cultural identity, articulated by various fractions of the broadly based Siraiki nationalist movement, whose 'principal demands are that Siraikis should be acknowledged as a nationality, official documents should be written in Siraiki, and Siraiki areas should vote on the basis of ethnicity' (Rahman, 2000: 185). As is the case with Urdu/Sindhi speakers in Sindh province, the Siraiki language movement has a political base. It represents a collective struggle against socioeconomic inequalities grounded in an unequal distribution of power and resources amongst the Siraiki people who are a minority group in the southern region of Punjab province (Rahman, 2000). This struggle is articulated around language rights and political self-determination.

The cohesiveness of the Pakistani 'nation' is also contested by the presence of diasporic peoples living within its boundaries. As stated earlier, these arose from Partition, which generated mass transmigration amongst Muslims from India to the newly formed Pakistan. Those who migrated from India, the *mohajirs*, had played a defining role in the establishment of the country. However, since they were not native to the region, they had no cultural base in the new national state, a factor that has posed a threat to social equilibrium within some states. As is discussed earlier, previously stable language regions such as Sindh province were expanded significantly by the *mohajirs* who, themselves, were a significant language group (largely Urdu speakers). The social cohesiveness of Sindh province is also fractured by Punjabi and Urdu speakers who migrated from the United Provinces (Uttar Pradesh), Delhi, Hyderabad, Central Provinces (Madya Pradesh), Ajmer, Rajputana (Rajastan), and Bihar (Ahmed, 1998). The fact that Sindhi speakers now comprise only twenty per cent of the population of Karachi (Engineer, 2000), the capital city of the province, has created ethnic tension amongst the different ethnolinguistic groups within the city.

Several language movements, for example, Bengali, Sindhi, Balochi, Pashto, Siraiki and Punjabi exist in the country, with varying degrees of intensity in their struggles to assert their ethnolinguistic rights (for a comprehensive discussion of these language movements and the politics in which they are enmeshed, see Rahman, 2000; see also the case-study of Pakistan in Chapter 7). These language-based struggles grounded in ethno-cultural nationalism, fracture the 'state's modernizing imperative of creating cultural uniformity through the hegemony of an urban Urdu-using culture' (Rahman, 2000: 251).

Evidently then, the idea of a cohesive 'nation' in Pakistan exists in tension; it does not represent a homogeneous Muslim nation under the hegemony of Urdu (Ahmed, 1998). In practice, it is a multinational state riven with fissures along cultural and ethnolinguistic lines, some of which have their origins in the transmigration that accompanied the partitioning of India and created the state of Pakistan. Traversed by ethnolinguistic contestation, elite group/social class interests, and social inequalities, language policy (as was the case earlier with postcolonial India) exists in tension and ambiguity. Indeed, the provinces, having distinct languages and cultures, would suggest that historically cohesive ethnolinguistic communities can be seen, effectively, as constituting separate 'nationalities' living within the broader framework of the Pakistani 'nation' state. At the same time, other minority languages and cultures of the diverse peoples living within their boundaries, contest the cohesiveness of the 'nationalities' of the provinces or sub-states. This dialectic of diversity, cohesion, struggle and redefinition is integral to the ethnolinguistic, cultural and sociopolitical integrity of the postcolonial 'nation' state in Pakistan. With regard to political modernization, whilst the 'people-nation' (see above) represents citizens who participate in the democratic process by voting in national, regional and local elections – the social, economic, educational and linguistic infrastructure to support the development of a strong civil society, has been undermined by long periods of political and social instability, and strong forms of political control inherent in successive military regimes. The latter, ironically, in several instances, had come to power to protect the state from the excesses of corrupt civil governments. An in-depth discussion of this issue lies beyond the scope of this book. The point that I want to make here is that political modernization in this unstable and uncertain context, remains an ongoing process of struggle, of self-definition and self-identification at the level of citizen and the state. The role and status of English, the excolonial language, in education in Pakistan is discussed later in the case studies in Chapter 7.

Sub-Saharan Africa

As is evident in the discussion so far, language occupied a central position in the struggle for independence in many decolonizing countries; it represented an important identity variable around which the idea of a postcolonial nation was articulated. As was the case with India and Pakistan, most postcolonial societies throughout Sub-Saharan Africa, opted to retain the colonial language as at least one of the official languages and, in many instances, it represented the only official language. This was the case despite the fact that colonial languages did not represent the primary means of communication amongst the people, and that some people lacked fluency in them. However, as is argued in Chapter 1, the arbitrary state boundaries that emerged from the Congress in Berlin in 1885, had resulted in countries comprised of various ethnic, linguistic, and tribal minority fractions contributing to conflicts and divisions which, potentially, could destabilize the emerging postcolonial state. In this situation, adopting an excolonial language, for many represented a common language, a 'neutral' means of communication (de Varennes, 1996) which could help to overcome ethnic differences, and thus to secure national unity as well as to maintain links with the international community. Moreover, the legitimation in colonial discourse, of Africa as a 'Tower of Babel' had legitimated the belief in a common, 'neutral', language as a means of integrating the various ethnolinguistic fractions into a unified nation. In addition, in the immediate aftermath of decolonization, national leaders were influenced by the widely held belief 'that the best way to (...) quick progress was to adopt or maintain the so-called "already developed" colonial languages, as the exclusive media of education' (Mateene, 1999: 176). The drive for rapid economic growth, and societal modernization, provided the main rationale for retaining colonial languages in education, over and above, the development and mainstreaming of local African languages.

Of course, the common claim of the neutrality of excolonial languages needs to be questioned on several levels, and, especially, in relation to their continuing status as official languages within many postcolonial contexts. Languages are not neutral artifacts; they are imbued with power and authority. As is discussed above, excolonial languages are grounded in the ideology of colonialism which is, fundamentally, that of subordination and domination. Official languages are located in institutions of power including key areas of administration, the judiciary and government as well as mass communication, and the university system. Postcolonial societies, in many instances, have also retained the Western-based judiciary, systems of administration, education and governance. Embedded in these formal structures, and the practices and processes through which they are constituted, official languages form an integral part of different countries' socio-political and economic infrastructure as medium of communication, social and political discourse. Indeed, many of the western-educated political leaders throughout Sub-Saharan Africa have continued to communicate in European languages with the populace, on radio and television (Obeng and Adegbija, 1999). This reflects a powerful form of symbolic violence through which the leaders, of previously colonized societies, have perpetuated the linguistic and cultural hegemony of the colonizers.

This is implicit in Leopold Senghor, the ex-president of Senegal distinguishing between two different forms of independence, namely, what he terms 'nominal' independence and 'real' independence. Arguing that '(w)e are the spiritual sons of France and good Africans don't break their family ties' (Senghor cited in Mansour, 1993: 121) he likened 'real independence to a child's slow evolution into adulthood' (Mansour, 1993). Similarly, the Organization for African Unity (OAU) did not adopt an indigenous African language or lingua franca, with interpreters, through which to conduct its business but rather chose to use excolonial languages such as French and English (Obeng & Adegbija, 1999). This contrasts somewhat with the various formal statements of intent surrounding language and culture in successive OAU documentation including, for example:

> There is no language which is basically more suited than another to be a mainstay of science and knowledge. A language translates and expresses the lives and thoughts of men (*sic*). From the time when our development was suspended (i.e. colonialism), our cultures

> trampled underfoot and the teaching of our languages often forbidden, it has been obvious that we must double our efforts to make African languages efficient instruments for our development. (OAU, 1969; *Pan-African Cultural Manifesto*, information in brackets added)

And:

> ... it is imperative to resolutely ensure the promotion of African languages, mainstay, and media of cultural heritage in its most authentic form. (OAU, 1976, *Cultural Charter for Africa*)

Later, in 1979, the *Meeting of Experts on the Use of Regional or Sub-regional African Languages as Media of Culture and Communication with the Continent* held at Bamako, Mali, was designed to 'bring about the effective promotion of the languages in literacy training efforts, formal education, administration and political life' (OAU, 1979), and to effect co-operation amongst African states in order to promote African languages spoken in two, or more, countries. In 1986 the OAU issued its *Language Plan of Action* which aimed to promote unity and multilingualism. It resolved:

(a) to encourage each and every Member State to have a clearly defined language policy;
(b) to ensure that all languages within the boundaries of Member States are recognized and accepted as a source of mutual enrichment;
(c) to liberate the African peoples from undue reliance on the utilization of non-indigenous languages as the dominant, official languages of the state in favour of the gradual take-over of appropriate and carefully selected indigenous African languages in this domain;
(d) to ensure that African languages, by appropriate legal provision and practical promotion, assume their rightful role as the means of official communication in the public affairs of each Member State, in replacement of European languages, which have hitherto played this role;
(e) to encourage the increased use African languages as vehicles of instruction at all educational levels;
(f) to ensure that all the sectors of the political and socio-economic systems of each Member State is mobilized in such a manner that they play their due part in ensuring that the African language(s) prescribed as official language(s) assume their intended role in the shortest time possible;
(g) to foster and promote national, regional and continental linguistic unity in Africa, in the context of the multilingualism prevailing in most African countries.

This plan of action was prepared by a meeting of linguistics experts in July 1985 at the OAU Inter-African Bureau of Languages in Kampala, Uganda (Mateene, 1999). The relative failure of these initiatives, lay in the lack of guidelines for implementation, the top-down nature of the initiatives lacking grassroots involvement and, as we can see above, in the fact that the old colonial languages continued to prevail within the discourse framework of the OAU itself (see Chapter 8 for further discussion). Whilst excolonial languages might have been useful in facilitating communication in a functional sense, these actions and choices have served to reinforce the high status of excolonial languages, historically, in official discourse. The effects are powerfully ideological – the colonial linguistic hierarchy has remained largely intact. Indeed, the incorporation of excolonial languages into the quotidian practices and processes of institutions and society serves to reinforce, and reproduce, the cultural hegemony of colonialism. Imbued thus with potent social, economic, political and cultural power, excolonial languages are seen as representing symbolic capital through which it is assumed that ordinary people can accumulate social prestige and secure economic advance. In this regard, the fear that education in native African languages prohibits employment and social mobility has potent hegemonic value (Mateene, 1999). Ordinary people, consequently, have continued to place a high value on acquiring these languages, and retaining them in education as language mediums for teaching and learning. As a result, local languages as a cultural and economic resource have remained under-developed. Although many radio and television stations now transmit in a variety of local, and regional African languages, and newspapers and popular magazines are also produced in different African languages, there is a paucity of textbooks and literature being produced in African languages for the mass market (see case studies, Chapter 6). In spite of growing attention amongst international donors, the dearth of high quality learning materials remains a matter of serious concern (Brock-Utne, 2000; Montagnes, 2000). Educationally, this is regrettable since the availability of books has been shown to be the single most consistently positive school factor in predicting academic achievement (Lockheed, 1993; Henevald & Craig, 1996). Unequal supply and distribution as well as lack of quality of language teaching and learning resources influence not only who can access information and knowledge but, ultimately, also who can participate in discourse within different domains of power.

Politically, the continued use of European languages in parliament, and local or district government has served to distance the majority of the people further from taking active part in public proceedings. This undermines possibilities for building a strong civil society. Obeng and Adegbija express the view that:

> Although in some countries competence in a European language is no longer a requirement for active participation in high levels of government, government business continues to be done primarily in the European languages. This by implication suggests that politicians or potential politicians without communicative competence in an official language are officially still excluded from holding political office. (Obeng & Adegbija, 1999: 360)

This, in effect, prevents effective political representation of rural communities, since only those with the requisite language skills and cultural capital, would be able to hold political office. Indeed, those who are elected might not necessarily be the most suitable candidates in relation to providing voice to the experiences of rural communities, and to articulate their concerns in a meaningful way. Although some improvements have taken place, generally, with regard to civic representation, the continued predominance of proto-elites in government indicates that the divide between elite groups and ordinary citizens, to a significant extent, has remained intact in many postcolonial societies throughout the region.

Summary

What then has been the impact of language on political modernization, at least for the postcolonial societies discussed here? Although local languages feature centrally in the discourse on nationhood, colonial languages have continued to be emphasized as key elements of modernity. Thus they continue to represent social and economic progress and, implicitly, access to life chances and upward social mobility. Their retention within the social and political infrastructure has meant that they have retained their political and economic exchange power. They, largely, have continued to shape the aspirations, expectations, hopes, dreams and desires of postcolonial citizens with regard to obtaining a job within the national and international labour market. Moreover, whilst policy often advocates language maintenance, the gap between policy principles and implementation has remained wide in most of the societies discussed here.

Modernization and human resource development: Issues of language and literacy

As could be seen in the discussion above, language and education played a central role in the postcolonial state's policy drive for economic and societal modernization. Derived from the concept of social modernization that occurred during the development of capitalism in Western Europe during the 18th and 19th centuries, modernization underscored industrialization and urbanization, the weakening of traditional ties and the development of the political construct of the secular modern nation state. Scientific and technological modernization underpinned the accelerated economic growth model of development which emphasized the need to increase levels of the Gross National Product (GNP) through higher levels of productivity facilitated by the maximization of human capital. Human capital theory as applied to education for development originated within the discourse of Theodore Schultz, the American agricultural economist. Schultz (1963: 10) argued that 'the economic value of education rests on the proposition that people enhance their capabilities as producers and as consumers by investing in themselves and that schooling is the largest investment in human capital'. The idea was that higher levels of investment in human capital would ultimately yield dividends within the labour market. During the period of decolonization, investment in education, viewed in modernization discourse as investing in human capital, became the primary basis of securing economic growth. Language and literacy were implicated in the development of skills and knowledge amongst the labour force, thus stimulating possibilities for increased production, raised incomes as well as economic and social mobility. The underlying principles of modernization theory included the drive for rapid technological and scientific development in order to 'catch-up' with the already industrialized economies of the developed world (Morley & Rassool, 1999).

Within the discourse of UNESCO, the 1960s were declared the First Development Decade, the beginnings of postcolonial economic, political and cultural development. However, 'political sovereignty did not necessarily bring with it economic independence' (Bernstein, 1983: 221). Instead postcolonial development took place within the context of crisis in the international capitalist economy. The post-war economic boom of the 1950s and 1960s came to an end in 1974 following the OPEC oil crisis of 1973, catapulting the world into a deep recession. This had a particularly negative effect on emerging postcolonial societies who had borrowed heavily from the World Bank/IMF to sustain development initiatives. Many postcolonial countries had accrued debts to the level of 38% of the GNP, and with falling commodity prices, high levels of inflation and a decrease in export markets many were unable to service their debts.

By the 1980s World Bank loans were tied in with stringent controls or conditionalities through its Structural Adjustment Programmes (SAPs).

These macroeconomic management strategies were aimed at reducing imbalances in the economy and correcting policy biases to establish the basis for sustained economic growth. Within the neo-liberal policy framework of the World Bank, this involved market and price liberalization, monetarist fiscal policy, and currency devaluation to support exports. Thus whilst many postcolonial societies adopted models of government based on socialist centralization, their development priorities were shaped by external influences inherent in the funding processes of the World Bank/IMF. Postcolonial societies were therefore from the beginning, part of the global political and economic landscape in which they were set in competition with other, more powerful, states. And thus the unequal power relations of colonialism were perpetuated.

Other political outcomes, for example, the predominance of one-party states in many Sub-Saharan countries, resulted in unequal representation for the different ethnolinguistic groups. This, combined with the history of political instability amongst different language groups, subsequently contributed to ethnic conflict throughout various regions. Moreover, dogged by military rulers, frequent *coup d'états* and civil wars during the 1970s and 1980s, many postcolonial societies, especially those throughout the Sub-Saharan region, were in a state of sustained economic, social and political crisis. Consequently, their development trajectories are significantly different from those of the modern nation states of Western Europe that emerged during the period of the Enlightenment. As we could see in the discussion earlier, the Western European nation state had emerged as part of a self-defining process within the context of the burgeoning industrial capitalism, and, on the capital derived from colonial trade, could build a cohesive social infrastructure. This included the introduction of state-sponsored mass schooling to meet the skills and knowledge needs of the developing capitalist economy and civil society. This was not the case in emerging postcolonial societies where a history of under-investment in education and social infrastructure had resulted in an under-developed human resource base in relation to both the labour market and civil society. Postcolonial societies therefore had multiple needs to address urgently as necessary prerequisites for social development to be able to take place.

As was the case with the project of building the nation state in 19th-century Western Europe, policy drives for cultural homogenization and having a common language were central also to the postcolonial development paradigm. Seemingly then, modernization engenders assimilation. Education in ex-colonial languages both ideologically, and in practice, constitutes learning through the medium of a foreign language. Although local languages do feature in primary education, they are not used as languages of teaching and learning in secondary and tertiary education. This signifies continuity of erstwhile colonial educational policy and practice. In consequence, 'whilst language is supposed to help in bringing education closer to the learner, (. . .) the lack of integration of educational goals with the cultural context and African values has contributed to the present educational crisis in Africa, in which education is geared mainly to the (re)production of ruling elites' (Hameso, 1997: 5). In this sense, it could be argued that the mirror image of postcolonial development reflects a copy of the colonial master in language, aspirations, and disposition and, as such, the postcolonial imaginary is self-negating. The ideology of excolonial languages in relation to their historical legacies as well as their potential impact on shaping worldviews or cultural hegemonies remains of major importance in the debate about the relationship between language and social and economic development in postcolonial societies. Overall, the debate about linguistic diversity and its role in education as an economic resource, its centrality to the development of civil society, and the possibilities for cultural transmission has remained at the margin of political discourse. These issues are discussed again in the case studies in Chapters 5, 6, 7 and also in Chapter 8.

Conclusion

This chapter argued that postcolonial societies as politically independent, sovereign states entered the global arena at considerable political, economic and cultural disadvantage. Much of this can be ascribed to the cumulative structural and cultural effects of colonial policy and practice on colonized societies over a sustained period of time. Colonial policies had ensured that there was no direct link between modern and traditional economic, sociocultural and political structures. Social structures, practices and processes put into place within the colonies were based primarily on those that had evolved historically within Western Europe. Moreover, as can be seen in Chapter 1, 19th-century colonialism was steeped in the ideology of the intrinsic cultural, 'racial', political and economic 'superiority' of Western European societies. Accordingly, the structures, practices and processes put into place within the colonies did not build on the knowledges, or the ways of knowing and doing intrinsic to the social organization; its traditional cultural base. They were foreign constructions imposed on societies having their own distinctive cultural histories, languages and ways of life. Colonial regimes did not develop the social and political infrastructure; neither did they harness the complex cultural networks through which local ways of life had been sustained historically.

They did, however, ensure the development of a powerful military machine dependent on imported technology (Elaigwu and Mazrui, 2003), and arms expenditure constituted a major portion of the colonial state's budget. The hegemony of the coercive state is an enduring legacy of colonialism as is evident in the proliferation of military regimes in many postcolonial societies, as is the case in Sub-Saharan Africa and South Asia.

Furthermore, instead of encouraging local production, colonial capitalism had ensured that colonies became captive import markets for goods for everyday consumption such as food products, candles, soap, and matches manufactured within metropolitan countries (Adu Boahen, 2003). Colonies, in turn, became major exporters of raw materials and other cash crops suited for the export market. This prevented many countries, particularly throughout the Sub-Saharan region, from developing the capacity for agricultural production to sustain their own populations. Under-development and unequal trade relations were therefore integral to the colonial project.

By the time of decolonization during the 1960s a new political and economic dynamic had already been established within the global terrain. Metropolitan states were not only disengaging politically from their colonies; they were also doing so economically. They were starting to move away from trading with primary producing countries located within their excolonies. Instead, excolonial states were placing greater reliance on cheap synthetic raw materials produced in industrialized countries. This realignment of metropolitan import markets, in favour of European states, had a devastating effect on the already underdeveloped economies of emerging postcolonial states. By now many were suffering from imbalances across different sectors of the economy, for example, the predominance of agricultural production dependent on export markets and, related to this, agriculture as the major provider of employment. These factors, combined with the high level of state investment required to develop a self-sustaining social infrastructure including, for example, housing, education, health and transport systems, presented major problems to the burgeoning postcolonial state. It was therefore not surprising that postcolonial countries entered the international arena with qualitatively lower levels of GNP, in comparison with their industrialized counterparts in the west. Together, these factors give some indication of the negative effects that the systematized underdevelopment of human and cultural resources had on the potential of postcolonial societies to sustain economic, political and social development as sovereign states operating within an increasingly international global cultural economy.

Whilst many postcolonial societies inspired by Marxist revolutionary theories adopted models of government based on socialist centralization, their development priorities were shaped by external influences inherent in the funding processes of the World Bank/IMF. Postcolonial economies were thus, from the beginning, part of the global political and economic landscape, in which they had to compete with other politically and economically more powerful states. This means that they were unable to disengage fully from the excolonial state; thus the cultural and economic dependencies set up during the colonial period were perpetuated.

Colonial language relations represented subtle means of control contributing to cultural disadvantage within postcolonial societies. Language plays an important role in the transmission of culture including group/social values, beliefs and aspirations – and, therefore, the ways in which societies historically produce and reproduce themselves. As such it is, simultaneously, a potent identity variable, and a source of cultural power. Linguistic imperialism (Phillipson, 1992, 1997) ensured that local cultural traditions and aspirations were replaced by the cultural hegemony, the values and belief system of the colonial 'mother country'. The effect of this was that by the end of the colonial period most of the new local political leadership, even though they might have engaged in anticolonial struggle were, nevertheless, imbued with a Western European cultural outlook and belief system. Many of them became advocates for retaining colonial languages within formal, official domains. Evidently then, since many of them were alienated from their own cultural roots, they devalued their own cultural languages, beliefs and values, and gazed upon Europe as the ultimate cultural source and model of modernization. Since colonial education generally took place in languages that were not an integral part of the 'social character'[2] (Williams, 1961: 3) it not only marginalized local languages, it also undermined the social, cultural and educational experience of learners. As can be seen again in the case studies in Chapters 5, 6 and 7, excolonial languages in most instances came to share equal status with national languages in most postcolonial contexts. In many instances, local languages were relegated largely to informal domains. Thus they have remained under-developed as cultural, political and economic resources.

Fifty years after decolonization, it is evident that retaining excolonial languages as the medium for official discourse did not empower postcolonial societies, nor did it facilitate their integration into the international system of nation states as equal partners. Instead, they are screened out economically by unequal trade agreements within the context of key defining economic/political ensembles such as the World Trade Organization (WTO), North American Free Trade Agreement (NAFTA) and the European Union (EU) (see also Chapter 8). Where local languages *were* used in education during the early years of postcolonial development, as was the case in Tanzania and Madagascar, they now have been replaced by the excolonial language (Prah, 2000). This is common practice at higher levels of education, for example, secondary school where learners have to make the transition to excolonial languages as mediums of teaching and learning. Excolonial languages then act as powerful screening mechanisms with regard to access to appropriate levels of cultural capital to be exchanged within the labour market. The availability of appropriately skilled workers, in turn, impact on national income. In other words, although language in itself is not responsible for national development or under-development, it does play an important role in contributing to the cultural capital that a society has available to exchange within the global labour market. Languages used in education, also demarcate those who have access to high status knowledges, and thus occupy powerful positions within society.

However, this is not to argue that learning and teaching should take place only in African or South Asian languages to the exclusion of ex-colonial languages and, particularly, English. Postcolonial societies are locked into the international system comprised of interlocking, interdependent, politically defined nation states grounded in competitive economic processes. It follows then that education for development does need to take account also of the significant role that some languages, notably English, play within the global cultural economy. These issues are discussed in further detail in Chapter 3, and again in Chapter 8.

Notes

1. Acculturation refers to the modification of a culture through contact with another, different, culture; people are socialized into the beliefs, values, awarenesses and behaviours of the dominant culture. It is a complex process involving different levels of destruction, domination, resistance, accommodation and incorporation.
2. Williams (1961: 146) defines the 'social character' as constituting not only behavioural norms and attitudes but also 'a particular system of values, in the field of group loyalty, authority, justice, and living purposes.

Chapter 3

The Global Cultural Economy: Issues of Language, Culture and Politics

This chapter examines the complex geopolitical[1] arena within which language operates in the contemporary world. The aim here is to examine the ways in which technological, economic, cultural and political shifts taking place within the global terrain, intersect with the legacies of colonialism within developing countries. Maintaining the focus on past-present influences adopted in Chapters 1 and 2, the discussion begins with a critical assessment of the concept, practices, processes and discourses of globalization within an historical perspective.

What is Globalization?

The concept of globalization as a political, economic, and cultural process is not new. As we could see in Chapters 1 and 2, colonialism represented a globalizing process, *par excellence*, disrupting as it did economic, political and cultural relations of discrete polities, and supplanting them with those of the external colonial state. Colonialism as a political, economic, and cultural force laid claim to territories, subjugated peoples, their cultures and languages, and restructured colonized polities and economies in the name, and interest, of predatory colonial 'super-states'. The colonial project was motivated, to a significant extent, by the drive for modernization, the rise of capitalism, the production needs of industrialization and the need to expand markets. Moreover, colonial rule enabled the political power of the colonizing state to be extended to colonies governed locally by subcolonial states – thus setting up a two-tier system of domination and control as the over-riding mode of governance. Colonial conquest secured almost unlimited economic and political power for colonizing states.

Colonialism and development

As is argued in Chapter 2, the large-scale, and long-term, oppression and exploitation of colonial rule facilitated the modernization of Western European imperial states. In other words, these states not only governed the colonies, but also became the locus of development benefiting either directly, or indirectly, from the economic exploitation of the colonies. Some of the major benefits included the modernization of the infrastructure of both state and society within colonizing states, particularly, France and Britain. Provision of resources to facilitate the introduction of compulsory mass schooling – and through this to strengthen civil society[2] (Williams, 1961) – helped to put into place important building blocks for the Western European liberal democratic nation state during the late 19th century. Increased levels of individual and societal literacy enabled colonizing states to accommodate the skilled and semi-skilled labour requirements of the burgeoning industrial economy.

Modernization also extended to the colonies, allowing social, economic and political infrastructures to be put into place, mainly in urban areas where they served to facilitate governance and the colonial trade. However, the infrastructures put in place, did not support the economic and political enfranchisement of colonized peoples, as is often assumed in discussions of the inherent benefits of colonialism. Colonialism's broad sphere of influence within countries across the world ensured that the Western European model of development, ultimately, became the universal definer of social, economic and political progress throughout the colonies. In the process, local cultures, social and political ways of life, and historically grounded infrastructures were subjugated and, in some cases, completely eradicated. Globalization during this timeframe (i.e. the ideology, practices and processes of colonialism) effectively set in train the systematic political, economic and cultural disfranchisement of colonized peoples – and, *de facto*, the historical process of structured under-development in colonized polities. Language played a key role in this process.

Linguistic and cultural imperialism

Again, as is discussed in Chapters 1 and 2, the languages of colonizing states represented official languages within the colonies. They played a major role in integrating colonized peoples into a common worldview, grounded in a belief of the inherent superiority of the colonial rulers and their cultures. Although colonial languages were not always imposed, the fact that they predominated in formal sociocultural, economic and political domains, imbued them with significant economic and symbolic power. Their incorporation into the technologies, processes and procedures of social and political institutions, allowed linguistic norms to be established within society and culture. Chapters 2 and 6 provide some insight into the ways in which hegemonic forms of control captured the imagination, and penetrated the consciousness of many colonized peoples – and in doing so – contributed very powerfully to symbolic violence (Bourdieu, 1991).[3]

Language in education also played an important role in facilitating colonial governance. In providing the vehicle through which selected forms of cultural knowledge and awarenesses were developed, colonial languages mediated a hegemonic consciousness grounded in mental subordination to colonial culture, and the power of the colonial state. Where they were integrated into educational processes and institutions, colonial languages served the hegemonic function of, at least subliminally, capturing 'the mental universe of the colonized, the control, through culture, of how people perceived themselves and their relationship to the world' (Ngũgĩ, 1993: 442). Implicity then, it sought to render colonized peoples as compliant, docile bodies. These factors represent the essence of 'governmentality' (Foucault, 1991). However, this is not to argue that these meanings succeeded entirely in securing docile subjects, that there was no contestation of colonial hegemony, or selective adaptation. In many instances, on group and individual level, colonial meanings were reinterpreted, reworked, and incorporated into an alternative ideological framework centred on self-empowerment. Aspects of contestation, redefinition and reflexive self-definition in relation to language choice and language use will be discussed later in Chapter 8.

Yet, at the same time, there *is* a dialogical relationship between the discourses of colonialism, and the contemporary phase of globalization. Meanings constructed around the inherent social, cultural, economic and political superiority of Western culture and politics, have been circulating historically within discursive policy terrains, notably, within colonial policy frameworks.

Intertextuality

As was the case with the development of industrial capitalism in Western Europe during the 19th century, the current phase of capitalist expansion is grounded in discursive forms of power, extending beyond the nation state. This is represented, for example, in the globalization of international trade, financial and commodity markets as well as the export of language and culture on a global scale. Continuous interconnectedness between countries and continents, at different levels, is a defining aspect of the new phase of globalization. Supported by symbolic (e.g. world languages) and physical infrastructure (e.g. transport, information or banking systems) facilitated by microelectronics technology, states and societies are becoming 'increasingly enmeshed in worldwide systems and networks of interaction' (Held and McGrew, 2003: 3). As such, dynamic flows of people, trade and capital as well as the global diffusion of culture through mass communication practices and processes have engendered new space-time geometries (Castells, 1996; Held and McGrew, 2003). These factors support the argument that language and communication practices and processes, lie at the centre of the interactive global cultural economy. Discussing this further, the next section begins to outline the contours of the interactive global cultural economy, in the aftermath of the world economic crisis of the early 1970s (see also Chapter 2). The latter refers to the period of fundamental economic and social restructuring that took place in many industrialized countries, in order to manage their particular national economic crisis.[4] This discussion highlights significant macro-level change processes during the late 1970s, and identifies key aspects of the global cultural economy.

Mapping the Global Cultural Economy

By the late 1970s many governments in industrialized countries, *inter alia*, the Conservative Government in the UK, and the Republican Administration in the US, were beginning to adopt a radically new approach to economic management as a means of boosting stagnant economies. Neo-liberalism emphasizes the free-market as primary regulatory mechanism, and argues for minimal state intervention in the economy (Friedman, 1982; Hayek, 1978). The ascendancy of neo-liberal ideology within many industrialized societies in the west, at the time, coincided with the emergence of new microelectronics technology effecting fundamental changes within the economy, culture and society. New flexible production regimes facilitated by microelectronics technology enabled mass production of low cost, differentiated, quality commodities to be sold to an increasingly discerning consumer base within the global market (Rassool, 1993, 1999). The capacity of the new technology to facilitate rapid capital transfer altered international banking and commodity markets, generating the development of flexible capital accumulation strategies able to operate across different countries and continents (Castells, 1996; Hoogvelt, 2001). This includes organic international trade taking place on financial markets, banking and commodity markets. Together, these developments heralded a new discursive phase of capital accumulation for countries that had the necessary social (e.g. business and trade networks) and cultural capital (e.g. high skills levels) as well as a political and economic infrastructure enabling them to participate within the redefined global economy.

What distinguishes this new phase of globalization from earlier epochs, are not only the organic forms of financial and cultural exchange made possible by microelectronics technology, but also the *speed* at which this can take place across countries and continents. Together, these developments have reshaped the economic, cultural and political basis of industrialized societies, catapulting them into a dynamic, interactive, global cultural economy. However, as can be seen below, this seemingly unfettered capital accumulation process has built-in inequalities. This is the case, particularly, in relation to development possibilities within countries having fewer linguistic, cultural and economic assets, and capabilities that can be exchanged within the global market.

There also are broader changes that have taken place altering, fundamentally, the way in which countries are represented within the global terrain. Of significance to the discussion here, are the ways in which the emergence of global political, cultural and economic networks, practices and institutions have transformed the distribution, organization and exercise of power.

Transnational governance and economic relations

The rapid production of a diversity of quality goods at competitive prices, and the infrastructure to transport goods, capital and services securely, and quickly, across countries and continents, have contributed to the fact that national economies are locked into a highly competitive global market. In order to increase their market share as well as to buffet themselves against shocks in the market, national states have increasingly opted for integration into larger regional economic power blocs (e.g. the European Union [EU], Common Market for Eastern and Southern Africa [COMESA] and the Economic Community of West African States [ECOWAS]). These, together with the predominance of strategic global economic regulatory institutions (e.g. World Bank/IMF, WTO), have decentred the nation state as the primary locus of economic power. Table 3.1 provides a schematic overview of important globalizing processes and institutions within the global cultural economy.

The examples in Table 3.1, give an indication of the extent that the global terrain is defined by a diverse range of political and economic communities existing within a complex, interlocking network of power relations extending across national boundaries. Looked at from the

Major Protracted Refugee Situations[1]

Table 3.1 Examples of major political and economic definers in the global economy

Globalizing institution/ processes	*Examples*	*Roles/functions*
Transnational Corporations	Microsoft McDonalds British Petroleum Toyota Union Carbide	Private economic institutions dominating investment, business, manufacturing production, and trade in countries throughout the world
International Financial Institutions (IFIs)	International Monetary Fund World Bank	Global macroeconomic management. Regulate and provide financial aid for development projects within countries experiencing balance-of-payment difficulties; nominally, promote financial stability and liberal trade within the global economy by imposing market-driven policies on domestic economies
Global Informational and Capital Networks	Internet International Stock Exchanges International Mass Media International Banking	Facilitate information, cultural and capital flows within and across countries and continents
International Free Trade Organizations and Agreements	World Trade Organization (WTO) Organization for Economic Cooperation and Development (OECD)	Trade regulation – emphasis on removal of exchange restrictions and tariff reduction on goods and services including intellectual property rights to facilitate investment as well as trade across national borders – obtained through complex trade negotiations

(*Continued*)

Table 3.1 *Continued*

Globalizing institution/ processes	***Examples***	***Roles/functions***
	General Agreement on Trade and Tariffs (GATT) Regional Trade Agreements	
International and Regional Political Systems/ Organizations and Economic Power Blocs	United Nations Organization (UN)	Comprises at least 15 agencies involved in human rights, fostering cooperation and social, cultural, economic development of nations; other concerns include the environment, poverty reduction and fighting diseases
	North Atlantic Treaty Organization (NATO)	Strategic geopolitical ensemble Maintains security of member states (North American and European) through political or military means
	European Union (EU) North American Free Trade Agreement (NAFTA) Common Market for Eastern and Southern Africa (COMESA) Economic Community of West African States (ECOWAS)	Regional Trade blocs. Facilitate regional political and/ or economic integration

perspective of industrialized pre-1994 OECD[5] (i.e. industrialized largely Western, including Japan) countries, this interactive global terrain, are regarded as having a common worldview, sharing common purposes and therefore relying on mutual cooperation. In practice, though, these contexts are in competition with each other within the economic sphere.

Neo-liberal ideology espouses a normative prescription for economic recovery, which includes the formula of privatization, trade liberalization, low inflation and the reduction of fiscal deficits. Implicit in this economic policy formula, is the assumption that the path of development is the same for every country. It takes for granted that countries already have established coherent social, legal, political and economic infrastructures. The discussion below highlights the extent to which these meanings contrast with existing realities within developing countries.

The neo-liberal policies of the World Bank/IMF, centred on fostering macroeconomic stability by controlling inflation, reducing fiscal deficits, deregulating markets and introducing trade liberalization, have had a major impact on social policy frameworks within developing countries. Neo-liberal policies have been transferred to developing countries since at least the early 1980s, through the structural adjustment programmes (SAPs) of the World Bank/IMF. The underlying principle was that only those countries that subscribed to neo-liberal policies, would invite foreign direct investment (FDI), and through this, countries would be able to procure access to global markets and technology. These policy meanings were given global scope in the discourse of the 'Washington Consensus'[6] (Williamson, 1993). The incorporation of the principles of the 'Washington Consensus' into the WTO discourse framework, consolidated the shift to a neo-liberal economic policy approach underpinning a *globalized* development paradigm. As is argued earlier, it advances a formulaic solution to the diverse problems within a global cultural economy, which is constituted in discursive histories, cultures and power relations.

The primacy of the market as regulatory mechanism, decreasing the role of the state in the economy, and creating 'a free-market economy', represents an important tenet of neo-liberalism. Another key principle is that markets are neutral and fair regulatory mechanisms. In practice though, they are complex constructions operating within a discursive and inherently unequal terrain.

Market irrationalities

The idea of the market represents 'a social protocol that structures labour, consumption, leisure, and many forms of custom and culture'

(Harrison, 2004: 1039). In practice, this means that markets are constituted in a complex set of social and power relations. Markets also differ according to their contexts, and the interests or 'needs' that drive them. According to Harrison

> Real markets only exist because social groups engage with them. This is not merely that people enter the market as buyers and sellers of commodities and labour power; it is also that people enter markets as representatives of corporate bodies or social groups/classes. (...) (Harrison, 2004: 1040)

Markets then are socially produced. Grounded in social, political, economic and cultural practices and processes they are constituted in discursive power relations – and thus, they are not neutral mechanisms.

Labour markets interface with equity issues in different ways. For example,

- those who are employed;
- those who are not employed;
- those who are employable;
- those who are unemployable;
- those who have different income levels; and
- differential conditions, and terms of employment, extended to workers in different sectors.

Worker employability depends on the cultural assets and capabilities, including the skills, knowledge and languages that can be translated into purchasing power (Nayyar, 2002), or can be exchanged within national as well as international labour markets. Markets also are underscored by power interests. This is reflected, for instance, in barriers of entry set up in international trade agreements in which powerful states fix markets, or erect barriers to trade, to serve their own national interests.

What these arguments highlight is that the market is imbued with an ideology grounded in economic expediency. They also highlight that in relation to economic globalization, there is no level playing field. 'Free' trade agreements emerging from negotiations within the framework of, for example, NAFTA and the WTO largely benefit the advanced economies of already powerful countries (see also GATS in Chapter 8). This unfair trade agenda resulting in inequitable trade subsidies, opening up markets to the products of industrialized countries, whilst closing theirs to the products of poorer countries, has exacerbated trade deficits especially throughout the Sub-Saharan region (Stiglitz, 2002). This, in turn, results in lower levels in the gross domestic product (GDP) of developing countries and, therefore, influence possibilities for social development and, subsequently, their ability to repay their debts. As a result, they are caught in a relentless debt and poverty trap. This globalized development policy approach, has had devastating effects on the sociocultural and economic base of many postcolonial societies. Issues related to *linguistic markets* within the global cultural economy, will be discussed in Chapter 4.

In contrast to the prevailing emphasis on market driven economic development within the World Bank/IMF and the WTO, the UN agencies embody the principles of human rights, education and culture. Focused mainly on social aspects of development, their emphasis is on promoting co-operation, sharing and partnership. The United Nations Educational, Scientific and Cultural Organization (UNESCO), historically, has played a key role in initiating, and funding, language and literacy projects and programmes. Of these, the *Experimental World Literacy Programme* (EWLP) (1969–1971), the UNESCO *World Languages Report* (2001) and the UNESCO supported project *International Clearinghouse of Endangered Languages* (Skutnabb-Kangas, 2000) represent major initiatives. Similarly, the United Nations High Commissioner for Refugees (UNHCR) and the United Nations Children's Fund (UNICEF) are underpinned by humanitarian principles centred on fostering the human rights of children. In addition, there are other significant UN organizations working in the social and cultural sphere, including the UN Permanent Forum on Indigenous Issues, and UNESCO initiatives such as its Convention on Cultural Diversity.

Within dominant discourse, globalization[7] is represented as a neutral process constituting a free-flow of people, capital, culture and resources within a homogeneous, integrated, cohesive global 'space'. In practice though, as is indicated above, the concept of globalization *per se* exists in tension. As was the case with the previous phase of globalization (i.e. colonialism) it is contested on different levels and within various arenas.

Contesting globalization

National identity

Held and McGrew (2003: 41) suggest that whilst 'governance is becoming increasingly a multilevel, intricately institutionalized and spatially dispersed activity, representation, loyalty and identity remain stubbornly rooted in traditional ethnic, regional and national communities'. In Europe this is the case, for example, in the reassertion of nationalism in contemporary Wales, Catalonia and the Basque region in Spain as well as tensions between individual European states, in spite of the formation of the European Union. In this sense, the idea of the European Union as a cohesive economic bloc exists in tension. On the other hand, the breakdown of the Socialist Eastern Bloc has resulted in the separation of Czechoslovakia into the, respectively, Czech and the Slovak Republics. Similarly, the former Soviet Union divided into fifteen autonomous states,[8] whilst the former Yugoslavia dissolved into five autonomous states.[9] There are ongoing struggles for independence amongst minority peoples throughout this region. Many of these, are articulated around the issue of language and national identity, as is the case with the Chuvash, Bashkirs, Tatars and Mari in the contemporary Russian Federation.[10] Germany and Yemen, on the other hand, were reunified after years of existing as separate sovereign states (Docquier & Marfouk, 2004).

In the case of Sub-Saharan Africa, many postcolonial states have been riven by political conflict. Many of these situations, at least in part, are connected with the arbitrary state boundaries drawn in the Scramble for Africa (1884/1885), or in the case of South Asia, at the partitioning of India (1947) discussed in Chapters 1 and 2. As a result of intermittent social and political conflict, many countries within the Sub-Saharan region (e.g. Democratic Republic of Congo, Rwanda/Burundi) and in South Asia (e.g. Kashmir, Pakistan[11]) have remained economically fragile, and politically unstable. These examples give credence to the argument that different sets of changes are taking place within the global terrain, and that each of these, are driven by their own particular historical, social and geopolitical circumstances. Together, these factors fracture the idea of a stable, cohesive, integrated global cultural economy.

The notion of economic globalization is contested also by Hirst and Thompson (2004), who argue that the idea of free capital markets and capital flows is fundamentally flawed. These writers suggest that the major economic powers, including the G3 economies, namely, Japan, Europe and the US have the capacity 'to exert powerful governance pressures over financial markets and other economic tendencies' (Hirst & Thompson, 2004: 2). There is some evidence to support this argument in my earlier discussion of the impact of the WTO and the World Bank/IMF on policy directions, and their influence on shaping national development possibilities within developing countries. There is also further evidence to support Hirst and Thompson's argument in the critique provided earlier in the chapter, of the inequalities that inhere in the power dynamic of the market itself. It was argued then that the neo-liberal emphasis on the primacy of the market can reinforce inequalities, marginalization and exclusion of countries, resources, language and culture and people. This confirms the argument made earlier that the notion of a coherent, homogeneous, and stable global cultural economy exists in tension. It is contested also by political reassertions of nationalism in different parts of the world, the building of regional political/economic power blocs as well as unequal international trade relations.

Transnational power ensembles

On this evidence then, economic globalization is asymmetrical and inherently contradictory. For example, the WTO discourse portrays its primary role as being to ratify international trade agreements between countries and regions, at least theoretically, aiming to create a level playing field. Yet, in practice, the WTO is also 'involved in the supply of services through the presence of commercial enterprises in foreign countries' (Shukla, 2002: 267), authorizing it to enter the domestic policy terrain on a variety of issues. This means that it cannot be seen as a neutral force. Moreover, global economic institutions such as the World Bank/IMF, as well as biases inherent in regional and international trade agreements, pursue narrow power interests. They serve primarily to legitimate the models of development of Western advanced economies which, in turn, often conflict with traditional cultural mores, traditional patterns of language use, as well as development needs and priorities within poorer countries.

As is discussed above, transnational power ensembles such as the Organization for Economic Co-operation and Development (OECD), World Bank, International Monetary Fund (IMF), and the World Trade Organization (WTO) represent global structures of economic regulation. However, given the extent of their influence on national economic policies they, indirectly, also represent global processes of political governance. The increasing involvement of supranational agencies such as the World Bank/IMF within national policy arenas, have altered the institutions of governance within some nation states, subordinating them to the exigencies of these external powers. Regarding the impact of World Bank/IMF structural adjustment programmes on developing countries:

> (d)ebtor nations forego economic sovereignty and control over fiscal and monetary policy, the Central Banks and the Ministry of Finance are reorganised (often with the complicity of the local bureaucracies), state institutions are undone and an 'economic' 'tutelage' is installed. A 'parallel government' which bypasses civil society is established by the international financial institutions. (Chossudovsky, 1997: 35)

As such, new global networks of power providing legitimacy to selective perspectives of progress and development are challenging the sovereignty of the modern nation state. In the case of postcolonial/developing countries, globalized forms of power playing a key role in influencing, or rather, defining national development policy, serve to undermine the role of the state. Thus they call into question the basis of governance within those societies.

Cultural hegemony

Furthermore, the large scale export of, mostly American, commodity culture through a globalized mass media has consolidated the hegemony of Western consumerism in which people (despite their differential levels of income and social conditions) aspire to, largely, ephemeral needs and wants within an ever-evolving global consumer market. Projected into people's everyday lives via multimedia mass communication technologies (e.g. the Internet, satellite, digital and cable television networks), it has the potential to reshape individual, and collective cultural aspirations within poor countries, orienting their gaze towards the economically advanced North, and away from their own cultural knowledges, values and linguistic heritage. Such shifts in cultural aspirations reflect broader economic and political power imbalances. As was the case with the growth of commodity markets and the rise of a mass consumer culture during the period of industrial capitalism[12] – at least until the crisis of Fordism during the 1970s – it also plays an important role in shaping the needs, wants and desires of consumers living within a commercially fetishized, politically and economically 'benign global community'. The latter thus represents a de-ideologized cultural space. In practice though, as is discussed earlier, inequalities often are *created* within the very processes of globalization (Massey, 1999). Implicit in the globalization process is the potential for exclusion, marginalization and polarization because investment resources, growth and modern technology tend to be concentrated in a few (industrialized) countries (Khor, 2001). Many countries, particularly those throughout the Sub-Saharan region, lack the levels of human resource power and the quality of social, economic and political infrastructure needed to support modern forms of development.

Table 3.2 highlights the *economic* aspects of globalization. In order to obtain a broader perspective of changes taking place within the global cultural economy, I now turn to another significant globalizing process, namely, the continuous transmigration of peoples across countries and continents. Again, transmigration is not a new phenomenon. Transmigration and the creation of ethnolinguistic diasporas which, in turn, alter the sociolinguistic and cultural base of the adoptive socio-political context is intrinsic to the human experience. For example, during the period of the 1880s (i.e. around the time of the Scramble for Africa, and Macauley's

Table 3.2 Key issues related to the concept of economic globalization

• Globalization is not new. It is intertextually linked with previous globalizing processes including successive colonialisms, for example, the period of colonialism that coincided with industrial capitalism during the late nineteenth century – until decolonization in the 1950s. Language played an important role in the political, hegemonic and economic project of colonialism. • Contemporary globalization is grounded in interconnectedness made possible by microelectronics technology. The interactive nature of the global cultural economy places language and communication at the centre of the new development paradigm. • Globalization is constituted in discursive forms of power that reside within transnational institutions such as the World Bank/IMF, the WTO and transnational corporations. The ideology of neo-liberalism embedded within these organizations is transferred to the socio-political and economic base of individual countries within the global terrain. This has had a deleterious effect on possibilities for economic and social progress in developing countries. Some of this relates to the inherent inequality of the market mechanism. Transnational agencies such as the World Bank/IMF and the WTO not only exercise economic regulatory power but also governance globally. These factors impact on development possibilities in individual countries. • Globalization is a contested concept; it exists in tension and contradictions.

Education Minute in India discussed in Chapter 2), the UK represented a country with a high level of *emigration* with at least 200,000 people per year leaving for the colonies, or the US. These discursive people flows effectively created an English language diaspora. Since English represented the official language of colonial governance and trade, it assumed a position of power and status[13] within the colonies. As could be seen in Chapters 1 and 2 the influence, historically, of this English diaspora on the cultural base of colonial and subsequently postcolonial societies, has been significant. At the same time, as is discussed in Chapter 2, African ethnolinguistic diasporas were generated within neighbouring countries throughout the Sub-Saharan region as a result of the boundaries drawn at the Congress of Berlin in 1885. These generated complex language tapestries within the new, reconstituted, political entities.

Transmigration

Postcolonial transmigration

The creation of new transnational ethnolinguistic diasporas were intensified again during the period of *decolonization* in the 1960s, when refugees fled to neighbouring countries throughout the Sub-Saharan region. Refugees from northern Angola fled to the Republic of Congo, from eastern and southern Angola they fled to Zambia and Botswana, and from Mozambique people migrated to Tanzania and Zambia (UNHCR, 2000). Similarly, Ewe refugees from Ghana fled to Togo after the plan to reunite those who had been split between Ghana and Togo during the late nineteenth century, failed. Civil wars in the Republic of Congo resulted in people fleeing to various countries including the Central African Republic, Burundi, Sudan, Uganda and Tanzania (UNCHR, 2000). Others fled elsewhere, to Europe, and the United States. Chapter 2 also discussed the ethnolinguistic diasporas created within the newly formed Pakistan, as a result of the transmigration of diverse groups of people from India, in the wake of Partition in 1947. Elsewhere in the industrialized world, the late 1940s and 1950s were marked by political refugees from, for example, Poland and Hungary fleeing Soviet occupation, settling in the West. Overall, these movements of people represented transmigration in response to a complex range of *political* factors.

The late 1950s and 1960s also marked a period of major *labour* migrations within the global terrain. Amongst these, mass transmigrations of labour took place from:

- Latin America, East and Southeast Asia to North America;
- North Africa, Southern Europe and Turkey to Western Europe (notably the different nationalities who comprised the *gastarbeiters* in Germany);
- countries across the world to the Middle Eastern Gulf states to work in the booming oil industry;
- the Caribbean Islands to the UK, invited mainly to work in the service industry, and thus to fill skills gaps in the labour market;
- Hong Kong to the UK to work in the catering industry.

In the case of Britain during this period, the arrival of immigrants from excolonial countries created a racist backlash, and generated a national debate in education about language provision for linguistic minority groups. Much of this debate centred on the 'linguistic deficits' of immigrant children in schools which were associated with cognitive, cultural and social 'deficits' (Rassool, 1998). This was followed by second and third generation settled Asians (largely Indians) in East Africa transmigrating to the UK, notably those expelled by the Idi Amin regime in Uganda as well as those migrating from Kenya. In the UK they joined other transmigratory groups, for example, the Vietnamese refugees, referred to at the time as 'boat people', consisting largely of ethnic Chinese, and later, Cambodians who had fled the Khmer Rouge – and later still, from South Africa, Chile and Argentina. Collectively, these groups represented political refugees who had been forcibly displaced as a result of sustained political conflict and instability in their countries of origin.

Transmigration has intensified in recent years, in response to various push factors within many postcolonial states, making it once again, a significant factor within the changing global context.

Transmigration and contemporary global change

In addition to capital flows, the global terrain is defined also by global flows of people comprising 'tourists, immigrants, refugees, exiles, guest-workers and other moving groups and persons' affecting 'the politics of (and between) nations to a hitherto unprecedented degree' (Appadurai, 1993: 329). Globalization discourse articulated from the perspective of economically advanced countries, depict these 'ethnoscapes' (Appadurai, 1993) as representing a dynamic free-flow of people grounded in the adoption of travel as a popular lifestyle choice related either to work or leisure pastimes. Implicit in this particular idea of cross-border movement of people and the cultural exchange that it engenders, are the notions of choice and freedom. This view contrasts somewhat with the tendency of countries in Western Europe, Australia and North America to circumscribe, through selective immigration laws, the transmigration of people from developing countries. Most of these people flows centre on pursuing jobs within economically more favourable contexts. Others are fleeing conflict, poverty, civil wars and political instability within their countries of origin. Within dominant discourses that surround contemporary flows of refugees or asylum seekers, these categories of description have been emptied of meaning. Imbued with 'otherness' linguistically and culturally, they represent the new 'enemy within' (Hall *et al.*, 1978) challenging the, socially constructed, culturally homogeneous societies in the North and, moreover, the much vaunted 'civilized' basis and economic security of 'developed' countries.

Whilst these diverse flows of people from postcolonial/developing countries to Europe, Australia and North America receive much attention in social and political discourse, the impact of transmigration on the economies and social base of *developing countries* (and their political implications) is less well publicized. This silence is significant. As can be seen below in Tables 3.3, 3.4 and 3.5 most of the world's refugees originate from, and have settled in developing countries.

Table 3.3 Protracted refugee situations

Region/country of asylum	*Origin*	*UNHCR status*		*Total*	*Percentage assisted*
		Assisted	*Not-assisted*		
Burundi	Dem. Rep. of the Congo	13,000	27,000	41,000	32%
Central African Rep	Sudan	36,000	—	36,000	100%
Chad	Sudan	55,000	55,000	110,000	50%
Dem. Rep. of Congo	Angola	43,000	81,000	120,000	36%
	Sudan	11,000	34,000	45,000	24%
Rwanda	Dem. Rep. of Congo	35, 000	—	35,000	100%
United Rep Tanzania	Burundi	320,000	170,000	490,000	65%
United Rep Tanzania	Dem of Congo	150,000	—	150,000	100%
Central Africa and Gt. Lakes		**670,000**	**370,000**	**1,000,000**	**67%**
Djibouti	Somalia	25,000	—	25,000	100%
Ethiopia	Sudan	95,000	—	95,000	100%
Kenya	Somalia	150,000	—	150,000	100%
Kenya	Sudan	63,000	—	63,000	100%
Sudan	Eritrea	73,000	35,000	110,000	66%
Uganda	Sudan	180,000	20,000	200,000	90%

(Continued)

Table 3.3 *Continued*

Region/country of asylum	*Origin*	*UNHCR status*		*Total*	*Percentage assisted*
		Assisted	*Not-assisted*		
East and Horn of Africa		**620,000**	**55,000**	**670,000**	**93%**
Zambia	Angola	72,000	87,000	160,000	45%
Zambia	Dem Rep of Congo	54,000	4,000	58,000	93%
Southern Africa		**130,000**	**91,000**	**220,000**	**59%**
Cameroon	Chad	—	39,000	39,000	0%
Côte d'Ivoire	Liberia	74,000	—	74,000	100%
Ghana	Liberia	42,000	—	42,000	100%
Guinea	Liberia	89,000	60,000	150,000	59%
Guinea	Sierra Leone	15,000	10,000	25,000	60%
West Africa		**220,000**	**110,000**	**330,000**	**67%**
AFRICA		**1,600,000**	**620,000**	**2,300,000**	**70%**
Algeria	Western Sahara	160,000	10,000	170,000	94%
Egypt	Occupied Palestinian Territory	—	70,000	70,000	0%
Iraq	Occupied Palestinian Territory	—	100,000	100,000	0%
Islamic Rep of Iran	Afghanistan[2]	830,000	—	830,000	100%
	Iraq	150,000	—	150,00	100%
Pakistan	Afghanistan[3]	1,120,000	—	1,120,000	100%
Saudi Arabia	Occupied Palestinian Territory	—	240,000	240,000	0%
Yemen	Somalia	59,000	—	59,000	100%

(Continued)

Table 3.3 *Continued*

Region/country of asylum	*Origin*	*UNHCR status*		*Total*	*Percentage assisted*
		Assisted	*Not-assisted*		
CASWANAME		**2,300,000**	**420,000**	**2,700,000**	**85%**
China	Viet Nam	11,000	290,000	300,000	4%
India	China	—	92,000	92,000	0%
	Sri Lanka	—	61,000	61,000	0%
Nepal	Bhutan	100,000	—	100,000	100%
Thailand	Myanmar	120,000	—	120,000	100%
Asia and the Pacific		**230,000**	**400,000**	**670,000**	**34%**
Armenia	Azerbaijan	50,000	190,000	240,000	21%
Serbia and Montenegro	Bosnia and Herzegovina	100,000	—	100,000	100%
Serbia and Montenegro	Croatia	190,000	—	190,000	100%
Europe		**340,000**	**190,000**	**530,000**	**64%**
TOTAL		**4,500,000**	**1,700,000**	**6,200,000**	**73%**

[1]Refugee situations numbering 25,000 or more persons by the end of 2003 which have been in existence for five or more years. Industrialized countries are not included. Numbers rounded to two significant figures. Totals may not add up due to rounding.
[2]UNHCR estimate. This figure is currently being reviewed by UNHCR and is expected to be revised upwards in 2004.
[3]UNHCR estimate. This figure does not include Afghans in urban areas and is currently being reviewed by UNHCR.
Source: (UNHCR, 2004, used with permission)

Table 3.4 Main countries of asylum 2002

Asylum country	*Begin 2002*	*Asylum country*	*End 2002*
Pakistan*	2198.8	Islamic Rep. of Iran*	1306.6
Islamic Rep. of Iran*	1868.0	Pakistan*	1227.4
Germany	903.0	Germany	980.0
Tanzania (United Rep.)	646.9	Tanzania (United Rep.)	689.00
USA*	515.9	USA*	485.2
Serbia and Montenegro	400.3	Serbia and Montenegro	354.4
Dem. Rep. of Congo	362.0	Dem. Rep. of Congo	333.0
Sudan	347.9	Sudan	328.2
China	295.3	China	297.3
Zambia	284.2	Zambia	260.7

*UNHCR estimate
Main asylum countries, 2002 (1 × 1000)
Source: UNHCR Statistical Yearbook (2002)

Table 3.5 Main countries of origin – Refugees 2002

Origin	*Begin year*	*Origin*	*End year*
Afghanistan*	3834.7	Afghanistan*	2510.1
Iraq	581.7	Burundi	574.5
Burundi	554.1	Sudan	508.7
Sudan	490.7	Angola	435.3
Angola	471.2	Somalia	431.2
Somalia	441.5	Occ. Palestinian Terr.	428.8
Bosnia and Herzegovina	423.7	Iraq	421.7
Dem. Rep. of the Congo	393.9	Dem. Rep. of the Congo	420.9
Viet Nam	353.7	Bosnia and Herzegovina	406.8
Occ. Palestinian Terr.	349.2	Viet Nam	373.8

*UNHCR estimate
Main refugee nationalities, 2002 (1 × 1000)
Source: UNHCR Statistiacl Yearbook (2002)

Transmigration and developing countries

According to the UNHCR (2002: 16) 'at the end of 2002, almost one quarter of the world's refugees was hosted by two countries: the Islamic Republic of Iran (1.3 million) and Pakistan (1.2 million)'. For some, transmigration is a short-term phenomenon. In the case of Iran and Pakistan, for example, at least 2 million Afghan refugees had returned home by the end of 2002. Other situations have remained unresolved for long periods of time, in some instances, up to 20 or 30 years. This has been the case with Ethiopian refugees in Sudan as well as the Palestinian diasporic peoples. The Palestinian Diaspora represents the world's biggest refugee population spread across the world – the largest number (3.6 million) residing in Jordan, Syria, and Lebanon (UNHCR, 2000; see also Table 3.3). Protracted refugee situations in which people remain in a long-term and intractable state of limbo, live in situations where their 'basic rights and essential economic, social and psychological needs remain unfulfilled after years of exile' (UNHCR, 2004c: 1). These transmigratory groups often remain trapped in a vicious cycle of dependency. Table 3.3 provides recent UNHCR (2004c) data on major protracted refugee situations currently in the world.

The transmigratory groups represented in Table 3.3, reflect ongoing political conflicts in particular regions of the world, which have remained largely unresolved. The long-term settlement of large groups of displaced peoples, presents complex problems to be solved by social policy within host societies, often with support from the UNHCR and other non-government organizations (NGOs). Transmigration has exerted immense pressure on the economic base of receiving countries in the developing world, of which, many have under-developed social infrastructures. Provision for refugees, and scope for their social and economic integration in protracted situations, vary amongst different countries. According to the UNHCR:

> In some cases, prospects for local integration are minimal, requiring the international community to continue to provide assistance on a daily basis; in others, refugees have become economically self-sufficient, largely because the host society has provided access to land or the labour market. (UNHCR, 2004c: 2)

Protracted refugee situations in *receiving* countries tend to perpetuate poverty, as very few refugees are enabled to become economically productive in a significant way. Some of this relates to the lack of access to formal education. This and their temporary situation prevent them from contributing significantly to the GDP of receiving countries.

Refugees, generally, not only lack sustained income and assets, they are also voiceless and powerless in relation to the institutions of state and society within receiving societies (UNHCR, 2004c). This means that although they occupy geographical areas, they do not necessarily inhabit a political or cultural space formally. Since they are not embedded in the social structure of the host society, they would have access to fewer resources and opportunities available, to maintain their languages within formal domains. This has implications for long-term language maintenance and development.

Nevertheless, as is argued in Chapter 2, transmigration does not engender a unidimensional process of change affecting only receiving countries, involving cultural adaptation only amongst transmigratory groups; it impacts also on the socioeconomic and cultural base of countries of origin. In general though, already industrialized societies seem to gain most. For example, whilst OECD countries show the largest gains in relation to the inflow of high skilled immigrants, developing countries face a 'brain drain' situation. Docquier and Marfouk's (2005: 1) research indicate that 'in proportion to the educated labor force, the highest skilled (e)migration rates are observed in the Caribbean, Central America, Western, Middle and Eastern Africa'. The mass exodus of skilled workers from these, already under-resourced, societies impacts negatively on the domestic labour market. It creates major skills gaps in the labour force, since most of those who transmigrate on a voluntary basis, tend to be workers who have skills and professional qualifications suited to the labour market needs in their destination countries. Lowell and Findlay (2003: 11) in a recent ILO Report highlight the negative impact on developing economies arguing that 'high levels of skilled emigration slow economic (GDP) growth and, adversely affect those who remain. As a consequence poverty and inequality are likely to increase'. These people flows are underscored by high levels of demand for education in the, already powerful, languages of their target countries. This, in turn, plays a major role in shaping the language and literacy aspirations within society as a whole and, especially, those of socially mobile groups – thus creating a cycle of cultural/linguistic disempowerment with regard to countries of origin.

Yet, at the same time, the outflow of workers can also generate cultural capital and economic growth in *sending* countries, as migration opportunities tend to increase people's investment in human capital (Docquier and Marfouk, 2005). In other words, in order to gain access to jobs elsewhere, people are prepared to invest more in their education. This suggests that people's learning ambitions, and aspirations, are shaped also by the job opportunities available within the global labour market. This is confirmed by the International Organization for Migration (IOM) (2003) which maintains that 'prospects of working abroad have increased the expected return to additional years of education and led many people to invest in more schooling, especially in high demand areas' (cited in Docquier and Marfouk, 2005: 3). Nevertheless, whilst beneficial to individual workers and receiving countries, if current patterns of migration are sustained, in the long-term this could impact negatively on the social and economic base of developing countries. UNDP (2001) projections indicate that, 'under new US legislation, about 100,000 software professionals are expected to leave India each year over the next three years. The emigration of those professionals costs $2 billion a year for India' (cited in Docquier and Marfouk, 2005: 3). Similarly, the large scale emigration of a wide range of high skill professionals from a newly emerged postcolonial society, such as South Africa, potentially has a negative impact on development within that context. South Africa still has the task of alleviating historically derived economic, educational, linguistic/cultural and social inequalities – the heritage of Apartheid policy and practice (see case-study of South Africa in Chapter 7).

Transmigration and developing countries

The discussion thus far, indicates that transmigration is a dynamic global phenomenon that continuously transforms the sociocultural base of national states across the world. Tables 3.4 and 3.5 provide recent evidence from the UNHCR showing the extent to which socially displaced peoples have taken refuge, not only in metropolitan countries, but also in countries throughout the developing world. Implicit in this are the ever-changing linguistic landscapes generated by contemporary people flows within the global terrain, and the problems raised for education, and language-in-education policy in receiving countries.

Tables 3.4 and 3.5 also show the dynamic nature of the people flows. Patterns of migration tend to vary from year to year. Provisional UNHCR statistics of refugee populations, for example, suggest that by the end of 2003 there was a *decrease* of approximately 920,000 refugees globally (UNHCR, 2004a). Yet by 2004 some individual countries reported an *increase* in their refugee population. This included refugee populations in 'Yemen (10,000), Rwanda (7200), Egypt (3400), Ethiopia (2700), Zambia (2200), Ecuador (1500), the United Republic of Tanzania (1200) and Malaysia (1000)' – representing 33,800 refugees in total during the first nine months of 2004 (UNHCR, 2004b: 3). Moreover, Afghan refugees have, since at least the late 1970s, transmigrated to, *inter alia*, Pakistan and Iran; refugees from Democratic Republic of Congo transmigrated to 'Zambia (+15,500), Rwanda (+8000) and the United Republic of Tanzania (+2600), refugees from Indonesia (+8800) and Myanmar (+3800) in Malaysia, Burundi refugees in Rwanda (+2900) and Somali refugees in Yemen (+2100)' (UNHCR, 2004b: 4). These examples give some indication of the organic nature of the continuous mass movement of people, and the ever-shifting cultural, religious and linguistic landscapes that they engender. These transmigrations also suggest that people, generally, tend to seek refuge in neighbouring countries, or those with which they share common historical, cultural, linguistic or religious links. In this regard, excolonial countries represent popular choices.

On the face of it, the economic and geopolitical aspects of globalization discussed so far, may seem far removed from the issue of language. The concluding section below discusses some of the ways that this dynamic people and cultural flows, in effect, are *central* to furthering our understanding of the unique and discursive ways that language *per se* features in the world today. The *first* issue relates to historical continuities in language policies in postcolonial societies.

Conclusion

Historical policy continuities in postcolonial societies

We saw in Chapter 2, the extent to which many postcolonial countries have continued to maintain excolonial languages as the official medium of communication. This has conflicting sociocultural and political implications revolving around issues related, on the one hand, to the maintenance of national identity, and on the other hand, concerns about the potential reinforcement of cultural and linguistic imperialism. The predominance of excolonial languages within official domains and in urban areas, and lack of policy and infrastructural support have contributed to the benign neglect of local languages. The under-supply of trained language teachers and educational provision[14] generally within rural areas has impacted negatively on levels of literacy in both local and excolonial languages. High levels of proficiency in excolonial languages thus reflect the distribution of sociocultural and economic resources within society. The subsequent under-development of human resources, through lack of adequate educational and linguistic infrastructure, has implications for the capability of many of these societies to sustain adequate levels of economic and social development. These issues have been made more problematic within the interactive, technologically driven, global cultural economy within which language *per se* has become a commodity.

The second issue relates to the direct involvement of global policy-defining agencies in the economies of individual countries, their long-term impact on development trajectories, and the ways that they influence language possibilities.

Global policy impacts

As is discussed earlier, the increasing intervention of the WTO in domestic policies and its potential for reshaping local development priorities. Similarly, the conditionalities of structural adjustment programmes of the World Bank/IMF provide universal templates for social development within different countries. This enables them to exercise considerable power over the economic and social policy frameworks of aid receiving countries. These imposed economic policy constraints, impact on levels of access to education, as well as the availability of appropriate teaching and learning resources. In this regard, despite the World Bank's notional support for education in indigenous languages, the trend has remained in favour of continuing support for excolonial languages. Roy-Campbell explains the indirect impact that IMF conditionalities have had on the language question in Tanzania:

> The language question, though not overtly addressed by the IMF and the government in their liberalization policies, was affected in the move away from Education for Self Reliance. While the decade following the introduction of Education for Self Reliance was marked by efforts to prepare for Kiswahili medium instruction at all levels of education in Tanzania, the decade of structural adjustment and IMF conditionalities was marked by efforts to rehabilitate English as a viable medium of instruction for post-primary school education. This was despite the fact that Kiswahili was the language most commonly used in other public domains of Tanzanian life, with the exception of international trade, commerce and tourism. (Roy-Campbell, 2001: 114)

The predominance of excolonial languages as medium for teaching and learning, in many postcolonial societies, serve as exclusionary mechanisms since very few people, particularly in rural areas, have access to these languages (or adequately to their own) in their schooling. Moreover, the introduction of school user fees has had a major impact on the possibility of parents to continue to keep all their children in school for the duration. Parents carry the burden of having to pay also for textbooks, equipment, examination fees as well as stationery. High levels of poverty mean that high levels of dropouts, even at primary school level, are commonplace in most developing countries. In addition, the irregular payment of teachers has led to mass disaffection which, in turn, has contributed to a rise in under-achieving schools in countries throughout the Sub-Saharan region. Together these factors influence possibilities for generating an adequate supply of human resources, to sustain social and economic development within these societies. They also influence possibilities for these countries to participate, effectively, in the global cultural economy.

Language as a global economic resource

The third issue relates to the integral role that language itself plays within the global cultural economy.[15] This refers to the integration of language and communication into the flexible production process, interactive textual environments such as the Internet, financial and commodity markets, and the predominance of 'world' languages (i.e. excolonial languages, and especially English) as a means of communication within official and public contexts (e.g. trade, geographically dispersed work places, travel) within the international terrain. Within the technologically driven 'knowledge' economy, information also represents an end-product, for example, computer software environments/infrastructures such as *Microsoft*, software packages, network systems, and intellectual property rights. Although some of these 'language practices' are intangible, they nevertheless constitute a commodity, an economic asset with an exchange value. In particular, the language interface of software programmes has implications for the relative power and status of individual languages. Although there are developments in relation to extending the range of language interfaces on the Internet, the emphasis has, to a significant extent, remained in favour of 'world' languages (see also Chapters 4, 7 and 8).

Mass transmigration

Fourth, as is discussed earlier, the increase in mass transmigration of various groups of people within, and across, countries and continents is bringing into contact different cultures, religions and languages as an integral part of everyday life. Present-day people flows, represented in the uncertain and often temporary lives of refugee groups throughout the world (see discussion above and Tables 3.4 and 3.5), call into question our theorization of their language entitlement, cultural, entitlements, assets and capabilities (i.e. knowledge and skills) – and, at the same time, the complex ways in which they engage with the issue of language within their redefined lives.

The centrality of language to the experiences of transmigratory groups, especially refugees within developing countries was highlighted. However, the language needs of migratory groups within developing countries rarely feature in contemporary discourse on language and education within the 'global cultural economy' (see Chapter 4). There clearly is a need for receiving countries, as well as international non-government organizations (NGOs), to be cognizant of the language needs of refugee groups in relation to providing them with appropriate forms of cultural capital that could be of benefit to the economies of receiving countries or, potentially, for the development of the economies of sending countries upon their repatriation. How effectively this can be addressed within constantly changing ethnolinguistic and political landscapes globally, remains problematic.

Table 3.6 highlights some of the key questions that surround language within the global cultural economy. Together, these questions highlight

Table 3.6 Language issues within the global cultural economy

- Which languages represent cultural capital to be exchanged within the global market?
- Which languages are imbued with symbolic power within the international arena? That is to say, whose languages are valued and therefore supported within the world today?
- What are 'world languages' and how do they relate to the global market?
- How does this relate to social and economic development within postcolonial societies?
- How do 'world languages' impact on national and ethnic identity within these contexts?
- Given their influential position within the global terrain, what are the possibilities for postcolonial societies to maintain and develop the languages of minority groups as effective cultural, political and economic resources?
- What are the socio-political, cultural and economic implications for postcolonial societies if already powerful languages are legitimized in social policy frameworks, to the exclusion of local languages?
- Given the interactive nature of information technology and its integration into cultural, political and economic processes, what is the status and significance of multilingualism within the global cultural economy, and how does this relate to language and development in developing countries?
- What are the language implications for transmigratory groups?

At the same time,

- How do people define themselves linguistically with regard to (a) cultural maintenance, and (b) accessing power and resources in their everyday lives?
- What are the long-term implications of these individual, institutional and national language choices collectively for the maintenance of cultural and political identity as well as the economic development of postcolonial societies within the broader context of the global cultural economy?
- What are the issues for education and its role in social, economic and political development?

the necessity to broaden the analytical framework within which the relationship between language and power within the global cultural economy (see Chapter 4), and their impact on development possibilities in postcolonial societies is considered. This also includes the need to focus on possibilities of self-identification[16] in relation to the need for countries to participate equitably in global economic, cultural, and linguistic markets. Some of the questions raised here will be examined further in Chapter 4, which focuses on the material ways in which language features within the interactive global terrain.

Notes

1. The concept of 'geopolitics' here refers to the dynamic interaction between geographic, political, economic and cultural factors and their collective impact on individual countries or regions.
2. In Britain the Reform Act of 1867 enfranchised urban workers; the Reform Act of 1884 extended the vote to all males who either owned, or rented housing. Women obtained universal voting rights on an equal basis with men only in 1928.
3. The subconscious process by which oppressed groups engage in disempowering actions and through this collude in their own dispossession.
4. Factors that underpinned this economic crisis include high levels of unemployment due to the erosion of the manufacturing base, the export of production to South East Asia, the impact of the OPEC oil crisis on national economies and the coming on stream of new production technologies and new work practices.
5. Mexico joined the OECD in 1994, the Czech Republic in 1995, Poland in 1996 and the Slovak Republic in 2000.
6. The 'Washington Consensus' refers to 'the 1980s–1990s ideology of the World Bank, International Monetary Fund, US Treasury Department, Federal Reserve Board and assorted Washington think-tanks funded by large corporations and banks, as well as institutions outside Washington like the World Trade Organization and sundry conservative university economic departments modelled on the Chicago School (Bond, 2000: 156). Thus according to Stiglitz (2002: 6) it refers to the agreement 'between the IMF, the World Bank, and the US Treasury about the 'right' policies for developing countries'.
7. As can be seen in the earlier discussion, globalization is a contested concept. Definitions of globalization vary amongst the disciplines and also depend on the ideological framework in which they are articulated. In other words, they derive from the discourse in which they are situated as well as the site from which they are articulated. For our purposes here the idea of globalization incorporates the dynamic interaction between culture, economy, history and politics within the global arena – and the complex relations thus produced within and across countries and continents.
8. Armenia, Azerbaijan, Belarus, Estonia, Georgia, Kazakhstan, Kyrgyzstan, Latvia, Lithuania, Moldova, Russia, Tajikistan, Turkmenistan, Ukraine, Uzbekistan.
9. Bosnia, Serbia, Croatia, Herzegovina and Montenegro.

10. The Tatar Autonomous Soviet Socialist Republic (TASSR) was formed in 1920. The peoples of the USSR were ranked in the following way: (1) 15 Soviet Socialist Republics, (2) 20 Autonomous Republics, (3) eight Autonomous Regions, (4) 10 Autonomous Areas, (5) peoples having no state organisation. In the Russian Soviet Federative Socialist Republic, there were: 16 Autonomous Republics (including Tatarstan), five Autonomous Regions and 10 Autonomous Areas. The Tatar ASSR's claims to independence began with the demand to raise its status to that of the 15 highest-ranking Republics of the USSR (Davis *et al.*, 2000).
11. In the case of Pakistan, for example '(t)here have been five periods of full or partial martial law, lasting 18 years, six abortive coups and three periods under state emergency. Only one president has completed his term, prime ministers have been dismissed eight times, one prime minister was assassinated, one executed and eight parliaments have been prematurely dissolved' (Thomas, 1997).
12. For example, the post-Second World War, Fordist hegemonic project which encouraged workers to aspire to become home owners as well as mass consumers of services and commodities.
13. See the example of Dr Abdurahman in South Africa in Chapter 2.
14. For example, school buildings, textbooks, furniture, writing equipment, curriculum and syllabuses, monitoring and assessment procedures (see Chapter 4).
15. The concept of the 'global cultural economy' here refers to the complex global interplay between the economy, culture and politics and the power relations in which they are constituted.
16. The concept of self-identification derives from Giddens and refers to the discursive 'self' as is 'routinely created and sustained in the reflexive activities of the individual' (Giddens, 1991: 52). Within this context it is extended to the reflexive process in which postcolonial societies are continuously redefining themselves in relation to their colonial pasts. Thus it denotes a continuous process of 'becoming'.

Chapter 4

Language in the Global Cultural Economy:[1] Implications for Postcolonial Societies

This chapter builds on key issues related to the complex changes taking place within the interactive global cultural economy discussed in Chapter 3. In particular, it examines the political economy[2] of language within the world today, placing emphasis on postcolonial societies in Sub-Saharan Africa, and South Asia. An underlying principle is that, because of the dynamic and discursive forms of interaction taking place within the global terrain, language as a social practice does not centre only on the languages spoken, levels of literacy, and/or the representation and identity of language groups within particular societies. Although these factors are indisputably important, the unprecedented extent that language is now integrated into economic, cultural and political processes means that, discussions about language in the world today should be concerned also with how power is exercised through language within, and through institutional, societal and global power processes. Using the relationship between language, economy and human resource development as a recurring theme, the chapter examines the central role that language and communication plays in the interactive global cultural economy. As a starting point, the next section looks at the complex ways in which language is related to the economy.

Language and Economy

Cultural capital: Skills, knowledges and awarenesses

Language, as a means of communication, features as a central variable within different sectors of the modern economy including business, trade, manufacturing and culture industries as well as the service sector. Language and communication skills and knowledges, for example, are central to the redefined technological labour process in which expertise is dispersed horizontally within integrated work teams. This mode of work organization referred to as *flexible specialization* (FS) (Piore & Sable, 1984; Tomaney, 1990), integrates different skills and knowledge expertise. This means that designers might have to communicate amongst different experts and with those involved at different levels of production, management as well as marketing. Flexible production often relies on expertise that is geographically dispersed across regions, countries and continents as people work together on international projects. The centrality of communication to the FS-based production process suggests that individual and group language exchanges taking place within these contexts represent valuable forms of cultural capital.

Moreover, as is discussed in Chapter 3, the capability of microelectronics technology to produce a diverse range of quality products has generated discerning consumers and competitive commodity markets as a result of cheaper products continually entering the global marketplace. Within this terrain, advertising, product presentation, management and marketing have become new core areas within the redefined labour market. These changes in the nature of work and the work process, have generated labour market demands for new sets of technological and business knowledge, problem solving skills, 'multiliteracies' (Gee, 1996) and communication competence[3] as well as worker awarenesses of the labour market, and work process (Rassool, 1999). Together these factors signify a language-based economy placing high reliance on a range of sophisticated linguistic skills, discursive knowledges, and worker awarenesses, which play an important supporting role in the capital accumulation process. These, essentially, higher order language and communication skills can be categorized as follows:

- multilingualism;
- information processing skills;
- knowledge of different subject registers;
- subject knowledges;
- inter-cultural communication skills, awarenesses and knowledges;
- data handling;
- decision making skills;
- problem solving skills;
- research skills;
- analytical competence;
- interpreting meanings;
- oracy skills (speaking and listening).

Linguistic flexibility incorporating language fluency and discourse/communicative competence, in this context, can be seen as being integral to the notion of individual worker capability. If this is the case then the extent to which a society can participate in the global cultural economy, depends significantly on its levels of *linguistic capability* in addition to its productive capacity, collectively, and individually. A society's linguistic capability includes the collective and individual accumulated stock of language and communicative competence – the cultural capital – to exchange within different sectors of the global labour market. This includes, for example, negotiations taking place within the financial and business sectors, the interpersonal and intercultural communication skills and knowledges required within the service sector and, as is discussed above, those employed in the production process.

Physical assets: Resource supply

Building a country's linguistic capability, as part of its collective cultural capital, therefore, contributes to its productive capacity. This has major resource implications for education at different levels including:

(1) Macro-socio administrative aspects, for example, language-in-education policy frameworks and guidelines for implementation, teacher education (initial and in-service), teacher supply as well as curriculum planning and organization taking account of the actual languages chosen nationally/regionally/locally for teaching and learning as well as the macro-system and protocols for assessment. Country-wide sociolinguistic surveys, sociocultural profiles providing information of cultural 'ways of thinking' and 'ways of knowing' as well as literacy mapping to inform policy making also represent important planning resources (see also below).

(2) A wide range of teaching and learning resources such as writing materials, textbooks, videos, video recorders, computer software (and hardware), audio recorders, thesaurus, translations, interpreters, and dictionaries in the range of languages identified in the policy framework (Coulmas, 1992).

(3) Coherent and effective educational infrastructures to support the educational process as a whole, and language development in particular; in other words, the operational aspects of putting language-in-education policy into practice. This includes micro-level administrative, management, assessment, monitoring, and planning institutions, resources (including staffing), practices and processes.

(4) Physical structures such as school buildings and classrooms that are functional and easily accessible (see also Mali and Pakistan case studies in Chapters 5 and 6).
(5) Adequate transport systems to enable learners to access schools.

Although under-resourced education systems prevail in many societies, including those with advanced economies, they do, for various reasons (see Chapter 3), tend to be concentrated in developing countries. Poor enrolment, attendance and retention as well as under-resourced education systems (e.g. textbooks, writing materials, teacher supply, buildings and equipment) are major factors impacting on possibilities for these countries to develop an adequately skilled, differentiated, skilled labour supply.

Whilst this is the case for settled communities within their countries of origin, these factors impact in a major way also on the lives of refugee groups, living in camps within receiving countries whose social infrastructures are under-developed and therefore, cannot deal effectively with the additional pressures placed upon them (UNHCR, 2003).

Refugee groups

It is commonplace in many developing countries, especially those throughout the Sub-Saharan region, rural areas in India, Pakistan and Thailand for teaching and learning to take place in classrooms that are located outside – under trees. According to recent UNHCR information on refugee education in developing countries, during the 2002/2003 period:

> more than one-third of all classes were classified as temporary or open-air structures (. . .) The highest proportion of temporary or open-air classrooms is found in Thailand (100% of the 1530 reported classrooms), Nepal (88% of the 775 classrooms) and Tanzania (14% of 1010 classrooms). (UNHCR, 2003: 3)

Nearly half (45%) of the temporary, or open-air classrooms are in UNHCR provided schools (UNHCR, 2003). In most instances, pupils from refugee groups living in camps, in effect, exist outside formal educational policy provision within receiving countries. Needless to say, these gaps in provision fail to maximize the potential of refugee groups to acquire appropriate forms and levels of cultural capital to exchange in the formal labour market of the receiving country – and thus to contribute to its GDP. In many cases refugees are prevented from being productively employed.

Skills and knowledges accumulated in exile could also facilitate their economic and social reintegration into their countries of origin – and in the process, contribute to their home economies. Ideally, it would therefore be useful to have coherent educational structures for refugee populations that also cater for language maintenance programmes. This is pertinent especially where cross-border transmigration takes place sporadically because of political instability in sending countries as has been the case, for example, in Ethiopia, southern Sudan and Democratic Republic of Congo over the past four decades.

Also embedded in decisions about the basic requirements for language education provision in general, are power related factors. These include, for example, which languages would be endorsed by policy and, therefore, are imbued with political status and economic currency.

Policy/power dimensions

As is discussed in Chapters 1 and 2, because of their association with political power, and their integration into the economic and cultural practices and processes of colonized societies, colonial languages were imbued with potent symbolic and economic power. Colonized peoples were obliged to use colonial languages in formal contexts if they were to be able to access jobs and services. Whilst education through the medium of the mother tongue, at least during the early years, represented the norm within many of the colonies, the transitional model of bilingualism adopted was grounded in assimilationist ideology. This ensured that a subtractive bilingualism predominated. Colonial languages generally supplanted local languages within formal domains. As a result, the development of local languages,[4] the lexical modernization[5] of local languages, within colonized societies was constrained in relation to developments in society, culture and the modern world.

Languages sanctioned by policy, invariably, are those already used within formal domains such as the labour market, the Church, judiciary, governance and formal civic arenas. These high status languages represent the means by which power is exercised through relations of dominance established within the social terrain. As such, they constitute power/knowledge discourses (Foucault, 1980) embodying both meaning *and* social relationships. In other words, meanings do not arise exclusively from language *per se*, or language use, but also from institutional practices, power relations, social position, status and individual and group habitus which, together, shape and influence subjectivities. For postcolonial societies this, at least subliminally, influenced the extent to which their colonial heritage impacted on the language policy decisions that they made after independence, and the systems that they subsequently put in place to support educational access through different local languages. Chapter 2 provided an indication of the extent to which excolonial languages have retained their high status as medium of communication within official/formal domains, including in education. This, in turn, has impacted on societal levels of literacy and, *de facto*, the relative skills of workers entering the labour market. These problems, in many postcolonial societies in Sub-Saharan Africa and South Asia, have remained largely unresolved; indeed, they have intensified in recent years as a result of developments within the interactive global cultural economy.

Global Linguistic Markets

Within a dynamic sociocultural and economic terrain in which 'world' languages are regarded as vital economic resources, which languages should be supported in education, and how this can take place effectively within developing countries are complex issues to be addressed in social policy. It is now commonly accepted that all languages have intrinsic value as cultural, economic and political resources. However, this does not necessarily mean that they all have parity socially, economically, culturally or politically. Since language and communication are central to trade and business negotiations at both macro- and micro-levels, some languages are imbued with more economic power than others within the global terrain. Some languages are also politically more valuable, and socially useful, than others. Different *linguistic markets* prevail, in which some languages, and forms of language use, have more currency and exchange value than others.

What are linguistic markets?

In order to examine the role that language and socialization play in social and cultural reproduction, Bourdieu (1977, 1991) introduced the concepts of *linguistic capital, linguistic markets* and *linguistic habitus.* Bourdieu argued that linguistic exchanges are embedded within a complex network of power relations. Utterances are always produced within a particular field, space or market[6] through which social meaning and value are attributed to the language exchange. In producing an utterance within a particular context, he suggested, the speaker makes a bid for social authority, and the recipient or audience decides, to what degree, to recognize that claim to authority (Bourdieu, 1977). Bourdieu introduced the concept of *linguistic capital* to describe the respect, or authority enjoyed by a speaker within a particular interactive context. Within a linguistic market, 'people undertake speech production with a certain "anticipation of profit", or anticipation of the expected reception of one's words ... linguistic capital is created, adapted, asserted, and re-evaluated through linguistic encounters' (Bartlett, 2003: 2). Although meanings and power relations are negotiated within every linguistic encounter, in sanctioning particular 'norms' of language use, linguistic markets dictate the nature of the linguistic capital required in the linguistic exchange. Those with high levels of linguistic capital, suited to dominant language markets, speak with 'command' and, as such, have power to influence the outcomes. As can be seen later, the ability to speak Standard English carries more weight in social and institutional discourse, within global policy defining sites, than is the case with other national languages.

Whilst Bourdieu's theory refers to individual speech acts, it also incorporates national or group languages, different subject registers and discourse styles. The rest of this chapter draws on the concepts of 'linguistic market' and 'linguistic capital', and uses them in a broader economic sense to explore the material base of language within the global cultural economy. Using these concepts provides a useful means of engaging with the relationship between micro- and macro-linguistic markets as well as formal and informal linguistic markets, including how language use is linked with social, political and economic processes nationally, and internationally. In a more general sense, it also provides insight into the status, role and use of various languages by different groups of people in relation to language markets that prevail within the global cultural economy. Through this it allows us to discuss issues linked to the relative power of languages in the global cultural economy.

Languages and macro markets

Language popularity follows *market trends*. As countries improve their economic status, making them important trading partners within the global economy, their languages gain in value within the international language market. Coulmas (1992) provides the example of Japan during the early 1980s, when the popularity of learning Japanese increased sharply as the yen rose against the US dollar. This was the period when Japan assumed a leading position within the world economy; it represented a successful capitalist economy. Japanese business organization and work practices (e.g. *kaizen* or continuous improvement, just-in-time [JIT] strategies and Total Quality Management [TQM]), represented successful models of production and management. These models were incorporated into the work practices of Western companies and, later, also education (Morley & Rassool, 1999) in order to maximize labour efficiencies and cost effectiveness. Japanese language and culture thus represented useful cultural capital at the time.

Earlier examples include the rising popularity of Arabic as a business language, following the oil boom during the 1950s and 1960s. Currently, Mandarin Chinese is in ascendance in response to China gaining in importance as a world trading partner and, potentially, a vast consumer market which is still largely untapped.

World events also impact on the popularity and status of languages as was the case with Russian during the period of the Cold War – and more recently, with ongoing political turmoil in the Middle East, Arabic. Whilst there is a novelty value attached to the current popularity of Arabic as a study subject amongst university students (Anthes, 2002), it is also linked more pragmatically with emerging employment possibilities within the labour market particularly in the media, government, sales and marketing, and the business sector (see also language courses on the Internet below).

Language markets and the 'knowledge economy'

On a different level, many countries with advanced economies are increasingly 'going offshore', tapping into a vast supply of low-skilled, low-paid labour located within developing countries such as India, Romania, the Philippines, China and Bulgaria. At the time of writing, UK-based insurance companies such as AXA, BUPA, Prudential and the Royal Sun Alliance have moved some of their information services to India, where the Call Centre industry has in recent years been growing at a rate of 60% per annum (Datta, 2004). In India, employment in this sector increased from one and a half million to more than 2 million by the end of 2004. Revenues from this sector increased 'from $565 million during the 1999–2000 period to more than $3 billion by March 2004, and are projected to increase beyond $10 billion by 2006' (Datta, 2004: 2). Underpinning this, are labour costs at an, approximately, 85% lower rate than in the UK, with Indian Call Centre staff earning on average between £1500 and £3000 a year, as opposed to the UK norm of £8000–£12,000 per annum (Advanced Workplace Associates, 2002).

Language plays a major role in facilitating this global outsourcing of labour. In the case of India, the labour pool comprises mostly graduates, who are fluent in English because they were educated in this language medium at least since their secondary school years. Working in call centres is referred to as 'voice-based' work, and requires harmonization of vocabulary and delivery. This, in turn, relies on short-term training programmes centred on teaching communication skills, knowledge of intercultural communication, voice training and depending on the employing company, either British-English or American-English enunciation. This is reinforced in the workplace by the use of prepared scripts enabling Call Centre workers to maintain the required discourse style. These strategies conform to the particular linguistic capital demanded by the market (see Bourdieu above). There are also subtle identity adjustments to be made, as many of these workers are encouraged to adopt English/American names[7] so that clients based in the English speaking world, can relate to them more easily. Here then, we have macro linguistic markets within which fluency in British, or American Standard English as well as knowledge of American/British culture, represents potent linguistic capital. The possibility for workers to exchange their accumulated linguistic capital (in this instance, English) within the global labour market, thus enables countries to make use of new work opportunities that arise within the global cultural economy.

Seemingly then, these new employment opportunities play a significant role in creating possibilities for developing countries rich in cultural capital, to diversify their economies by extending their service sector, and to some extent, also their business sector – and through this – to enter the global economic market. It is also helpful in channeling workers into new areas, and new opportunities, especially in situations of large numbers of over-credentialized workers as is the case in India, and Pakistan, as well as countries faced with high levels of skilled worker unemployment. In these circumstances, linguistic capital plays a strategic role in economic management within affected societies. The implications of this for national language policy in postcolonial/developing countries are discussed later.

Job outsourcing is expanding also into higher level 'knowledge-based' work, for example, processing insurance claims, accountants being subcontracted by auditing firms in the UK or US, architects, computer programming, financial analysts, and medical services such as radiology (Engardio *et al.*, 2003). In the case of medical services, radiologists and surgeons from countries such as South Africa, Germany and Australia, for example, undertake work in the UK for short periods every year. The incentives of high incomes, and favourable pound sterling exchange rates, make this a popular choice amongst medical specialists from these countries. These workers represent a growing number of 'work' tourists or 'short-term' economic migrants, employed sporadically to clear backlogs (see also below).

International job outsourcing is influenced by high levels of fluency in the languages of *labour exporting* countries. The UK tends to outsource to English speaking (excolonial) countries such as India, Ireland, the Channel Islands, South Africa, Malaysia and the Caribbean. French companies have Call Centres in Mauritius, and 'German multinationals from Siemens to roller-bearings maker INA-Schaeffler are hiring in Russia, the Baltics, and Eastern Europe' (Engardio *et al.*, 2003: 2). As mentioned in Chapter 3, the UK has at least since the late 1950s, also imported labour from English speaking excolonial countries, to work in their domestic service sector, mostly the National Health System (NHS) and the public transport system. As stated above, this has intensified in recent years by subcontracting expertise from other countries within the international arena on a short-term basis in order to help National Health Trusts[8] meet treatment/service targets. The key issue here, is that the services rendered by these out-sourced workers benefit, to a large extent, the GDP and national well-being of recruiting Western societies and, to a lesser extent, that of their own countries. This fluid process of labour transfer reinforces the high status of English, thus providing incentives for young people throughout the world to aspire to become fluent in this, economically powerful, language.

What does this suggest with regard to the status, currency and, therefore, the long-term maintenance of local languages within formal domains in postcolonial developing countries? What are the implications for appropriately diversified labour supply and, consequently, the development of different economic sectors within these countries? This question is significant since, as can be seen in the discussion so far, labour migration to some degree is a response to fill existing skills gaps within advanced but under-resourced economies.

Labour and immigration flows

OECD countries since, at least the 1990s, have been adjusting their immigration policies to facilitate inflows of highly skilled professionals, within selected areas of the economy, aimed at 'attracting a qualified work force through the creation of labor-shortage occupation lists' (Docquier & Rapoport, 2004: 5). Reporting on their research, these writers argue further that '(i)n all OECD countries, the proportion of skilled immigrants originating from low-income countries has increased, especially in North America, with notable increase of high-skilled immigration from Asian countries' (Docquier & Rapoport, 2004: 7). As mentioned in Chapter 3, in these situations poverty-stricken countries tend to lose out, as a result of the effects of the 'brain drain', as their more qualified workers transmigrate to areas with particular labour shortages. These contribute further to the North/South knowledge, and by implication, also economic divide. Figure 4.1 provides insight into the level of labour force migration that has taken place in Africa during the past decade.

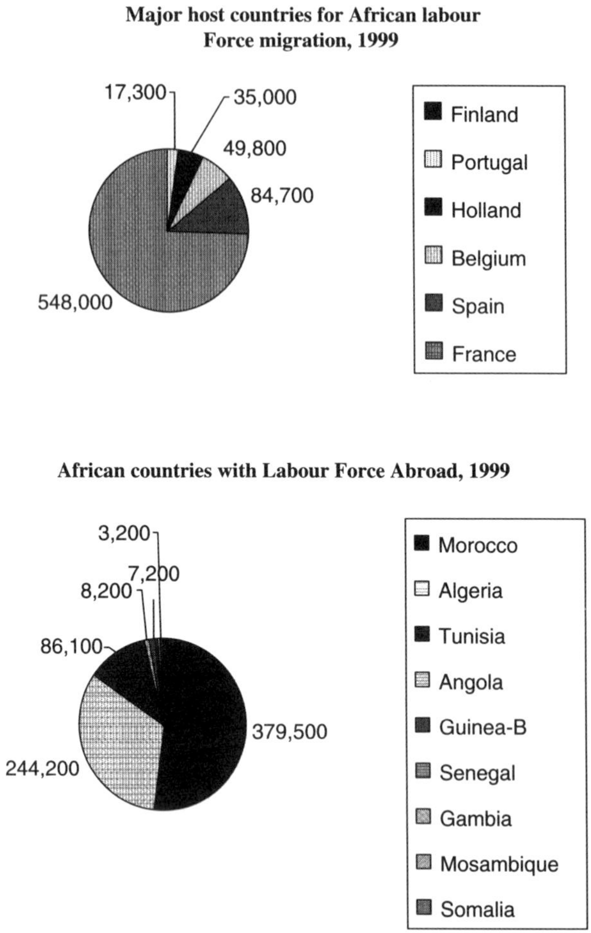

Figure 4.1 African labour force migration, 1999. *Source*: Grantmakers concerned with immigrants and refugees (GCIR), 1999 (cited in Dzvimbo, 2003: 9) printed with permission from GCIR)

What are the implications of labour force migration for continued qualified labour supply within postcolonial/developing countries, and their ability to sustain social and economic development? This question is pertinent, especially, in relation to the possibilities for developing countries to diversify their economies within sectors relying on high-skilled labour, particularly in the evolving technology-based global economic market as well as the expansion of the service sector. Moreover, what then are the implications for national language-in-education policy within these societies, with regard to (a) the need to support local languages at higher levels of education in order to maximize human resource development – and (b) thus to reinforce the economic and social infrastructure? Given the infrastructures provided by wealthy multinationals, and the consumer culture that they promote as part of the company work experience, what are the possible long-term impacts on the aspirations, and behaviours of individual workers, and through that, the local linguistic and cultural base? What is the future for local, less powerful, languages in these situations?

In addition, as can be seen in the example of India above, there are also issues related to comparative salaries of workers in developing countries. Those who possess the requisite linguistic capital (i.e. 'world' languages) within the global labour market would earn more and, therefore, would be able to support wealthier lifestyles, than those who work in different, less well-paid, sectors of the national economy. Lifestyle changes amongst young people within non-Western, culturally more traditional societies, also have the potential to create intergenerational conflict. This happens when there are perceived threats to the maintenance of a sustainable cultural ecology of the community/society. The concept of 'cultural ecology' here refers simply to the traditional ways of life including local languages, and the sociocultural, and political environment in which they are embedded. The impact of environment on language and, vice versa, is accepted common knowledge (Mühlhäusler, 1996).

These are complex issues that are only beginning to emerge and, therefore, it is difficult to predict the nature of the dynamic interplay of factors within individual countries, and in the global arena. As such, we can identify trends, but cannot anticipate outcomes. What is significant though, is that the developments associated with the international outsourcing of jobs discussed here, support my argument earlier, that within the contemporary world, language *per se* represents a potent form of cultural capital; it is situated at the heart of the global cultural economy.

Language and national income levels

The economic strength/buying power/exchange value of a language can be gauged by a country's national income, its Gross Domestic Product (GDP), and also the extent that language users 'trade their goods and services internationally'. This indicates the extent to which countries participate in the global cultural economy (Graddol, 1997: 29). If we apply this argument to developing/postcolonial countries throughout Sub-Saharan Africa, or South Asia, which provide the general focus of this study, then we can conclude that their low levels of GDP, reflect the low economic status of their languages within the international terrain, and vice versa. These local languages are further marginalized in contexts where excolonial languages still constitute the official languages (see Chapter 2).

Number of language users

Languages also increase in value as the number of speakers/users rise, particularly within formal contexts. As can be seen above, current trends indicate that English has gained in importance as a business lingua franca internationally, whilst 'the use of German and French are almost exclusively confined to trade within Europe' (Graddol, 1997: 29). This suggests that English predominates within the international business domain, whilst a small selection of Western European languages, have more purchasing power within a smaller regional trade environment. This would also be the case with 'languages of African intercommunication' (UNESCO Regional Office for Education in Africa, 1985 cited in Skutnabb-Kangas, 2000: 43) such as Kiswahili in East Africa, Yoruba in West-Central Africa, and Hausa in North-African regions.

Whilst English as a world language, may be the preferred linguistic currency at macro-level business, communication at the level of production and institutional management may depend more on fluency in a local or regional language (Graddol, 1997, 2006). As is argued earlier, the centrality of information and technological capability to modern capital accumulation regimes, as well as the integration of communication into the technological production process, means that the ability to generate, access and use knowledge and information now represent key skills areas in relation to human resource development. In other words, language and communicative competence *per se* is important. Fluency in several languages as well as having different forms of linguistic capital such as appropriate discourse style/strategies suited to specific language markets would be of greater value to workers operating within local and regional contexts, than would fluency in excolonial languages.

Knowledge exchange

Educating specialist workers overseas, especially in Western Europe and the US, is another strategic human resource development choice in postcolonial/developing countries, aimed at yielding major dividends to national economies. These opportunities to study in other countries enable professionals to acquire new skills and knowledges that, ultimately, contribute to economic and social development in their countries of origin. For example, at Microsoft's Beijing research lab 'one-third of the 180 programmers have PhDs from US universities. The groups helped develop the "digital ink" that makes handwriting show up on Microsoft's new tablet PCs' (Engardio *et al.*, 2003: 3). Another strategy is to establish higher education links between countries enabling an ongoing process of knowledge sharing to be sustained. This is the case, for example, in China where Motorola US has established its own corporate university working in partnership with local universities (Yan, 2004). This is also the case, where knowledge exchange takes place in externally funded university projects based in developing countries. The primary emphasis, in these instances, is on capacity building for human resource development, that is, developing adequate education and training infrastructures to support the development of generic worker skills and knowledge. 'World' languages, especially, American English, currently occupy a dominant position in this knowledge exchange.

The Political Economy of 'World' Languages

What are 'global'/'world' languages?

The notion of 'global' or 'world' languages has obtained potent hegemonic value within the global cultural economy. It is assumed that we all know what 'world' languages are, that they are indisputably 'world' languages, and that they are inherently superior to other languages. Because we do not question their intrinsic value, they exist as commonsense, self-evident, taken-for-granted 'truths'.

In a functional sense, we could argue that 'world' languages transcend national boundaries. That is to say, they are understood, and serve, communication purposes within and across different geographical contexts, by large groups of people. This would suggest that the conferment of 'world' language status is based, largely, on the fact that these languages are incorporated into institutions and social processes of different societies and cultures. This would also refer to other languages of wider communication, such as Kiswahili throughout major parts of Sub-Saharan Africa, Malay in South East Asia, Bislama in the Pacific Islands, Hindi in India and, at least theoretically, Urdu in Pakistan (see Chapter 7). In practice though, only a select few languages have the status of powerful 'world' languages conferred upon them. Most of these are excolonial languages as is the case, for example, with English, Spanish and French. 'World' languages then are integrally linked with global economic, cultural and political power institutions, practices and processes.

The adoption of English as the dominant language interface of the Internet, its spread as a business lingua franca, its centrality to American popular culture, especially films, computer and video games, music, and the international media as well as its association historically with colonialism, have consolidated its status as a 'world' language. Figure 4.2 shows the extent to which English predominates on the Internet.

There is, of course, an overlap between English, and non-English languages represented in Figure 4.2. For example, in countries commonly regarded as English-speaking such as the US, Canada, Australia and the

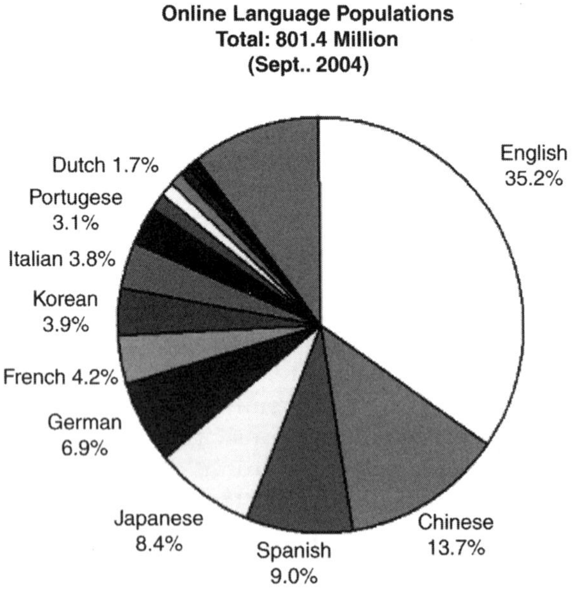

Figure 4.2 Languages used on the Internet. *Source*: Global Internet Statistics (http://www.glreach.com/globalstats/ (printed with permission)

UK, English does not, necessarily, represent the family language in some households. As a result of transmigrations of peoples from different countries, English within these contexts combines with a variety of other languages spoken in the home and community. The significance of the information in Figure 4.2 though, is the *absence* of the languages of Africa and South Asia which can be attributed to the lack of a coherent technological infrastructure within these countries (see Chapter 6 for current situation in South Africa). This means that fewer people are able to access the Internet as well as the fact that their languages do not feature significantly within this arena. According to UNESCO's *Initiative B@bel*:

> Today, more than 90% of content on the Internet exists in only 12 languages, so many users of the 6000 languages in the world are overlooked by this important communication medium. (UNESCO, 2002)

Moreover, as could be seen in Chapter 2, excolonial languages have remained the official/national languages within many postcolonial societies. These languages, therefore, are fully integrated into social, economic and political infrastructures and, in the process, subjugate local languages. As is argued earlier, the fact that these languages themselves are imbued with cultural capital has meant that they have acquired high exchange value within the labour market. Their appropriation by elite groups in postcolonial/developing countries, through privileged access to education, historically, has contributed to the development of knowledge (and power) hierarchies between different social groups. The drive for literacy in powerful 'world' languages, as well as the lack of policy support for minority language maintenance programmes in education, has relegated many local languages to low status, domain-specific, oral usage. These factors have contributed to political, economic and social disparities between elites and other social groups and, therefore, represent an inherent threat to social equilibrium.

Language elites

According to Myers-Scotton (1993: 156), 'what sets elites apart from non-elites is their frequent use of the (non-native) official language, both for business and in their private life' (information in brackets added). Excolonial/'world' languages thus become important social markers and 'serve as models for the aspiring masses'. As a result, 'it is now possible to talk of a special social "class" of Nigerians, comprising members from various ethnic and linguistic groups, for whom the "public", and indeed prominent use of English exists as one of their salient status symbols' (Aghcyisi, 1977: 99; cited in Myers-Scotton, 1993: 156).

Fluency in English, within this context (and French or Spanish in others), has become associated with 'being educated' and, therefore, is seen to represent a prerequisite for upward social mobility. That this is the case is due, mainly, to the fact that tertiary education is provided through the medium of English (French and Spanish) in most of these societies (see case studies in Chapters 5, 6 and 7). These Westernizing practices, and cultural aspirations, have long-term implications as they play an important role in shaping the social character – the social habitus – and, in the process, reinforce existing unequal language (and economic, political and cultural) relations. The valorization of excolonial languages, in their redefined status as 'world' languages, contributes to the self-marginalization and, in many instances, the demise through benign neglect of local languages. Again, this represents 'symbolic violence' describing the ways in which people collude willingly (consciously or unconsciously) in their own dispossession (Bourdieu, 1991). In Bourdieu's terms then, the intellectual elites in many postcolonial societies still have a colonial, that is, a Western European cultural habitus. Sadly, this has remained an enduring legacy of colonial hegemony and, in this regard, many postcolonial countries have yet to decolonize culturally and intellectually (Brock-Utne, 2000; Ngũgĩ, 1993).

Linguistic choices also have practical implications for education. In cases such as those discussed here, they often translate into unequal allocation of teaching and learning resources, in favour of 'world' languages, at the expense of educational support for indigenous languages. To emphasize my earlier argument, language and therefore educational elites, invariably, become the political elites who, in turn, reinforce the use of excolonial languages within official domains. Thus they perpetuate existing sociocultural, economic and political inequalities.

As can be seen earlier in Figure 4.2 English currently represents the 'world' language, *par excellence*, of the global cultural economy.

Complexities and ambiguities related to English as a 'world' language

English as a 'world' language has to be viewed in relation to two different phases of globalization. As is argued earlier, the predominance of English as the preferred 'world' language is to a great extent due to its historical links with British colonialism. English became embedded in the sociocultural base of colonized societies. Interacting over time with different cultures and experiences, it evolved in different ways within colonial and, subsequently, postcolonial societies. English language has not remained uncontested or unchanged within these contexts; rather, it has existed in a continuous dialogue with the languages and cultures within society (Canagarajah, 1999, 2005). English therefore has adapted to local use, incorporating local words and meanings giving rise to the development of different varieties of English, or different 'Englishes' (Kachru, 1982) existing alongside local language varieties. Thus we have, for instance, American English, Filipino English, Indian English, Canadian English, South African English, Pakistani English, etc. each replete with their own lexicon (see also Chapter 8).

English as counter-hegemonic discourse

Ironically, English was also used as a medium of communication through which discourses challenging the hegemony of colonialism[9] were articulated in India, the Caribbean, Africa and elsewhere. This counter-hegemonic discourse is an ongoing process, as is evident, in the rich tapestry of postcolonial literature that has entered mainstream publishing in recent years. In these instances, postcolonial writers[10] use English as a medium through which they explore their historical pasts and re-interpret their peoples' experiences, within their own frames of reference, in their own words and voices.

In South Africa (see also case study, Chapter 6) during the period of Apartheid rule, English represented a significant means by which the oppressed peoples of that country chose to 'disidentify'[11] (Pecheux, 1982) and contest the mental, cultural, economic and political subordination that constituted Apartheid policy and practice. In becoming a weapon against Apartheid hegemony, English language use empowered people in their everyday lives, by enabling them to defy the discriminatory and exploitative policies that dehumanized them. This was particularly significant, since the drive for the *dominance* of Afrikaans within the public domain formed a central part of everyday life, especially in rural areas. Thus whilst Dr Abdurahman's celebration of English discussed in Chapters 2 and 6, reflects the extent to which colonized peoples were incorporated into the colonial hegemonic project, in practice, English language use at the time, and throughout the years of anti-Apartheid struggle, represented a double-edged sword in South Africa. That is to say, whilst as a colonial language, it was inextricably linked with colonial domination, it was re-interpreted and given new, empowering meanings and inserted into the anti-Apartheid struggle. Thus, it also served as a vehicle for generating counter-hegemonic discourse.

Together, these factors highlight the need for a textured view of the different roles that English has played historically within different sociopolitical situations.

Decolonization and language policy choices

In the period following decolonization ex-colonial languages were seen as representing a pragmatic means of:

- overcoming linguistic/cultural/ethnic cleavages within society, and providing a neutral means of building a cohesive, integrated pluralistic nation;
- providing access to the global economic and political arena;
- facilitating economic, social and political modernization.

During this period, English (and French/Portuguese) was seen, largely, as providing a neutral means of integrating discursive ethnolinguistic elements into a coherent multi-ethnic 'nation'. As such, the adoption of English (and French/Portuguese) represented a state management strategy positioned within the broader nationalist project of postcolonial rulers. Yet, although articulated within an ideological framework centred on nation building, in practice, English (and French/Portuguese) was imbued historically with superior cultural, political and economic value and status. As a result, the adoption of excolonial languages as official languages in most postcolonial states, in effect, subjugated local languages within formal domains, relegating them to informal spheres of interaction, serving thus to undermine their intrinsic cultural, economic and political value.

Postcolonial policy approaches placing an emphasis on social equilibrium through the adoption of excolonial languages as a common language, sacrificed existing cohesive nations such as the Ewes, Oromo, Ibos and Hausas which constituted smaller ethnolinguistic units within countries. Although most postcolonial societies have instituted one, or more, dominant local languages as a/the national language/s (see de Varennes, 1996; Skutnabb-Kangas, 2000: 297–311), adopting the excolonial language within the official sphere as a long-term policy strategy, to the exclusion of a diversity of local languages, has failed postcolonial societies politically, economically and culturally. The outcome of this policy approach has been an under-developed and under-resourced local language infrastructure, low levels of literacy in general, and the under-development of local languages within many postcolonial societies.

The renewed valorization of English as a 'world' language has a dialogical relationship with earlier status definitions of English as a colonial language. As such, it remains linked largely with elite groups, and political systems that still exclude most of these countries' people from the full range of educational, citizenship and economic opportunities (see case study of Pakistan in Chapter 7). As is argued earlier, poverty and under-developed educational systems remain major exclusionary mechanisms in developing/postcolonial countries. In many instances, the majority of the population is excluded from the educational process. In rural areas this is related, to a significant extent, also to a lack of policy recognition of the educational value of local languages. This, in turn, contributes to unequal resource provision ultimately resulting in low levels of literacy in local languages, excolonial languages or English as a 'world' language. Clearly then, the under-development of local language infrastructures, and lack of policy support for their inclusion in education, represent an uneconomical approach to countries' human resource development.

The 'worldliness' of English

As is argued earlier, within the contemporary world, the status of English as a 'world' language, is increasingly also related to the impact that American popular culture (e.g. film, video and music), multimedia technologies, and their concomitant ideologies of consumerism, have had on the imaginations, aspirations, expectations, dreams and desires of large groups of people within different sociocultural and economic contexts, globally. This underlines what Pennycook (1995: 35), drawing on Said's (1983) concept, terms the 'worldliness' of English, which is to say, it is *in* the world and, at the same time, 'inextricably *bound up with* the world' (my emphasis). As such it forms an integral part of the complex sociocultural, economic and political fabric of late modernity.[12]

English is used in most formal contexts within the global political and business arena. Although interpreters are used within international forums, English now represents the preferred language medium, in which most transactions take place within transnational business organizations, as well as political/economic ensembles such as the World Bank/IMF, the WTO and to a large extent, also in the European Union (EU) (Phillipson, 2003). Official discourse is produced in English first, and then is translated into different languages (Buck, 2002) within these contexts.

Moreover, Phillipson (2003) highlights increases in Britain's share of the global market in international students. Phillipson argues that:

> Universities must produce the post-colonial, post-national global citizens who are competent to work in English for transnational corporations, finance houses, and international bureaucracies. In 2001, the number of foreign (overseas/international) students in the UK was

220,000 of whom 132,000 were Europeans; 565,000 foreigners (overseas/international students from elsewhere in the world) attend language schools in Britain each year. (Phillipson, 2003: 77; information in brackets added)

This market trend in English as an Additional Language (EAL) signifies the continuing ascendancy of English in the world, supported, largely, by British universities, global cultural industries such as the British Council, and also as part of existing degree programmes within traditionally non-English speaking countries (Phillipson, 2003; Yan, 2004). The latter example gives some indication of the ways in which individual countries are adjusting to language market demands within the global cultural economy.

As is argued throughout the book, now, more than ever before, language is organically linked with discursive power processes and, as such, the structural power dynamics of societal, and global language relations, remain important. It therefore is significant, that although transnational organizations such as the World Bank/IMF, verbally acknowledge the significance of local languages to social development they, nevertheless, continue their support for excolonial languages in tertiary education. They do so by leaving silences on language policy issues at this level (Mazrui, 1997). In practice, this represents *informal policy*, reinforcing a linguistic hierarchy with historical links to colonialism. This lack of official support for local languages, within major policy defining arena, continues to contribute in a major way to the eradication of many existing ethnolinguistic landscapes. In doing so, it is complicit in the process of 'linguicide' (Skutnabb-Kangas & Phillipson, 1995).

Challenging the hegemony of English as a 'world' language

Yet at the same time, the capillary ways in which power operates through language in the global cultural economy, emphasize the importance of taking account also of *human agency* and *self-definition*. Together, these concepts refer to the ever-present possibilities for challenging, and fracturing, power-based definitions by re-interpreting, and repositioning meanings, and inserting them into alternative discourses centred on empowering individuals or groups within the processes of everyday living. This was evident in the example of Apartheid South Africa discussed above (see also Chapters 6 and 8). These concepts are grounded in Giddens' (1984) structuration theory, which suggests that the contemporary social order represents an advanced stage of capitalism which he refers to as 'high' – or 'late' modernity. Within this context, Giddens argues, modern institutions have a dynamic and global impact that hitherto has been unprecedented. Instead of representing a linear process of homogenization, the effects of globalization are complex and fluid. Giddens suggests, for example, that the discursive and dynamic interaction of cultural, economic, and people flows, within the global terrain, undermines the idea of mass cultural standardization or homogenization. In fact, globalization generates greater cultural diversity, because of people and culture flows globally. As the hegemony of the older national states is reduced, it has resulted also in the reassertion of local cultural identities. There is evidence of this in the examples in Chapter 3 of the affirmation of Catalan, Basque, Welsh, Czech and Slovakian national identities. This is also the case, in the reassertion of separate national identities amongst countries previously incorporated into the Former Soviet Union (FSU). The same is also the case, with the rise of religious, political and cultural fundamentalism, as people seek recourse to the security of linear cultural 'truths' embedded in rigid frameworks, as a response to the chaos and fragmentation of life in 'late modernity'. There is, therefore, an inner tension in the local/global dialectic, having different expressions within contexts defined by different geopolitical and historical power relations. I return to the idea of 'self-definition' in relation to language and definitions of power within the global cultural economy again in Chapter 8.

This tension is also reflected in the complex sets of language choices that prevail within the global cultural economy. Whilst, as is indicated earlier, English undoubtedly is in the ascendance as an international medium of communication, it does not mean that the situation necessarily will remain static, that the hegemony of English as a preferred 'world' language will not be contested in the future by other international languages – particularly across geopolitical regions. We can, for example, speculate about the rise in the market value of Mandarin Chinese within the South East Asian region, and the Pacific Rim[13] countries, in relation to the vast commodity market that China represents – as well as the potential for China to emerge as a significant global economic power in the future. Already China is offering special incentives for investors throughout the region through its Special Economic Zones and Open Coastal Areas.

Similarly, local languages also flourish in informal markets, such as popular music and the performance arts catering for the different ethnolinguistic diasporas globally. UNESCO's *Initiative B@bel* plays a pivotal role in providing multilingual access to the Internet for developing countries in a bottom-up sense (see Chapter 6), thus contesting the hegemony of English.

The hegemony of English as the preeminent 'world' language is contested also on an everyday basis. Internet websites advertising services for the teaching of 'world' or 'global' languages, generally include a broad range of 'languages of the world' which, in addition to standard Western European languages also include, for example, a diverse range of languages such as Malay, Vietnamese, Basque, Czech, Polish, Indonesian, Byelorussian, Serbo-Croatian, different Sign languages and Hebrew. A simple Google or Yahoo search, yields advertising by a wide variety of language teaching companies offering tuition services for people working, *inter alia*, in business, banking, government, the hospitality industry, and the media. Others offer software programmes providing dictionaries in different languages, or offer translation and/or interpreting services. This gives an indication of the dynamic and highly profitable, global language industry that exists in the world today. It also indicates the existence of alternative minority language markets. Figure 4.3 represents an example of the type of language services offered on the Internet.

Here languages constitute a saleable commodity with regard to business and marketing, whilst for the clients they represent an investment in cultural capital which can then be exchanged within the global labour market. In an overall sense, macro and micro as well as formal (e.g. work, education, government institutions, business and industry), and informal (e.g. film, music, video and computer games and other language-based leisure commodities) linguistic markets constitute an important part of the global cultural economy. Language within these contexts represents largely a means to an instrumental end. It is also significant that these lists of business languages offered on the Internet reflect the relatively high economic position globally of the countries with which they are associated. Thus they tend to include European, South East Asian languages and Latin American Spanish. A Google and Yahoo search could not locate any African languages as part of the list of sought after

Global Languages Ltd was founded to provide a modern, comprehensive successful and cost effective language training service to the business community. Over the years we have achieved an outstanding level of success which has been reflected in the loyalty of our clients, the increase in the number of participants and the range of languages covered. Our clients are drawn from many business sectors, including Solicitors, Engineers, Media, Marketing, Information Technology, Banks and Government Offices. Our philosophy is that anyone, who seriously wants to or needs to, can learn a foreign language.

- **OUR AIM To offer a PERSONALISED and EFFICIENT service**

- **OUR STATEMENT We DELIVER our PROMISES**
- **OUR MISSION To do BETTER what you are already doing WELL**

Figure 4.3 Language services offered on the Internet. *Source*: Geo-languages.com (printed with permission)

business languages offered on courses advertised on the Internet (however, see Chapter 6 for developments in South Africa). This can be seen as reflecting their lower economic exchange value/currency in the global cultural economy.

In a broader sense though, the notion of a 'global', or 'world', language serves more than functional or instrumental purposes. For instance, the social arena is defined by discursive language markets. In addition to languages *per se*, these include also the *forms* of language embedded in institutions and social processes. That is to say, the specific language registers required within particular contexts of interaction, as well as the languages sanctioned by the state. These incorporate the languages and discourse used in macro-societal contexts such as trade, politics, education, business and the media, which, in themselves, represent particular forms of linguistic markets. As is the case with economic markets, discussed earlier, language markets are inherently unequal in that they ratify only particular languages/forms of language use as constituting primary cultural/symbolic capital. Since the global language market favours excolonial 'world' languages, and particularly English, they serve potentially to marginalize local/national languages by reducing their exchange, or purchasing value within formal domains. As was the case under colonialism, this shapes the language choices of people, in favour of economically powerful languages – and since language is intrinsic to culture – to some extent, also the lifestyles associated with them.

Together, these factors inhibit the development of local languages as cultural capital that can be exchanged within the global market. They also highlight the fact that neither the concept of 'world' or 'global' languages, nor the discourses in which they are grounded are neutral; they do not exist outside the field of power. The legitimation of 'world' languages in economic practices and processes, imbuing them with potent symbolic and economic power, serve to devalue local/national languages of postcolonial/developing countries, within particular spheres of interest. It is in relation to this, that the language dilemmas, already existing within postcolonial societies, have been intensified.

Implications for Postcolonial Societies

As can be seen above, excolonial languages now represent the major 'world languages', amongst which, English is presently in the ascendance. Based on this evidence, it could be argued that excolonial languages, and particularly, Standard English, represent preferred linguistic capital within the global cultural economy. If this is the case, then it raises major questions about the impact of geopolitical and economic shifts taking place within the international terrain, on the economic, sociocultural and political base of postcolonial societies/ developing countries. What, for example, does the ascendancy of economically powerful languages signify, with regard to setting national language policy priorities in relation to the sociocultural, economic and political goals of postcolonial societies? The discussion here (see Chapter 3) suggests that there are a growing number of economically disadvantaged, and linguistically/culturally disempowered, peoples living disparate lives within the global cultural economy. Others, although living in settled communities are, nevertheless, distanced from full participation, not only in the global cultural economy but, more significantly, within the borders of their own countries. Much of this is related to the lack of development of literacy in local languages spoken by people in their interactions within everyday cultural, economic and social domains.

Furthermore, fundamental changes taking place within the global labour market are impacting directly on employment possibilities, and economic development, within postcolonial societies. What are the implications of the labour market trends, discussed earlier in the chapter, for the motivation of students within postcolonial societies/developing countries, to maintain their own historically and culturally inherited languages? What incentives are there, especially for young people planning their future careers within what seems to be a growing international pool of labour supply, to maintain their ethno-cultural languages, and their cultural heritage? This question is significant, especially in developing/postcolonial societies with high levels of poverty and unemployment, where there is a growing trend of skilled labour outflows in search of jobs in the international labour market. How do developing/ postcolonial societies improve their economic status within the global cultural economy, without relinquishing their own languages and, implicitly, their cultures, and becoming subsumed by the dynamic of globalization?

Whilst the discussion, therefore, returns to questions about tensions between the local, and the global, it does so in a way that acknowledges complexities, contradictions, and ambiguities, in the way that we think about the issues that surround language within the global cultural economy, and their implications for policy and practice. At the same time, the role that structural power, embodied in organizations such as the World Bank/IMF and the WTO, play in shaping social, economic and cultural inequalities within countries remains significant.

Conclusion

This chapter focused on the political economy of language within the changing global cultural economy. It discussed the organic interaction between people, language, the economy, politics and culture within the global terrain – and their collective impact on societal development. It argued that within this interactive global context, discourses on the links between language and development, have to take account of the dynamic relationship between the economy, culture and politics, and the discursive power relations in which they are embedded.

The discussion, throughout this chapter, highlighted the ways in which excolonial languages, and particularly English as a 'world' language, have retained potent economic exchange value within the global cultural economy. Seemingly then, with linguistic markets, as is the case with economic markets, there is no level playing field amongst countries within the global cultural economy. Languages form an integral part of the competition globally for power and resources; in this contest less powerful, local languages are prone to being sacrificed, at least within official domains.

The discussion suggested that these issues need to be seen also, in relation to the ways in which the technological, economic, cultural and political shifts taking place within the global cultural economy, intersect with the legacies of colonialism, as well as the impact of the new imperialism through power ensembles such as the WTO and World Bank/IMF on language and development within postcolonial societies. It highlighted the fact that the unresolved language problems in postcolonial societies, throughout Sub-Saharan Africa and South Asia, have become more urgent to address, if these societies are to be enabled to participate more effectively within the global cultural economy.

Overall, the issues identified in this chapter, highlight the fact that problems related to language and development, are not exclusively related to the fact that English as a world language facilitates access to the global business environment. Rather, they also revolve around how best to support the development of the full economic, social and political potential of a society. The discussion throughout the chapter identifies the need to build, and sustain, the necessary educational infrastructure taking account of how, and in which domains, different languages are used within society, the purposes that they serve, and how these can be harnessed to support societal development. A multilingual policy that is informed by *actual language use* could therefore, potentially, be more profitable than a 'world' language versus local language approach set up in an unequal core-periphery relationship (see also Chapters 5, 6, 7 and 8). It suggests, instead, the need for a mixed language economy, representing the co-existence of languages for use in formal domains, and languages for informal domains. In other words, mixing ownership of individual language repertoires suited to informal markets, with languages regulated by formal markets. There is, therefore, a need to actively develop local languages as an integral part of national programmes for sustainable development. The significance of this stretches beyond economistic indicators of development; local community languages serve to weave the cultural patchwork/tapestry that, in turn, sustains the fabric of society as a whole. As such, they should be harnessed for social and economic development, despite the ever-growing pressures for fluency in 'world' languages to participate in the global cultural economy. I return to this point again later in Chapter 8.

In this regard, there is perhaps an ironic lesson to be learned from the struggle for 'Afrikanerdom' amongst the Dutch settlers in South Africa who, previously, had relied predominantly on Dutch as the language of written communication – and who were engaged in struggle against the hegemony of English. The valorization of Afrikaans as a distinct language, grounded in a distinct culture, lay at the centre of the burgeoning Afrikanerdom during the 19th and early 20th century. As such, in 1908 the Afrikaner far-right politician Dr D.F. Malan exhorted his people to:

> raise the Afrikaans language to a written language, make it the bearer of our culture, our history, our national ideals, and you will raise the People to a feeling of self-respect and to the calling to take a worthier place in world civilisation .... A healthy national feeling can only be rooted in ethnic [volks] art and science, ethnic customs and character, ethnic language and ethnic religion and, not least, in ethnic literature. (Cited in Prah, 2002a: 6)

Implicit in this, clearly nationalist, appeal is the significance of language planning as an integral part of the nation building process. Despite its nationalist rhetoric and, moreover, the fact that it later provided the rationale for the policy of 'separate development', that is, Apartheid, it does make a serious point that could be transferred to postcolonial societies rooted in the dichotomy of excolonial languages as the official language, and a dominant local language nominally representing a national language. A linear policy approach leaves a vast amount of potential cultural capital under-developed, to the detriment of society as a whole. Establishing policy norms for local languages, investing in both status and corpus planning, developing literacy in local languages, and incorporating them into the educational structure as well as the broader cultural and sociopolitical domains, serve an important role in raising the status of local languages (see Chapters 5, 6 and 8). Creating thus the material conditions for making possible the development of a philosophical base for the society in which the languages are grounded, in turn, contributes to developing the self-esteem, cultural empowerment, and identity of the people as a cohesive social entity. Again, this highlights the need for a coherent process of language planning to form an integral part of national development programmes (see also Chapter 8).

Before returning to these issues again in Chapter 8, Part II centres on the case studies of Mali, Pakistan, and South Africa provided in Chapters 5, 6 and 7. These chapters address some of the problems related to language and development, in postcolonial societies still struggling with unresolved national language policy, and social development dilemmas.

Notes

1. The concept of the 'global cultural economy' here refers to the complex global interplay between economy, culture and politics and the power relations in which they are constituted.
2. Political economy here is concerned, specifically, with the organic interaction between people, language, the economy, politics and culture within the global terrain, and their collective impact on societal development. The overall emphasis is on the historical power relationship between materially rich countries at the centre of the global cultural economy and their poor counterparts existing at the periphery.
3. Communicative competence here includes the ability to use language effectively within specific contexts including having knowledge of different discourse genre, discourse strategies, discourse styles as well as different languages.
4. This includes, for example, standardization of local languages, and harmonization of vocabularies across different cultural spaces.
5. This refers to the organic development of the lexicon of languages including new words and meanings that evolve as societies – and ways of living – change over time; the modernization of a language.
6. Bourdieu defined the concept of linguistic markets as a 'system of relations of force which impose themselves as a system of specific sanctions and specific censorship, and thereby help fashion linguistic production by determining the "price" (or value) of linguistic products' (Bourdieu & Wacquant, 1992: 145).
7. According to *The Observer* 29 May 2005 this strategy does not prevent call centre staff in India being racially abused by clients with comments such as 'you're a Paki, I don't want to talk to you, pass me to someone who can speak my language'. The article reports 'Shyamanuja Das, editor of *Global Outsourcing* magazine which published a study on the stress factors triggering resignations, said that hostility from clients was one of the factors which caused

workers to quit – 25% of those questioned said client vitriol was a major stress factor'.

8. The British National Health Service (NHS) has since the 1980s adopted neo-liberal policy strategies in which market forces play a major role. The restructured NHS comprise service units of Hospital Trusts. Sub-contracting services was an outcome of the overall rationalization of the National Health Service. Many Hospital Trusts find it difficult to meet their yearly targets because of under-staffing in key areas such as heart treatment and cancer care.
9. For example, in the work of Nehru, Gandhi, Raja Rammohan Roy, C.L.R. James.
10. For example, Arundhati Roy, Salman Rushdie, Woye Soyinka, Ngugi wa Thiongo, Yousuf (Joe) Rassool, Chinewa Achebe.
11. 'Disidentification' according to Pecheux (1982) represents the process by which people consciously work against their subjectification and thus to fracture hegemonic, disempowering meanings and practices.
12. 'Late modernity' refers to the contemporary world in which the transformation of space, place, and time as a result of technological development has contributed to a more fragmented social experience fraught with uncertainty, risk, ambiguity and complexity.
13. The Pacific Rim comprises South Korea, Singapore, Taiwan and Hong Kong. 'The Pacific Rim continues to gain strength in the global economy. From the colonization of the Americas to just a few years ago, the Atlantic Ocean had been the leading ocean for the shipment of goods and material. Since the early 1990s, the value of goods crossing the Pacific Ocean has been greater than the value of goods crossing the Atlantic' (geography.about.com).

Part 2

Case Studies

Chapter 5

Language and Education Issues in Policy and Practice in Mali, West Africa

MAGGIE CANVIN

Introduction

Since independence in 1960, successive Malian governments have struggled with the problem of raising the literacy rate of the people whilst contending with severe economic conditions. At independence the literacy rate (in French) was barely 10%, and, according to the 2000 census data, is now 19% in French or a Malian language (UNDP, 2004). Since the 1980s, concerns about the large number of students abandoning education, being excluded for failure, or retaking years in formal education, have led to experimentation with the use of Malian languages as the language of instruction. One language maintenance approach, which aims at functional bilingualism/biliteracy in a Malian language and French, is Convergent Teaching (Pédagogie Convergente). This approach is currently being implemented nationwide in the 11 Malian languages recognised for education out of the thirteen national languages so far recognised by the government. Almost a third of first cycle (Years 1–6) primary schools had made the transition by 2004. However, as we will see, there are challenges for educational planners attempting to implement a language policy that encourages the use of Malian languages in the school system.

A Sociolinguistic Profile of Mali

Mali, a former French colony, is one of the largest countries in West Africa and covers an area of just over 1,240,000 square kilometres, although it has a population of only 12 million inhabitants. Mounting economic difficulties led to a bloodless coup in 1968 and following this an authoritarian military regime took power and held it for 23 years. Following the revolution in 1991, Mali made the transition from a repressive military regime to a democratic republic. The country is now 'considered one of the most successful and promising cases of a democratic transition in contemporary Africa' (Charlick *et al.*, 1998: 11).

The language situation in Mali is moderately complex and is characterised by the coexistence of a large number of Malian languages together with French, the excolonial language. The country is landlocked being bordered to the north by Algeria, to the south by Côte d'Ivoire and Guinea, to the east by Niger and Burkina Faso, and to the west by Mauritania and Senegal. This large number of shared national borders has little relation to language boundaries. In fact, all but one of the 13 officially recognised languages of Mali are spoken in neighbouring countries (Coulibaly, 2003). This poses potential problems for harmonising orthographies where they have been developed separately on both sides of a national border for the same language group (see Table 5.1).

The country is divided administratively into eight regions plus the district of Bamako, the capital. None of the regional boundaries correspond to language group boundaries. There are many social and commercial connections between the various ethnic groups of Mali, and Bamanankan (also called Bambara) is the most commonly used lingua franca, being spoken by more than 80% of Malians as a first or second language in the central and southern areas of Mali (Coulibaly, 2003).

Forty-eight differentiated languages have so far been identified, which fall primarily into three major language families (see Table 5.2): Niger-Congo (40 languages); Nilo-Saharan (5); and Afro-Asiatic (3). The

Table 5.1 Officially recognised Malian languages that cross national borders

Country	*Language/s*
Algeria	Tamasheq
Mauritania	Hasanya Arabic, Fulfulde, Soninke
Senegal	Bamanankan, Fulfulde, Maninkakan (Malinké), Soninke
Guinea	Bamanankan, Fulfulde, Maninkakan (Malinké), Soninke
Côte d'Ivoire	Bamanankan, Mamara Sénoufo, Maninkakan (Malinké), Soninke
Burkina Faso	Bamanankan, Bomu, Dogon, Fulfulde, Mamara Sénoufo, Syenara Sénoufo,
Niger	Songhay, Tamasheq

Source: Derived from Coulibaly (2003)

Table 5.2 Language family affiliation

Atlantic	
Fulfulde, Maasina	Niger-Congo, Atlantic-Congo, Atlantic, Northern, Senegambian, Fulani-Wolof, Fula, West Central
Pulaar (Peulh)	Niger-Congo, Atlantic-Congo, Atlantic, Northern, Senegambian, Fulani-Wolof, Fula, Western
Pular (Futa Jallon)	Niger-Congo, Atlantic-Congo, Atlantic, Northern, Senegambian, Fulani-Wolof, Fula, West Central
Berber	
Arabic, Hasanya	Afro-Asiatic, Semitic, Central, South, Arabic
Tamajaq	Afro-Asiatic, Berber, Tamasheq, Southern
Tamasheq	Afro-Asiatic, Berber, Tamasheq, Southern
Dogon	
Dogon, Bangeri Me	Niger-Congo, Atlantic-Congo, Volta-Congo, Dogon
Dogon, Bondum Dom	Niger-Congo, Atlantic-Congo, Volta-Congo, Dogon
Dogon, Dogul Dom	Niger-Congo, Atlantic-Congo, Volta-Congo, Dogon
Dogon, Donno So	Niger-Congo, Atlantic-Congo, Volta-Congo, Dogon
Dogon, Jamsay	Niger-Congo, Atlantic-Congo, Volta-Congo, Dogon
Dogon, Kolum So	Niger-Congo, Atlantic-Congo, Volta-Congo, Dogon
Dogon, Tene Kan	Niger-Congo, Atlantic-Congo, Volta-Congo, Dogon
Dogon, Tomo Kan	Niger-Congo, Atlantic-Congo, Volta-Congo, Dogon
Dogon, Toro So	Niger-Congo, Atlantic-Congo, Volta-Congo, Dogon
Dogon, Toro Tegu	Niger-Congo, Atlantic-Congo, Volta-Congo, Dogon
Gur	
Bomu	Niger-Congo, Atlantic-Congo, Volta-Congo, North, Gur, Central, Northern, Bwamu
Koromfé	Niger-Congo, Atlantic-Congo, Volta-Congo, North, Gur, Central, Northern, Kurumfe
Mòoré	Niger-Congo, Atlantic-Congo, Volta-Congo, North, Gur, Central, Northern, Oti-Volta, Western, Northwest
Pana	Niger-Congo, Atlantic-Congo, Volta-Congo, North, Gur, Central, Southern, Grusi, Northern

(Continued)

Table 5.2 *Continued*

Gur (Continued)	
Sàmòmá	Niger-Congo, Atlantic-Congo, Volta-Congo, North, Gur, Central, Southern, Grusi, Northern
Senoufo, Mamara	Niger-Congo, Atlantic-Congo, Volta-Congo, North, Gur, Senufo, Suppire-Mamara
Senoufo, Sìcìté	Niger-Congo, Atlantic-Congo, Volta-Congo, North, Gur, Senufo, Suppire-Mamara
Senoufo, Supyire	Niger-Congo, Atlantic-Congo, Volta-Congo, North, Gur, Senufo, Suppire-Mamara
Senoufo, Syenara	Niger-Congo, Atlantic-Congo, Volta-Congo, North, Gur, Senufo, Senari
Mande	
Bamanankan	Niger-Congo, Mande, Western, Central-Southwestern, Central, Manding-Jogo, Manding-Vai, Manding-Mokole, Manding, Manding-East, Northeastern Manding, Bamana
Bankagoma	Niger-Congo, Mande, Western, Northwestern, Samogo
Bobo Madaré, Northern	Niger-Congo, Mande, Western, Northwestern, Soninke-Bobo, Bobo
Bozo, Hainyaxo	Niger-Congo, Mande, Western, Northwestern, Soninke-Bobo, Soninke-Boso, Boso, Eastern
Bozo, Jenaama	Niger-Congo, Mande, Western, Northwestern, Soninke-Bobo, Soninke-Boso, Boso, Jenaama
Bozo, Tièma Cièwè	Niger-Congo, Mande, Western, Northwestern, Soninke-Bobo, Soninke-Boso, Boso, Eastern
Bozo, Tiéyaxo	Niger-Congo, Mande, Western, Northwestern, Soninke-Bobo, Soninke-Boso, Boso, Eastern
Duungoma	Niger-Congo, Mande, Western, Northwestern, Samogo
Jahanka	Niger-Congo, Mande, Western, Central-Southwestern, Central, Manding-Jogo, Manding-Vai, Manding-Mokole, Manding
Jalunga	Niger-Congo, Mande, Western, Central-Southwestern, Central, Susu-Yalunka
Jowulu	Niger-Congo, Mande, Western, Northwestern, Samogo

(*Continued*)

Table 5.2 *Continued*

Mande (Continued)	
Jula	Niger-Congo, Mande, Western, Central-Southwestern, Central, Manding-Jogo, Manding-Vai, Manding-Mokole, Manding, Manding-East, Northeastern Manding, Bamana
Kagoro	Niger-Congo, Mande, Western, Central-Southwestern, Central, Manding-Jogo, Manding-Vai, Manding-Mokole, Manding, Manding-West
Maninkakan, Kita	Niger-Congo, Mande, Western, Central-Southwestern, Central, Manding-Jogo, Manding-Vai, Manding-Mokole, Manding, Manding-West
Maninkakan, Western	Niger-Congo, Mande, Western, Central-Southwestern, Central, Manding-Jogo, Manding-Vai, Manding-Mokole, Manding, Manding-West
Marka	Niger-Congo, Mande, Western, Central-Southwestern, Central, Manding-Jogo, Manding-Vai, Manding-Mokole, Manding, Manding-East, Marka-Dafin
Soninke	Niger-Congo, Mande, Western, Northwestern, Soninke-Bobo, Soninke-Boso, Soninke
Xaasongaxango	Niger-Congo, Mande, Western, Central-Southwestern, Central, Manding-Jogo, Manding-Vai, Manding-Mokole, Manding, Manding-West
Nilo-Saharan	
Songhay, Humburi Senni	Nilo-Saharan, Songhay, Southern
Songhay, Koyra Chiini	Nilo-Saharan, Songhay, Southern
Songhay, Koyraboro Senni	Nilo-Saharan, Songhay, Southern
Tadaksahak	Nilo-Saharan, Songhay, Northern
Zarmaci	Nilo-Saharan, Songhay, Southern

Source: Derived from Gordon Jr, 2005 (ed.) Ethnologue (15th edn)

largest group of these in Mali, the Niger-Congo family, can be further divided into three sub-families: Atlantic (3), Dogon (10), Gur (9) and Mande (18) (see Dumestre, 1994; Gordon Jr, 2005; also Table 5.2). Dogon is not yet fully classified. In addition to the 48 languages mentioned above, Ethnologue lists Bamako Sign Language and French as other living languages in Mali (Gordon Jr, 2005).

Population figures for language groups are difficult to estimate. The latest available figures for the population of each language group (see Table 5.3) show that the five largest language groups account for the languages used as mother tongues by over 47% of the population. Of the other 43 languages only two number more than 250,000 and 19 languages have between just 2000 and 50,000 speakers. This is based on a population of 11,956,788 (Gordon Jr, 2005). French remains the 'official language' of Mali and 13 of Mali's languages have been recognised by the government as 'national languages'.

For educational planners, one of the significant features of the linguistic landscape of Mali is that all the administrative regions are linguistically mixed. No one region contains only one language, and only a few languages are limited to one region. In addition, the small populations of some language groups have significance for educational provision as it is more difficult to provide teaching materials for them and to find teachers from those groups.

The Literacy Situation

Since independence Mali has struggled to raise its low rates of literacy and school enrolment. During the 1960s, as part of the 'rush for school' following independence, there was a steady increase in the enrolment rate from 12% in 1962 (66,208 children) to 20% in 1972 (229,879 children), although this rate of increase was slower than in other African countries (Toure, 1982). As part of the experimental world literacy programme (1969–1971) to eradicate illiteracy, Mali promoted a mass literacy campaign for adults in many of its languages (UNESCO, 1976). A pilot programme for this, PEMA (*un Programme Expérimentale Mondiale d'Alphabétisation*, pilot literacy programme), financed primarily by UNESCO, operated from 1968 to 1972 (Haïdara, 1998). This programme, although successful, was never fully developed, partly because it was impossible to demonstrate the 'social and economic returns that would satisfy orthodox criteria' (UNESCO, 2000). The trend of experimental programmes not being expanded, even though successful, has continued in Mali until the expansion of the most recent experiment, Convergent Teaching (*Pédagogie Convergente*).

Table 5.3 Language groups of Mali (ranked according to population size)

Language name	*Date of pop data*	*Number*	*% of pop*	*Regions where spoken*	*Regions where used for education*
Bamanankan	1995	2,700,000	22.4	Bamako, Ségou, Sikasso, Koulikoro, Kayes	Bamako, Ségou, Sikasso, Koulikoro, Kayes
Fulfulde, Maasina	1991	911,200	7.6	Tombouctou, Gao, Mopti, Ségou, Koulikoro	Mopti
Senoufo, Mamara	2000	737,802	6.1	Sikasso, Ségou	Sikasso
Soninke	1991	700,000	5.8	Kayes, Koulikoro	Kayes, Koulikoro
Maninkakan, Western	1993	626,800	5.2	Kayes	
Songhay, Koyraboro Senni	1999	400,000	3.3	Tombouctou, Gao	Tombouctou, Gao
Senoufo, Supyire	1991	364,000	3.0	Sikasso	
Tamasheq	1991	250,000	2.1	Kidal, Gao, Tombouctou	Tombouctou, Gao
Maninkakan, Kita	1998	200,000	1.7	Kayes	
Songhay, Koyra Chiini	1999	200,000	1.7	Tombouctou, Mopti, Ségou	
Tamajaq	1991	190,000	1.6	Kidal, Gao	
Pulaar	1995	175,000	1.5	Kayes, Koulikoro	
Senoufo, Syenara	1991	136,500	1.1	Sikasso	Sikasso
Dogon, Tomo Kan	1998	132,800	1.1	Mopti	

(Continued)

Table 5.3 *Continued*

Language name	*Date of pop data*	*Number*	*% of pop*	*Regions where spoken*	*Regions where used for education*
Dogon, Jamsay	1998	130,000	1.1	Mopti	
Dogon, Tene Kan	1998	127,000	1.1	Mopti	
Xaasongaxango	1991	120,000	1.0	Kayes	Kayes
Bozo, Tiéyaxo	1987	117,696	1.0	Mopti	Mopti
Arabic, Hasanya	1991	106,100	0.9	Kayes, Tombouctou, Kidal, Gao	
Bomu	1976	102,000	0.8	Ségou, Sikasso	Ségou
Bozo, Jenaama	1991	100,000	0.8	Mopti	
Duungoma	1991	70,000	0.6	Sikasso	
Dogon, Toro So	1998	50,000	0.4	Mopti	Mopti
Pular	1991	50,000	0.4	Kayes	
Jula	1991	50,000	0.4	no info	
Dogon, Donno So	1998	45,300	0.4	Mopti	
Tadaksahak	1995	30,000	0.2	Gao, Mopti	
Marka	1991	25,000	0.2	Mopti	
Dogon, Bondum Dom	1998	24,700	0.2	Mopti	
Dogon, Kolum So	1998	24,000	0.2	Mopti	
Bobo Madaré, Northern	2000	18,400	0.2	Mopti, Sikasso	
Mòoré	1980	17,000	0.1	Mopti	

(*Continued*)

Table 5.3 *Continued*

Language name	*Date of pop data*	*Number*	*% of pop*	*Regions where spoken*	*Regions where used for education*
Dogon, Dogul Dom	1998	15,700	0.1	Mopti	
Humburi Senni Songhay	1999	15,000	0.1	Mopti	
Kagoro	1998	15,000	0.1	Ségou, Koulikoro, Kayes	
Jowulu	2000	10,000	0.1	Sikasso	
Jalunga	2002	9,000	0.1	Kayes	
Bankagoma	1995	5,085	0.04	Sikasso	
Dogon, Toro Tegu	1998	2,900	0.02	Mopti	
Pana	1982	2,800	0.02	Mopti	
Bozo, Tièma Cièwè	1991	2,500	0.02	Mopti	
Dogon, Bangeri Me	1998	1,200	0.01	Mopti	
Jahanka	2001	500	0.004	Kayes	
Koromfé	No info	100	0.001	Mopti	
Sàmòmá	No info	6 villages		Mopti	
Bozo, Hainyaxo	No info	Villages		Ségou	
Senoufo, Sìcìté	No info	Villages		Sikasso	
Zarmaci	No info	Villages		Gao	

Source: Derived from Gordon, Jr, 2005, (ed.) Ethnologue (15th edn); Haïdara, 1998
NB: 1. Shaded cells indicate the language is used for education
2. The figure for Tiéyaxo Bozo is the aggregate figure for Tiéyaxo, Hainyaxo and Tièma Cièwè Bozo (information courtesy Thomas Blecke, SIL)

In common with many other African countries in the early 1980s, Mali experienced a period during which the literacy rate remained static, school enrolments reduced in number, and the number of children who abandoned school increased. This was partly attributed to a rebellion by parents against the economic and political system. They protested in one of the only ways open to them – by refusing to enrol their children in school. This ultimately added to the pressure for educational reform that was a significant factor in the revolution of 1991 (Lange & Diarra, 1999). Following the revolution, a review of the structures and organisation of education in Mali took place in 1991. This occurred within the political framework of the transition to a democratic republic. The review had, as its aim, basic education for the majority of the population (Ouane, 1995).

The literacy rate for all adults over 15 years was reported as 25% in 1991 (UNDP, 1999). However the 2000 census shows a drop to 19% (UNDP, 2004). The rate for 15–24-year-olds also shows a drop, from 34.9% in 1985 (UNDP, 1999) to 24.6% in 2000 (UNDP, 2004). These results are disappointing, but not unexpected following the pre-revolutionary revolt of parents mentioned above. However, the DNAFLA (*Direction Nationale de l'Alphabétisation Fonctionnelle et de la Linguistique Appliqué*, National Directorate for Functional Literacy and Applied Linguistics) adult literacy campaigns of the 1990s did increase the number of new literates and helped to prevent the figures being worse (Coulibaly, 2003). On a positive note, there has been a great increase in the number of children attending school and the gross enrolment rate has risen from 26% of school-age children in 1990 to 70.5% in 2003 of whom 60% are girls (IRIN, 2004; World Bank, 2005b). This may reflect the way that parental confidence in the government and the school system has increased since the revolution. The retention rate has also increased and by 1999, as compared with 1982, 28% more girls and 44% more boys reached the fifth year of the first cycle (UNESCO, 2000). This increased school enrolment and attendance should have a marked impact on the literacy rate within a few years.

Historical Language Policy Frameworks

The expansion of Islam into the area now known as Mali in the Middle Ages brought with it the religious use of Arabic in addition to the languages which already existed in the region. This has led to a significant literary history in Arabic through the development of Koranic schools (both formal and non-formal) and one of the earliest and greatest libraries in the world at Tombouctou (Bray & Clarke, 1986, cited in Easton & Peach, 1997; Toure, 1982). Aspects of Islamic culture have been incorporated into

Malian culture and have had a significant impact on language policy, and Arabic remains an important language in education and in society (Ministère de l'Education de Base, 1999). Both formal and non-formal Koranic schools are widespread, and the formal schools are incorporated into the education system, while still emphasising mastery of Arabic together with French (World Bank, 1999). By the mid-1980s one quarter of formal primary school students were in Koranic schools although that had dropped to 9% by 1998 (Bray & Clarke, 1986, cited in Easton & Peach, 1997; Lange & Diarra, 1999).

Under the French colonial system, which lasted from the end of the 19th century until 1960, Malian languages had no official status, had no formal written tradition and were relegated to domestic domains of use only. Language policy during this period was to use French as the medium of communication for all official business including education and commerce, apart from at local market level, with the exception of some Christian mission schools which used Malian languages, and Koranic schools which used Arabic (Haïdara, 1998). During the colonial period, in order to promote French culture through schooling, Malian culture was suppressed; the curriculum and examination structure mirrored that of France; and children were taught French literature, French geography and French history. The primary concern of colonial schools was the political and economic functions of education, so students were taught to read, write and calculate, so that they could become auxiliary staff and become the new elite who would consolidate French influence (Toure, 1982). However, the colonial schools were few in number, were for large regions of French West Africa, and were restricted in their intake to the children of the elite (Toure, 1982).

Contemporary Language Policy Frameworks

The continuing cultural influence of French colonisation is seen in Mali today in the structure of the education system and the prevailing influence and prestige of French as the official language (Toure, 1982). Formal education consists of nine years of primary education divided into first cycle (Years 1–6) and second cycles (Years 7–9); three years of general secondary education, or two or four years of technical and professional secondary education; and four years of post-secondary education. Large numbers of students drop out during the first cycle such that only half continue through to Years 7–9 (second cycle) (Ouane, 1995). The non-formal system consists of functional literacy classes for adults; and village development schools (*Ecoles Développementales Villageoises* [EDV]) and Centres of

Education for Development (*Centres d'Education pour le Développement* [CED]) for young people who have dropped out of school or who did not have the opportunity of attending school (Ministère de l'Education, 2001).

The contemporary political environment has been dominated by what is known in Mali as 'the crisis in education' (*la crise scolaire*) (Diakité, 2000). The current crisis has its roots in the formal education system inherited from the colonial regime but is considered by many Malians to have been exacerbated by government policy since independence. The power relationship between the State and the people is a pivotal issue. The main internal influence has been the way that secondary and tertiary students played a dominant role in the revolution. Since 1991, there has been a power struggle between the major organised student group, the Association of School Children and Students (*Association des Etudiants et des Elèves de Mali* [AEEM]), and the government. Student groups have felt frustrated by the government's inability to meet their demands for improvements to education. This frustration has been expressed through disruptive protests bringing the whole education system to a halt (Charlick *et al.*, 1998). In one period of six months in the academic year 2000–2001, I observed over 40 days teaching time lost to student strikes, which became progressively more violent (Canvin, 2003). Teacher's Unions have also expressed their frustrations about lack of progress in meeting their demands for improvements in pay and conditions by disrupting examinations and assessments. This disruption of education has had considerable impact on the provision of education and has lowered educational outcomes. The preoccupation of the government in coping with these disruptions has had an inevitable effect on its ability to bring about education reforms, including language reforms (Charlick *et al.*, 1998).

The power/authority relationship between the government and external agencies has also had an impact on language and education policy. The education system is dependent on financial and technical assistance from multilateral, bilateral and non-governmental agencies that naturally have their own agendas and economic interests. This can be seen, for example, by the impact of the structural adjustment policies imposed on Mali by the World Bank and the IMF. Structural adjustment policies are financial policy guidelines required of developing countries in order to qualify for international aid or loans. The language policy debate is situated within this power/authority relationship that, as Charlick *et al.* state:

> ... sets up conditions under which political leaders must weigh the consequences of failing to respond to internal demands versus those of antagonizing important donors. (Charlick *et al.*, 1998: 14)

The Use of Malian Languages in Education

After independence in 1960, a resurgence of the appreciation of Malian culture took place. This led the new government to consider using Malian languages for education as part of the process of de-colonisation (Toure, 1982). In the educational reforms of 1960 and 1962, schooling was made compulsory, co-educational and secular (Ouane, 1995; Traoré, 2001a). Language policy reforms were also on the agenda during that period, but, at that point, the emphasis was on responding to the parents' response to the 'rush for school' initiative by providing the infrastructure for expansion (Toure, 1982). The protocols for Malian languages to be officially recognised were set in process. From 1964 to 1978 various conferences and seminars were held in Mali, which considered how to raise the literacy rate and which further considered the language issue.

Two major educational debates, the 'General State of Education' (1989) between the leaders of the old regime and major donors, and the 'National Debate on Education' (1991) following the revolution, have taken place in Mali. The political education reforms that followed the revolution in 1991 resulted in education being seen as a much higher priority by the new government, and a new Ministry of Basic Education was founded. This set the scene for the response to the UNESCO/World Bank/UNICEF sponsored Conference on 'Education for All' of March 1990 held in Jomtien, Thailand and participation in the dialogue of poverty alleviation (Chambas *et al.*, 2000; Charlick *et al.*, 1998; Lange & Diarra, 1999). The provision of a basic education for all Malian children ('Education for All') is seen as contributing to development aims by alleviating poverty through providing education in a language that is understood.

The practical outcome of the debates since independence has been the establishment of two new education programmes for the first cycle of primary schooling using Malian languages. In 1979 a few 'experimental schools' were established. These schools used the Traditional French teaching methodology but with the commonly used French materials translated into Bamanankan, the most widely spoken Malian language. There was a transition to the use of French as the language of instruction from the third year. This programme was expanded to include Fulfulde, Songhay and Tamasheq in 1982.

Schools using the Convergent Teaching methodology were piloted in 1987 and since then all other experimental schools have been phased out. These schools use an interactive methodology, with an integrated syllabus related to everyday life. One of the aims of Convergent Teaching is language maintenance. Malian languages are used as the medium of instruction during the first six years of schooling (first cycle), with French being gradually introduced as an additional medium of instruction from Year 3. Initial teaching is in a Malian language known by the students. Oral French is introduced in Year 2 and written French in Year 3. Convergent Teaching schools started to be expanded nationwide from 1994 with a further expansion phase from 2001. The number of schools using the Convergent Teaching methodology have increased dramatically, from 241 out of 3082 primary schools (first cycle) in 1999/2000 to 1184 in 2001–2002 and the number is rapidly increasing (Coulibaly, 2003; Ministère de l'Education, 2001).

In Traditional French first cycle primary schools, which are still in the majority, French is used both as the medium of instruction and as a subject. The linguistic aim of these schools is for the students to have good spoken and written French in order to pass on to the second cycle and from there on to secondary education. French is taught by a process of osmosis through immersion in the language. In consequence, a lot of classroom time is allocated in the first two years to drilling the students in French. There is no use of written Malian languages in the classroom. However, they are used orally in order to assist students to understand what they are being taught.

As an example of this, in a recent study I conducted in Mali:

> One Year 5 teacher said, 'I resort to Bamanankan because they all understand that', and a Year 4 teacher said, 'I act things out to make myself understood and as a last resort I use Bamanankan'. (Canvin, 2003: 186–87)

In addition to state primary schools, part state-funded Catholic schools, founded in the colonial period, private basic schools, established in 1983, and private non-religious schools, established in 1994, all offer education only in French (Lange & Diarra, 1999). Private community schools, run by non-governmental organisations mostly use French, but the language of instruction is decided by the community. Hadrassa (Koranic) private schools, established in 1982, use Arabic and French as the languages of instruction.

All students take the same examination in French at the end of the sixth year regardless of which school they have attended. In addition to this, students in Convergent Teaching schools take an extra examination in the Malian language in which they were taught. With the exception of a few private schools, all students who continue schooling go to the second cycle of primary education (Years 7–9) in a state school. From the beginning of the second cycle all state schooling is currently in French.

Some specific comparative testing of students in Convergent Teaching schools and students in Traditional French schools was carried out by IPN (*l'Institut Pédagogique National*) in 1998 and 1999. This evaluated the standards of second and third year students in Mathematics and French in the Dogon language area (1998) and in the Songhay, Tamasheq and Soninke language areas (1999). The results of the tests showed that on average students taught by the Convergent Teaching method in all four languages did better in both subjects than those taught only in French (Ministère de l'Education Nationale, 2005a).

One way to compare the efficacy of the two systems is to consider the results of the examination at the end of the sixth year which gives entry to the seventh year (second cycle). Comparative results published by the National Examination Centre (*Centre Nationale des Examens et Concours de l'Education*) show that students from Convergent Teaching schools have achieved better results consistently than students from Traditional French schools (see Table 5.4). The table shows the percentage of students who passed the examination out of the number of students who took the examination. An improvement can be seen in the pass rates for both Convergent Teaching and Traditional French students between the 2000 and 2005 examinations (Ministère de l'Education Nationale, 2005b). There are no available breakdowns of the results by the language used for Convergent Teaching

Table 5.4 Comparative success rates for the end of the first cycle of primary education examination by region

	Convergent teaching		*Traditional French*	
Region	***2000***	***2005***	***2000***	***2005***
Bamako	75.54%	87.69%	56.75%	66.88%
Kayes	68.10%	82.16%	49.04%	60.92%
Koulikoro	92.90%	84.65%	61.00%	68.14%
Sikasso	65.10%	70.21%	46.03%	53.40%
Ségou	46.69%	75.57%	45.12%	54.18%
Mopti	79.22%	62.14%	51.03%	67.94%
Tombouctou	62.00%	76.68%	62.10%	75.62%
Gao and Kidal	59.56%	80.07%	53.51%	72.61%
National %	68.57%	79.01%	52.34%	62.22%

Source: Extrapolated from Traoré, 2001a and the published results for 2005 (Ministère de l'Education Nationale, 2005)

and the aggregated results in some regions, such as Mopti, may be aversely affected by recognised teaching difficulties for some Malian languages such as Dogon and Bozo, which have significant varieties (Zono, 2002).

In the non-formal sector, basic education schools called 'village development schools' (EDV), established in 1992, and 'Centres of Education for Development' (CED) established in 1994, are mostly in rural areas. These schools do not go beyond basic and vocational education and mainly use Malian languages whilst introducing the students to French (Lange & Diarra, 1999).

A major initiative in the recent debate about education reform in Mali was the policy developed in 1995, after much discussion, to try to integrate all these different kinds of primary schools into a coherent structure using the principles of Convergent Teaching. The New Primary School (*Nouvelle Ecole Fondamentale* [NEF]) was intended to:

> create a school which would be more closely linked to the community and to its cultural values by encouraging the use of maternal languages as well as French (and for the Medersas [Koranic schools], Arabic) and by linking the school to the development of the community. (Charlick *et al.*, 1998: 17)

Although officially adopted, according to Charlick *et al.* (1998), this reform failed to be implemented widely for a number of reasons:

- it was felt by many that the impetus for the reform did not originate in Mali;
- the use of many non-qualified teachers in the system who would be given 'training on the job' through new training centres was not popular;
- the decision to have a planned success rate of 85% was severely criticised;
- the curriculum was highly unconventional merging informal and formal education; and
- it was a reform of the primary education system only.

The NEF programme was formally abandoned only a year after its inception, but the new 10-year programme, PRODEC (*Programme décennal de développement de l'éducation*, 10 year development programme for education 1998–2008), adopted many of its ideas in 1998. This programme has become well established and has tried to answer the criticisms made against the NEF programme while expanding the use of Malian languages in primary schools and their intended continuation into secondary school (Charlick *et al.*, 1998).

Legal framework

The legal framework of the debate about using Malian languages in schools has been defined through a number of decrees, ordinances and laws. Two years after Mali gained independence, educational reform was undertaken and *Decree 235/PGRM of 4 October 1962* opened up the way for the use of Malian languages in the formal school system as the medium of instruction (Haïdara, 1998). Mali took part in pan-African meetings to decide on a unification strategy for African alphabets in 1966 (UNESCO/CLT/BALING, 1966) and again in 1978 (UNESCO, 1981). Following the 1966 meeting, the outcome for Mali was the first of several definitions in law codifying language policy. Through *Decree 85/PGRM of 26 May 1967* the alphabets for four of the principal languages of Mali, Bamanankan, Fulfulde, Songhay and Tamasheq, were formalised (DNAFLA, 1981; Ministère de l'Education de Base, 1999). At the 1978 pan-African meeting it was reported that research had been started in five other languages: Soninke, Bomu, Mamara Senoufo, Syenara Senoufo and Dogon (UNESCO, 1981). Article 1 of *Decree 159/PGRM of 19 July 1982* gave the status of 'national' languages (officially recognised languages) to the following 10 Malian languages and fixed their alphabets: Bamanankan, Bomu, Bozo, Dogon, Fulfulde, Mamara Senoufo, Soninke, Songhay, Syenara Senoufo and Tamasheq; with French remaining as the official language. It also made provision for research in linguistics and applied linguistics into all Malian languages and made it possible for them to have official alphabets as well. The use of Malian languages in the school system was further extended after this decree to include, in addition to the use of Bamanankan, Fulfulde to be used in the region of Mopti, and Songhay and Tamasheq to be used in the regions of Tombouctou and Gao (Haïdara, 1998: 6).

A political result of all this discussion about the role of language in education was constitutional amendment. The Constitution states in Article 2 that:

> all Malians are born and live free and equal in their rights and duties. Any discrimination based on social origin, colour, language, race, sex, religion or political opinion is prohibited. (Mali, Republic of, 1992)

Article 25 further states that:

> ... French is the official language. Law will determine the method for making official and promoting national [officially recognised Malian] languages. (Mali, Republic of, 1992)

Following this constitutional change, Article 12 of *Decree 93-107/P-RM of 16 April 1993* assigned the responsibility for the use of officially recognised Malian languages as the languages of instruction to the Ministry of Basic Education. The outcome of this was that from the academic year of 1994–1995 five Malian languages were used in schools together with French (Leclerc, 2003). A formal codification of the alphabets and spelling rules was produced by DNAFLA in 1993 (DNAFLA, 1993).

The number of officially recognised languages was increased to the current 13 by *Law 96-049 of 23 August 1996*, by adding Hasanya, Maninkakan and Xaasongaxango to the 1982 list. However, Hasanya and Maninkakan are not yet recognised for education. Thus, in principle, approximately two-thirds of children have the possibility of access to education in their mother tongue. The languages used are: Bamanankan, Bomu, Bozo, Dogon, Fulfulde, Mamara Senoufo, Songhay, Soninke, Syenara Senoufo, Tamasheq and Xaasongaxango, (language names as per Ethnologue 15th edition [Gordon Jr, 2005]). The shaded cells in Table 5.3 show the regions where some of these have been adopted for education.

A further recent codification of the law about the use of Malian languages for education occurs in *Law 99-046 of 28 December 1999*. Article 10 states that:

> Teaching will be carried out in the official language and in national [officially recognised Malian] languages. The method of using national and foreign languages in teaching will be fixed by order of the Ministers in charge of education. (Mali, République du, 1999)

Institutional change

A major emphasis of the legal reforms since independence was the necessity of encouraging scientific research into Malian languages, in order to use them for non-formal literacy classes as well as in the formal school system (Ministère de l'Education de Base, 1999).

Since independence, many educational facilities have been created to promote literacy and they have also been involved in the creation of language policy. From 1994 to 2001 a series of decrees, laws and ordinances pertaining to education and language were passed which resulted in structural change. *Law 00-048/P-RM of 25 September 2000* created a new National Directorate of Basic Education (*Direction Nationale de l'Education de Base* [DNEB]), *Ordinance 00-85 of 26 December 2000* ratified it, and *Decree 00-0526/P-RM of 26 October 2000* laid out its terms of reference. DNEB is responsible for interpreting, putting into practice and coordinating the national policies promoting the officially recognised Malian languages in formal and non-formal education (Coulibaly, 2003; Ministère de l'Education Nationale, 2004a).

Following on from the creation of DNEB, there was a massive structural reorganisation of institutions in 2001. This was in order to develop a coherent body dealing with Malian languages and to separate research on languages from their implementation in the school system. A new institute, the Institute of Languages (*l'Institut des Langue Abdoulaye BARRY* [ILAB]), was created through *Ordinance 01-044/P-RM of 19 September 2001*, its terms of reference being laid out in *Decree 01-516/P-RM of 22 October 2001* (Mali, République du, 2001a, 2001b). Many linguistic researchers from DNAFLA were transferred to ILAB, which promotes the use of officially recognised Malian languages in education and society by continuing research on Malian languages. It does this through: identifying languages and further developing the language map of Mali; collecting, transcribing and publishing texts; the systematic description of Malian languages; research on translation and interpretation between languages; expanding training programmes in the use of Malian languages; cooperating with other African countries on linguistic research; and the publication of research results (Mali, République du, 2001a). ILAB is also tasked with promoting linguistic cooperation between Mali and other African countries particularly with the neighbouring countries that share one or more of the 13 officially recognised Malian languages (Coulibaly, 2003).

Two other institutions have also been created to deal with the day-to-day running of education in the formal and non-formal sectors. The National Centre of Education (*Centre National d'Education* [CNE]) is primarily responsible for educational research and the evaluation of programmes, materials and pedagogy in the formal school system. The National Resource Centre for Non-Formal Education (*Centre National des Ressources en Education Non Formelle* [CNR-ENF]) is primarily responsible for coordination of programmes, training teachers, and the production of teaching materials in the non-formal sector. It provides an interface between agencies providing non-formal education and the government (Coulibaly, 2003).

Language Attitudes and Language Choices

Societal use of Malian languages

The debate on language and education, while expressed politically through legislation, is also expressed socially through attitudes towards languages and the choices that people make. Language choice is often a practical matter and is driven by social and economic necessity. We see this in Mali in the way that Bamanankan has become the most widely spoken language in the south of the country, and there are many second-language speakers. In addition, Bamanankan is now being used in some administrative domains which were previously French-only. In some domains, such as the law courts or government services, where French is used in written communication, oral communication in Malian languages, particularly Bamanankan, is permitted (Dumestre, 1994). There has been a deliberate policy of encouraging media production in Malian languages since 1972. At the moment there are radio programmes in the officially recognised languages and, on local radio, in some of the not yet recognised languages, and there are newspapers in Bamanankan, Fulfulde and Soninke (Coulibaly, 2003).

Parental choice

In principle, parents have the choice of which school their children should attend and therefore, at least theoretically, choice of the language of instruction. Within the formal and non-formal sectors, there are both state and privately funded schools offering education in French, Arabic and Malian languages. Factors that may influence parental choice include: the scarcity of schools in rural areas; the problem of parents moving to a different language area; the belief that going to a French-only school will give their children a better chance of employment; and religious concerns which prompt some parents to send their children to Koranic schools, which use French and Arabic.

There are also problems for Teachers who are assigned teaching posts outside of their language area. As one teacher said to me:

> Another problem we all fear as teachers is this. If a teacher is transferred to another region where a different language is used in the Convergent Teaching schools, how are his/her children going to cope in the Convergent Teaching system? (Canvin, 2003: 244)

Key Human Resource Development Issues

Economic issues

Despite political reforms, Mali remains one of the 10 least developed countries in the world (UNDP, 2004) and this has affected its ability to fully implement language policy reform, particularly through education programmes. The majority of the population live in rural areas with only 27% living in towns. The population is largely concentrated in the fertile south of the country, and this is reflected in the linguistic complexity of that region (DNSI, 2001). This, in turn, has an impact on both language policy and the provision of education.

A major economic factor that emerged after the colonial period was an acute shortage of trained personnel. All senior staff were French and this is reflected in the fact that at independence in 1960 for the whole population of 4,300,000 there were only three Malian veterinarians, eight medical doctors, 10 lawyers, seven engineers and three pharmacists. In order to promote national economic growth, the newly formed government found itself with the task of producing large numbers of trained middle and high-level personnel in all the professions (Toure, 1982).

In view of this, from the perspective of human resource development, the key issue since independence, and particularly since 1991, has been the restructuring of the power relationship between the educated elite and the ordinary people of Mali who had been denied education (Charlick *et al.*, 1998). It was thought that the provision of basic 'Education for All' would enable citizens to become active agents in social and economic development; and that the promotion of a policy for the development of human resources would alleviate the acute human resource shortage revealed on the departure of the French colonialists (Ouane, 1995). This is closely allied with the dialogue on human rights, which include language rights, and the dialogues on poverty alleviation and 'Education for All' (Ministry of Economy and Finance, 2002).

As Tollefson argued:

> Whenever people must learn a new language to have access to education or to understand classroom instruction, language is a factor in creating and sustaining social and economic divisions. (Tollefson, 1991: 9)

Language thus becomes a criterion for determining which people will complete the different levels of education and can be a way of rationing access to jobs with high salaries. In Mali, the mastery of French has been an essential prerequisite for both higher education and social and economic advancement. Whilst the expansion of the Convergent Teaching approach, providing as it does a transition to French from a known language and potentially allowing access to higher levels of education for more students, may improve their employment prospects, this is clearly not, in and of itself, sufficient. The pivotal question in all the education debate is 'education for what'? If all education does is prepare a student for the next level of education then it is not fulfilling the human resource development needs of the country, and is not preparing students for life.

Technological issues

A counter-balance to the emphasis on the use of Malian languages has been the cultural influence of global media in Mali. Radio, television, advertising and the increased availability of Internet access through cyber cafés in large towns have played a part in promoting the demand for the teaching and use of international languages, particularly French and English. Advances in technology and the global market mean that an increase in societal computer literacy is also becoming essential in order for Mali to compete in world markets. In the area of global communication there was a new emphasis on the recognition of Malian languages following the workshop on African Languages and the Internet in Bamako 2002. In that conference the use of African languages on the Internet was seen as strengthening social and economic development and the statement was made that:

> The protection and the promotion of the national [Malian] languages is an essential component of an inclusive information society and linguistically pluralistic information. (WSIS, 2002)

The Ministry of Education in Mali is aware of the need to develop human resource skills in the areas of global communication and technology. The Report from Mali to the 46th session of the International Conference on Education organised by UNESCO in Geneva in September 2001 stated that Mali intended to introduce data processing and computing from the first years of schooling using solar energy as the power source (Ministère de l'Education, 2001). How this will be carried out remains to be seen. A thematic meeting on 'Multilingualism for cultural diversity and participation for all in cyberspace' was held in Bamako in May 2005 (WSIS, 2005) which explored the technological issues. This meeting was pertinent to the UNESCO initiative of developing community multimedia centres in Mali (UNESCO, 2005) and the technological challenges of providing materials for development in Malian languages.

Health issues

A further key human development issue in Mali is that of health. According to UNDP (2002) 43% of children aged five and under in Mali are malnourished and underweight. This has inevitable impacts on the health of school children and educational achievement. The overall struggle against malnutrition in Mali, particularly in rural areas, is being addressed through a 10-year improvement plan (IMF, 1999).

Curriculum Issues and Teaching Materials

Curriculum issues

The new curriculum for the first six years of Basic Education (first cycle) has already been developed, and the new curriculum for Years 7–9 (second cycle) is in the process of being developed. Following a National Forum on the generalisation of the curriculum for basic education in 2004, the intent of the curriculum reform is to recognise Malian culture whilst promoting integration into the technical age (Ministère de l'Education Nationale, 2004b). The introduction of the new curriculum began in 2005 in Convergent Teaching schools and will be implemented progressively in all schools. The new curriculum integrates the methodology of Convergent Teaching with other educational methods and innovations currently being used (Ministère de l'Education Nationale, 2004b). In many areas schools serve multiple language groups and the language to be used in school will be set on a school by school basis after language survey, and after the communes have been consulted. In some cases the language of instruction will continue to be French (Ministère de l'Education Nationale, 2004b). The introduction of Malian languages is intended eventually to continue into Years 7–9 but as yet there are no materials or plans for this (Ministère de l'Education, 2001). The key curriculum issue will be that functional bilingualism is to be developed in French and a Malian language where possible, using an active methodology. In order to achieve this, French will be taught as a foreign language rather than by immersion, and both languages will then be used as the language of education in primary schools (Ministère de l'Education, 2001).

Teaching materials

In the traditional French approach the textbooks are of broader African application than just the Malian setting, which means that much of the culture of the students is ignored (Canvin, 2003). By comparison, in the Convergent Teaching approach, teaching materials are very varied. Visual aids in both the Malian language used in the school and French play a large part in the approach, and the classroom walls are a riot of colour because of the many posters hung on them. The materials and illustrations used in the Convergent Teaching approach are highly relevant to the lives of the students and use localised illustrations wherever

Figure 5.1 Convergent teaching classroom wall showing class library. *Source*: Canvin, 2003.

possible. The Convergent Teaching approach is a whole-language methodology. Teaching materials are produced in annual teachers' workshops and gathered from a number of sources, including French textbooks. Written discourse has a prominent role in the Convergent Teaching approach. A text is first written on the blackboard, and then, once it has been used, it is written on a sheet of brown paper that is hung on the classroom wall to provide a class library (see Figure 5.1, Convergent Teaching classroom wall showing class library) (Canvin, 2003).

Coulibaly (2003) reports that there are now 80 titles available in 11 Malian languages for Convergent Teaching schools where teachers also use Books 1–5 of the French series '*Rencontres*'.

The production and distribution of school textbooks has been a major issue since the reform of education in 1962. Initially textbooks were revised to reflect Malian culture and local publishing was encouraged. However, during the re-evaluation of educational costs as part of the structural adjustment policy required of Mali by the World Bank and the IMF in the 1980s, it was deemed too expensive to continue producing textbooks in Mali. Textbook production was transferred to France and Canada where textbooks were developed and produced for the whole of francophone West Africa. Consequently, local production of textbooks was restricted to small-scale experimental work in Malian languages (Brock-Utne, 2000). This had an adverse impact on language policy for education, as it limited textbook production in Malian languages and increased reliance on outside funding. In recent years, PRODEC has encouraged the pairing of Malian publishing companies with foreign publishing companies to produce textbooks. PRODEC proposed the 'renting' of books to students in order to provide a revolving fund managed by school governing bodies but it is unlikely to happen in practice (Charlick *et al.*, 1998). The lack of provision of materials for teacher and the insufficient number of books for students in both French and Malian languages is a problem in most schools at all levels (Charlick *et al.*, 1998; Kané, 2000). On a recent field trip I observed this lack of textbooks in a sixth year Traditional French class where only two students out of 113 had the textbook that the teacher was trying to teach from (Canvin, 2003). This problem is not confined to the Traditional French schools and Kané (2000) documents the lack of materials (for both student and teacher) in Convergent Teaching schools. Following the National Forum in 2004 the problems of development and distribution are being addressed and new textbooks are being developed to reflect the generalisation of the new curriculum. These are being developed and distributed progressively in Malian languages and French (Ministère de l'Education Nationale, 2004b). The materials for Years 1–2 were distributed in 2005, those for Years 3–4 will be distributed in 2006 and those for Years 5–6 in 2007.

Linguistic research on the 11 Malian languages recognised for education is being conducted by ILAB and other agencies thus providing resources for teachers. All of these languages have a standardised orthography and a bilingual dictionary with French except for Bomu, which is in progress. In addition, monolingual dictionaries are available in Bamanankan and Fulfulde. There are also grammars, storybooks and other materials in Bamanankan available in bookshops. Systematic grammatical descriptions have been completed by ILAB and others in Songhay, Soninke and Tamasheq, and summary grammatical descriptions in Bomu, Bozo, Mamara Senoufo and Syenara Senoufo (Coulibaly, 2003). However, it is rare to find these resources in the hands of teachers (Canvin, 2003). A result of this is, as Doumbia (2000) points out from his classroom observation, that even in Bamanankan, one of the most developed Malian languages, the grammar of the language is taught indirectly and not systematically as French grammar is taught.

Teachers and Classes

Classes

Class sizes in Mali were the highest in the world in 1996–1998. The average number of students per teacher in Basic Education rose from 48.5 in 1990/1991 to 79.5 in 1997/1998 (UNDP, 1999), although, according to the Ministry of Education (Ministère de l'Education, 2001) this reduced to 66 per class for the first cycle and 61 for the second in 2000. There are four reasons for this high pupil teacher ratio: the increase in the percentage of children of school age going to school; the number of children retaking years of schooling; the fact that the number of new schools and classrooms being built is not keeping pace with the increase in the school population; and the lack of qualified teachers. For example, in one Traditional French school I visited in my study in 2001, class sizes ranged from 113 to 172 with one class teacher. The problem is not limited to Traditional French schools because, as more parents are choosing to put their children in Convergent Teaching schools, overcrowding of these classrooms is also happening and I observed a second year class of 96 students. One head teacher had to resort to using one classroom for one year in the morning and for another year in the afternoon because he only had five classrooms for the six classes (Canvin, 2003). I believe these schools to be typical of many schools in Mali. One further point to note here is the condition of many of the classrooms that do exist. In my study I found that none of the first cycle classrooms I visited in Mali had an electricity supply, the insides of classrooms were very dark, and many badly needed repair. The head teachers were reduced to clustering around the one single window in their office in order to see to work (Canvin, 2003).

Teacher supply

The shortage of teachers in all primary schools (first and second cycle) contributes to the large class sizes already mentioned. To cope with this, many classes are divided in half and the teacher will teach one half in the morning and the rest in the afternoon. In addition, classes are often amalgamated to cover maternity leave or other teacher absences. Staff shortages occur despite the recruitment of temporary teachers and staff drafted in from other professions and given a short teacher-training course (Canvin, 2003). The massive expansion of the number of schools using the Convergent Teaching approach and the expansion to 11 of the officially recognised languages will lead to further problems of teacher supply, as there is a limited number of teachers from some smaller language groups.

The training and supervision of teachers

Teacher Training Institutes, IFMs (*Institut de Formation des Maitres*) train teachers for both the Traditional French approach and the Convergent Teaching Approach. This training can be of two or four years duration.

However, in practice, there are many teachers in schools who have not been trained at all or who have been given minimal training.

Until recently, Convergent Teaching schools were staffed by experienced teachers drawn from Traditional French schools and given additional training. In more recent years training for Convergent Teaching has been integrated into the normal teacher training programme. However, some teachers have only received a short course of training in Convergent Teaching. In-service training sessions are held every year during the long winter vacation, July to September, for all Convergent Teaching teachers. The training is conducted by experts in Convergent Teaching from various institutions. There are three levels of training. Each level consists of two sections: a Malian language section and a Convergent Teaching methodology section. In Level One, teachers are introduced to Convergent Teaching and transcription and writing in Malian languages. Those who are not able to read and write in the relevant Malian language are taught to do so. In Level Two, teachers are introduced to the teaching of oral French and their skills in writing in the relevant Malian language are strengthened through creative writing. In Level Three, teachers are trained to teach to the sixth year in the programme. Each level takes 20 days training although this is felt by Traoré (2001a) to be insufficient because it does not allow the teachers enough time to master the contents of both sections in the level. Training is also conducted at various times of the year for head teachers, educational advisors and regional staff. In order to meet the increased need for teachers, the training requirements for entry into teaching have been reduced and this will have an impact on the quality of teaching (Amadio, 2001). Efforts have been made to maintain teacher quality through an annual national level evaluation conducted by a team consisting of linguists and educationalists from the government agencies involved and other specialists. At a regional level there are quarterly and monthly evaluations by regional staff. In practice, in some regions of Mali this is extremely difficult to carry out because of the geophysical conditions and lack of transport links. School head teachers also carry out daily evaluations of their staff. The aim of this evaluation plan is to support the teachers whilst providing continuous feedback on performance (Haïdara, 1998; Traoré, 2001a).

Problems and Dilemmas

The postcolonial political debate has been centred on the design of an education system that is felt to reflect Malian culture whilst meeting the needs of the country for trained personnel. As is discussed above, these ideals have been expressed politically through education reforms, experimental programmes, literacy campaigns and changes in the legal framework enabling Malian languages to be used in schools alongside French. The main dilemmas for the government are how to raise the literacy rate, reduce the number of children who do not complete basic education, reduce the number of children who retake years of school, and meet the UNESCO 'Education for All' goals. This will need to be done within the constraints of the education budget, which has been severely limited by structural adjustment policies, or with the help of NGOs and bilateral agencies. The use of Malian languages in education is seen by many to be an essential tool in bringing 'Education for All' about. However, the provision of education in a language students understand is not as simple as merely officially recognising all or some Malian languages. Although the linguistic map of Mali shows some discrete language areas, there are many people in those areas whose mother tongue is different. This can make the provision of basic education in the 'mother-tongue' difficult, if not impossible, for all children, even if there is the political will. For many children, the choice of a Malian language as the language of instruction will result in an improved learning environment. However, if the switch to Malian languages is widely implemented, some children may come to school speaking the parental language, be taught in a different Malian language, and still need to learn French before progressing further in their schooling.

The new curriculum for basic education will require a reformation and restructuring of the teacher-training programme (Ministère de l'Education, 2001). The massive rise in school enrolments has had an impact on class sizes, adding to the already major problems of a lack of textbooks and teachers, and consequently exacerbating concerns about teaching quality. A further impact of the redesign of the curriculum and the innovative teaching methodology is the need for the training and retraining of school directors and pedagogical counsellors (Ministère de l'Education Nationale, 2004b; OPEC, 2000). As the curriculum reform extends to secondary schooling this problem will become more acute.

Future Developments

The problems that beset the education system are well known in Mali, and educators and politicians have been trying to find ways to improve the system over many years. The latest wave of reforms following the National Forum in 2004 (Ministère de l'Education Nationale, 2004b) shows a continued desire to achieve this whilst recognising the linguistic diversity of Mali as a strength that reinforces the ideals of democracy.

In the past, improvements and access to education have been seen as contributing to poverty alleviation, and resources from bilateral debt relief have been used to bolster the education budget. As Paul Boateng stated:

> To date, in Mali, resources from bilateral debt relief have led to more spending on education, with almost 2500 classrooms constructed, and almost 2000 teachers recruited and trained. This new commitment will allow more resources to be spent on poverty reduction. (HM Treasury UK, 2005)

Marouni and Raffinot (2004) corroborate this by confirming that recent reforms have increased the Basic Education budget allocation to 45% of the Education budgetary expenditure, and it is hoped that the recent debt relief innovation will continue to aid the reformation of the education system.

In order to address the known shortcomings of the education system, PRODEC and the National Forum on the Generalisation of the Curriculum of Basic Education have begun major curriculum reform. It is also planned before 2008 to improve teacher quality through the reform of the teacher-training programmes, to improve provision and distribution of textbooks, and to expand the Convergent Teaching approach (Ministère de l'Education Nationale, 2004b).

In published education plans Coulibaly (2003) states that the 11 Malian languages officially recognised for education will be used as the language of communication in pre-school education, and as the language of instruction together with French in first cycle schools. Teaching materials in the 11 languages will be used from the seventh year upwards and in addition the 11 languages will be used for oral explanation in all schools when needed. For Convergent Teaching students the fact that they have passed an additional examination in the Malian language in which they were taught will be included in the Basic Studies Diploma (*Diplôme d'Etudes Fondamentales* [DEF]) if they are successful in the sixth year. In non-formal education the following will be created: a certificate of literacy in an officially recognised language which will be recognised for employment; a certificate for non-formal facilitators; and a leaving certificate for students completing education at the Centres of Education for Development (CED). In addition, road traffic and other major signs will become bilingual; libraries in Malian languages will be built up; and there will be a greater diversification of newspapers and media using Malian languages (Coulibaly, 2003).

The future is encouraging, and I will leave the last word to Traoré (2001b) who sees the concept of primary schooling in Mali changing through the implementation of the Convergent Teaching approach.

> Convergent teaching, which is being spread across the country, is a new concept of schooling which can give Malian schools a new purpose. This is to educate independent, creative children rooted in their own culture, yet turned towards the future ... (Traoré, 2001b: 368)

Chapter 6

Language and Literacy Issues in South Africa

KATHLEEN HEUGH

South Africa is now 10 years into a new political dispensation, guided by a Constitution considered to be one of the most democratic or progressive of the modern world. Three-hundred and fifty years of colonial, postcolonial and finally apartheid rule were replaced in 1994 by the first democratically elected government of national unity. As has been the case elsewhere, the effects of colonialism, and in this case postcolonial developments peculiar to South Africa, have been well-documented by numerous authors. Structural inequities compounded over the three and a half centuries have presented enormous economic, educational and social challenges to the new government whose goals are rooted in societal equity. This case-study will identify some of the glaring difficulties facing the first post-apartheid government in relation to issues of literacy, language, education and access, and then assess the attempts to address these over the last decade.

Structural difference in South Africa has until fairly recently been most often identified along 'race' and class lines. Although the institutional use of Afrikaans as a language of vertical control[1] and political exclusion has been emphasized, less obvious has been the extent to which the role and use of language (especially English) more widely accentuates divisions between those with power, and those without. Dismantling the most obvious and blatant forms of exclusion began even before the transfer of power in 1994. While language issues were identified for attention in the interim Constitution of 1993 and the finalized version in 1996,[2] these have been largely underestimated and under-resourced. This is despite efforts of the Department of Arts and Culture,[3] which is responsible for language policy and management, and a statutory body, the Pan South African Language Board (PANSALB), which was set up in accordance with provisions of the Constitutions to promote linguistic equity and multilingualism and to protect language rights (see Alexander & Heugh, 1999). Quite simply, those who are literate and have the highest levels of education tend to be most proficient in Afrikaans and/or English. Those who have the least experience of, and success in formal education, and access to economic power or social services, continue to be speakers of African languages. This is a contemporary example of the reproduction of institutionalized postcolonial phenomena witnessed elsewhere (see Pennycook, 2002a, 2002b).

It should therefore be obvious that speakers of African languages are most likely to be unemployed, poverty-stricken and unable to access social services or claim their rights in terms of the Constitution. The ramifications of continued economic and educational inequality seriously compromise issues of citizenship, national development and social equilibrium. In order for this situation to be reversed, language and literacy concerns ideally ought to have been included as significant criteria in the grand ideas for economic and development planning of the new government. The Reconstruction and Development Programme (RDP) of 1994 and its successor, the Growth, Employment and Redistribution: A Macro-Economic Strategy (GEAR) of 1996 missed the opportunity to address the relationship between language issues and the economy in terms of domestic, regional and global interests. The national Department of Education after formulating a potentially enabling language-in-education policy (DOE, 1997) has both procrastinated and prevaricated over its implementation (Heugh, 2002). Government as a whole has thus far failed to take serious cognizance of the relationship between language and literacy on the one hand and social and economic development on the other hand.

Sociolinguistic Profile of South Africa

Linguistic communities in Southern Africa, as elsewhere, are mobile and, consequently, language profiles change over time. Mesthrie describes the language profile of the country thus:

> South Africa has been the meeting ground of speakers of languages belonging to several major families, the chief ones being Khoesan, Niger-Congo, Indo-European and (South African) Sign Language. (Mesthrie, 2002: 11)

The Khoe and San languages are now close to extinction while several Bantu languages of 'the wider Niger-Congo family' (Mesthrie, 2002), which include Nguni (Zulu, Xhosa, Swati and Ndebele), Sotho (North Sotho, South Sotho and Tswana), Tsonga and Venda, are spoken by the majority of the population. Trading and colonial interests have been largely responsible for Afrikaans and English becoming the dominant languages or languages of vertical power. They are usually identified as the languages of European origin although Afrikaans emerged only in the Cape and included not only Dutch, but also features of 'Malayo-Portuguese' spoken by slaves and 'KhoiKhoi' (Giliomee, 2003a: 4; see also Chapter 4). Yet there are small numbers of speakers of other European as well as Indic languages (e.g. Hindi, Gujarati and Marathi). Other African languages have resulted from recent patterns of migration from other parts of Africa, partly because many people assumed that post-apartheid South Africa would offer more promising opportunities than those in more poverty-stricken parts of the continent. In many instances, migration is a result of ongoing political conflict and war affecting many countries.[4] Such changes are altering South Africa's linguistic profile. The extent to which this is taking place has not yet been accurately assessed since those who arrive in the country 'illegally' do not volunteer such information for official purposes. There are, therefore, widely divergent official and non-official estimates of people with other languages of the African continent. The former Minister of Home Affairs responsible for immigration issues referred to 'millions of people' who are illegal immigrants (Buthelezi, 2002), and he subsequently admitted that 'we don't even know how many such people there really are' (Buthelezi, 2003).[5] A substantial number of foreigners come from the Southern Africa region and speak languages which are also used in South Africa. For example, speakers of Changana (Shangaan) in Mozambique find that speakers of Tsonga understand them easily; speakers of Sotho from Lesotho, Tswana from Botswana, and Swati from Swaziland are frequent visitors, if not immigrants. In other words, there are several cross-border languages which are used in regular communication. However there are many more languages, particularly from Central and West Africa, including Hausa, Kikuyu, Yoruba, Kirundi and Kiswahili, which have been recently introduced to South Africa.

The Constitution identified 11 official languages: those which had since the Union of South Africa (1909–1910) enjoyed official national status (Afrikaans[6] and English), and those which during apartheid years were given official homeland status (Zulu, Xhosa, Southern Ndebele, Swati, Southern Sotho, Northern Sotho, Tswana, Venda, Tsonga).[7] PANSALB was given responsibility for monitoring the official use of these languages and also to address the interests of speakers of Khoe, San, languages of religion and community languages. There is some contestation about the languages selected for official status. There are a number of small linguistic communities that believe they have been short-changed in the new dispensation. The Northern Ndebele people (*Ama*Ndebele) see their language, *Si*Ndebele, as distinctly different from, rather than included with, Southern Ndebele (*Isi*Ndebele). So while the latter was given official status, the former was not and this community has been contesting what it believes to be both exclusionary and a violation of language rights (Heugh, 2003).

There have been two national censuses conducted since the transfer of power in 1994, namely, in 1996 and 2001. These, together with a National Sociolinguistic Survey (PANSALB, 2000) have gathered information in relation to the language profile of the country. While sociolinguists understand that most people live in bilingual or multilingual contexts, the deposits of ideologies, perceptions and patterns of behaviour from the colonial and apartheid eras continue to exist under the new political dispensation. For example, the structural after-effects of separate development have so infused government bureaucracy in this country that the census data collection process replicates the former apartheid notion of ethnolinguistic and monolingual stereotypes. Thus while South Africans are often bilingual or multilingual in their homes, their immediate communities and in their places of work, the national census limited its concerns to the 'language most often spoken at home' (Statistics SA, 2003: 14). The PANSALB Survey, based on a sample of 2160, however, elicited far more complex data, including 'present main language', 'language used in childhood with parents', 'language used when talking to oneself', 'language of greatest fluency'; neighbourhood languages; languages used in education, for accessing various services, in the workplace, and in the immediate community; and languages 'mixed with home language' (PANSALB, 2000). Gaps in both sets of data include accurate figures for immigrants from other African countries and users of Sign Language(s) although PANSALB found that approximately 3% of households have one or more people who are deaf. By extrapolation therefore at least 3% of people are likely to use sign language (or signed languages) as their L1 (PANSALB, 2000: 170). Statistics selected from both sets of data collection procedures are presented in Table 6.1.

These statistics show several trends. The first is that Zulu is the strongest and most frequently used language in the country, and that although there is no obvious single lingua franca, Zulu, Xhosa, Afrikaans and English appear to be most in use. If one takes into account the close proximity and mutual intelligibility of the Nguni cluster (Zulu, Xhosa, Swati

Table 6.1 Home languages, languages of greatest fluency and main language used in neighbourhood[1]

	Census 2001	*PANSALB 2000*				
	Main language used at home	***Main language used at home***	***Language of greatest fluency***	***Main language used in neighbourhood 100%***	***2nd lang. Most often used in neighbourhood 60%***	***3rd lang. Most often used in neighbourhood 30%***
Zulu	23.8%	24%	22	23	13	12
Xhosa	17.6	16	16	15	9	11
Afrikaans	13.3	17	17	18	16	12
N. Sotho	9.4	8	7	7	6	4
English	8.2	9	10	12	27	15
Tswana	8.2	10	9	9	4	9
S. Sotho	7.9	7	6	7	6	12
Tsonga	4.4	3	4	3	6	4
Swati	2.7	3	3	3	3	1
Venda	2.3	2	2	2	1	2
S. Ndebele	1.6	1	1	1	2	2

[1]The sequence of languages listed follows that presented in the Census 2001 documentation.
(Data from Statistics SA, 2003; PANSALB, 2000: Tables 3A, 5A, 5E)

and Ndebele) and, similarly, of the Sotho cluster (S Sotho, N Sotho and Tswana), then about 50% of the population speak or can understand Nguni, 25% can speak or use Sotho, up to 18% use Afrikaans and up to 12% use English as either the home language or main language of local communication. English, however, significantly outperforms other languages as second or third alternative to the main language of local communication.

If one were to be concerned with development planning one would need to look at data distribution in terms of language fluency and use across provincial, rural-urban, gender, age and educational lines.[8] Language fluency data reveal insignificant differences in relation to gender. However, there are considerable fluency differences amongst age and education levels as well as in respect of which languages are most likely to be used for neighbourhood communication (see Table 6.2).

Public perception is so pervasive that often academics attest to the notion that English is *the* lingua franca (Young, 2001). It is however, undoubtedly the language most widely used by the political and economic elite (Alexander, 2000; Webb, 2002). Yet the PANSALB figures, which have yet to draw any scientific rebuttal, show that overall Zulu is the language of greatest fluency followed by Afrikaans and Xhosa. It is only at the highest level of education (Grade 12+ attained by 28.8% of adults over age 20) that Afrikaans and English outstrip Zulu, and then this is in equal proportions.[9] Thus public perception of the predominance of English, as recorded or presented by the media, senior members of the

Table 6.2 Language fluency and educational levels

	Educational qualifications			
Language of greatest fluency	***Total***	***0–Grade 5***	***Grade 8–9***	***Grade 12+***
Afrikaans	17	10	18	25
English	10	1	5	25
S Sotho	6	8	6	4
Tswana	9	13	12	2
N Sotho	7	8	7	5
Xhosa	16	21	15	11
Zulu	22	25	21	20

Data from PANSALB, 2000: Table 3G, p. 20

government, and top management of the private sector, reflects a reality pertinent only to a small percentage of the South African public. English has not yet been shown in any scientific study to outstrip other languages of the country in terms of levels of proficiency.

The figures in Table 6.3 show relative stability of language use and proficiency amongst some languages, and language shift in other cases. Of particular note is the apparent increase of proficiency in Zulu with a corresponding decline in English proficiency between the ages of 25–44, that is, during the most economically active period of people's lives. The increase in the use of Zulu can be accounted for in its role and function as a lingua franca in communal/hostel dwellings (PANSALB, 2000: 26, 35) and in the workplace. The decline of proficiency in English in the 25–44 age group can be accounted for through emigration of people highly proficient in English (English provides access to employment in other countries; see Chapter 4) and it should be noted that increasingly speakers of English as a second language comprise a significant proportion of emigrants (mainly to Britain, Canada and Australasia). The point at which the greatest proficiency in English is recorded (age 16–17) can be accounted for by the predominantly English as a Second Language (ESL) education system and, specifically, the small percentage of African language speaking students who have entered private schools. Given that the ESL education system is firmly in place for about 75% of students, and that school examinations are conducted through English for all students except L1 speakers of Afrikaans, it is surprising that so few L2 speakers record their language of greatest fluency as English. It suggests that the ESL-based system is not delivering the goods.

Table 6.3 Language proficiency in relation to age

Language of greatest fluency	*Total*	*16–17 years*	*18–24 years*	*25–34 years*	*35–44 years*	*45–54 years*	*55+ years*
Afrikaans	17	18	16	16	14	17	22
English	10	13	11	9	7	11	12
S Sotho	6	5	7	7	7	6	4
Tswana	9	12	9	7	8	12	10
N Sotho	7	3	7	5	9	10	8
Xhosa	16	17	15	16	15	17	18
Zulu	22	23	23	29	25	17	13

Data from PANSALB, 2000: Table 3F, p. 19

When the data on the main languages used for neighbourhood communication are examined across the provinces, it becomes clear that although Zulu is numerically the most widely spoken in the country, its use is limited to three provinces: KwaZulu-Natal (71%), Gauteng (26%), and Mpumalanga (38%). Afrikaans functions as a viable lingua franca across five and possibly six provinces: Northern Cape (71%), Western Cape (49%), Free State (28%), Gauteng (26%), Eastern Cape (18%), and Northern Province (11%). Xhosa functions as a lingua franca mainly in the Eastern Cape (71%) and Western Cape (31%). English does the same in three provinces: KwaZulu-Natal (23%), Gauteng (19%), and the Western Cape (18%). Again, despite the impression that English has come to function as the (pre)dominant lingua franca, the PANSALB statistics show that it can function as one of three lingua francas in the Western Cape and Gauteng as well as one of the two in KwaZulu-Natal. In other provinces it has limited utility for certain functions, in large towns or metropolitan centres. These tend to be high-level points of administration, education and the economy. A good example of this is in the case of the capital of the Northern Cape Province where fewer than 2.5% of people use English as their main language of communication and almost all of these reside in the capital, Kimberley, where they find employment in the provincial administration.[10]

Further data collected for the PANSALB survey show that whilst national government disseminates most of its messages to the public in English, a significant percentage of people do not understand this information and therefore are unable to insist on the rights enshrined in the Constitution. 47% of South Africans do not understand messages from government. If one discounts the 9% of L1 speakers of English and the highly bilingual Afrikaans-English speakers, then over 60% of people who are L1 speakers of African languages do not understand government. This ranges between 83% of Venda speakers to 43% of Xhosa speakers whose access to services is hampered (PANSALB, 2000: 139). Sixty-seven percent of rural people cannot access government information and this improves to 32% of urban dwellers (PANSALB, 2000: 143). Predictably, only 20% of those with the lowest levels of education (Grade 5 or less) access information compared with 86% of people who have Grade 12+ (PANSALB, 2000: 142).

Literacy levels

There is little doubt that literacy rates in South Africa are highly problematic. Firstly there are, as with the data on immigrants, partly unreliable and divergent sets of information. Official census figures are not likely to be accurate since many people, certainly in South Africa, are not willing to disclose their inability to read and write. A particularly optimistic figure is that 85% of those aged 15 plus are literate (SAIRR, 2002). However, as can be seen in Table 6.4, this figure is not borne out by other sources.

Harley's (2003) analysis of the 2001 statistics in relation to illiteracy, suggests that the slight decrease in percentage of functionally illiterate adults since the 1996 Census, is related to the fact that the census elicits data in relation to how many years of schooling adults have had. Thus young adults who were at school at the time of the 1996 Census, are now regarded as literate if they have spent at least eight years in school. More young people, a decade into the new political dispensation, are staying in school for longer periods. This does not, however, in Harley's analysis (and others below), translate into improved literacy achievement.

Harley's (2003: 10–11) discussion of the 2001 Census data shows that the proportions of adults who have had no education whatsoever has dropped slightly from 1996. In terms of actual numbers of people, there were 500,000+ more adults in 2001 who have had no education and 22.3% of African adults have had no education at all (Harley, 2003: 11). The increase in the number of citizens with no education reflects significant gender differences. Of those who had no education by 2001, 60% were women, 40% were men. The gendered difference is consistent also in the literacy data reflected in Table 6.4 above. This trend is especially worrying since although one of the underlying concerns of the post-apartheid government is gender equality, the educational circumstances of women do not reflect signs of improvement.

KwaZulu-Natal, Limpopo and Mpumalanga are the three provinces with the highest proportion and numbers of people without any education, and also a very high incidence of people living in rural areas. This is coupled with significant levels of unemployment, HIV/Aids and increase in Aids orphans. In sum, those who are most at risk educationally, economically and in terms of health are rural women, and this trend appears to be worsening rather than improving.[11] Altogether these factors have serious implications for the country's ability to sustain appropriate levels of human resource development required in the competitive and high skilled national and international labour market (see Chapter 4). These ultimately impact on the country's ability to sustain socio-economic development in the long term.

South African adult education experts consider that anyone with less than Grade 9 qualifications, normally achievable by age 15, requires some form of adult education. Rule (2003: 3) argues that 90.7% of rural

Table 6.4 Literacy data in South Africa

Data sources	*Overall level of literacy*	*Female illiteracy*	*Male illiteracy*
MarkData and PANSALB 2000, Table 16	43% over the age of 16 cannot read	46%	38%
SA Census 1996 (SAIRR, 2000: 112)	36% over the age of 20 are illiterate	55.48% of those who are illiterate are women	44.5% of those who are illiterate are men
SA Census 2001 (in Harley, 2003)	33.9% over the age of 20 are illiterate		

adults have had no formal training. Webb (2003: 90) referring to ongoing research of Hough and Horne (see Horne, 2001), suggests that only 5% of rural teacher trainees have the requisite English language literacy skills and that 51% of the Grade 12 school leavers who applied for admission to technikons[12] in 1990 had adequate ESL literacy levels (Grade 8 or above). Horne (2001: 41) shows that this had declined to 18% in 2000. Horne (2001) states that in another study only 2% of African language speaking students who applied to a formerly mainly 'white' metropolitan university in 2000, had ESL literacy levels expected of Grade 12 school leavers. In other words, although young people are staying in school for longer periods, there are alarming signs of poor literacy achievement and this is especially the case when the yardstick is English literacy.

Since 1999 a number of studies related to early literacy have been conducted or commissioned by the national Department of Education (DoE). A recent study conducted in 2001 and 2002 so troubled the DoE that it refused to release the findings.[13] Researchers commissioned by the Western Cape Department of Education have been prevented from disclosing the results of their provincial research conducted over 2002–2003. This is despite the fact that the literacy levels of Western Cape, along with Gauteng students, have been consistently the highest.[14] Nevertheless, newspaper reports on the study reveal that 46% of Grade 2 and 3 learners 'do not have sufficient literacy skills' for their grade level and students scored 30% overall in numeracy (mathematics) (Monare, 2003). These last statistics mirror closely those of a 1999 study conducted amongst Grade 4 learners as part of a joint UNESCO, UNICEF and DoE initiative. This study showed that students scored 48% for literacy and 30% for mathematics (numeracy) (Strauss, 1999: table C1).[15] The provinces with the highest concentration of rural people performed most poorly. Worst of all was Mpumalanga with a 33% score for literacy. Census 2001 shows that Limpopo (33.4%) and Mpumalanga (27.5%) provinces have the highest percentages of people with no education whereas Gauteng (12.6%) and the Western Cape (11.2%) have the highest percentages of people with tertiary education (StatisticsSA, 2003: 44–45).

Since the most recent literacy study involved young learners who entered the school system several years after the transfer of power, and subsequent to the introduction of new curriculum changes (see also below) phased in from 1998, it is difficult to account for the dismal literacy and numeracy performance.[16] However, as Bourdieu (1991) and many others have pointed out elsewhere, the effects of habituated state practices outlive the political lifespan of governments. One should therefore have anticipated that although literacy and educational levels might not improve immediately after the introduction of democracy, they would at least remain on a par with those during the last years of the former political dispensation. What one did not expect was a substantial decline in proficiency, which the current early and school leaving literacy trends show.

Language policy frameworks and their debates

Language policy has been a matter of contestation ever since the arrival of the administrators of the Dutch East India Company in the Cape in 1652. An initial policy of Dutchification had a serious and negative impact on the vitality of the Khoe and San languages spoken in the area at the time. Moreover, it neutralized the languages of slaves brought mainly from the Malaysian peninsula, as well as the languages of the German and French (Huguenots) and of other settlers in the Cape. Successive waves of British attempts to colonize, first the Cape and then Natal, were accompanied by Anglicization policies from the late 18th through the 19th centuries, culminating in the most strident version immediately after the Anglo-Boer War 1899–1901. A negotiated settlement (1909–1910) resulted in the Union of South Africa with two official languages, namely, Dutch and English. In 1925 Afrikaans replaced Dutch as an official language. State education provided to 'white' and some 'coloured' children was based on mother-tongue education (MTE) for primary school and usually a switch to English for Dutch/Afrikaans-speakers in secondary school during the 19th century. Missionaries offered limited education for African pupils and generally used mother tongue for four to six years followed by English medium. Bilingual Dutch/Afrikaans-English schools, especially at secondary level became increasingly popular in the second half of the 19th century and a policy of the two Boer republics prior to the Union in 1910. Bilingual education was so commonplace that a now well-known study was conducted in the late 1930s by E.G. Malherbe on the educational and social efficacy of various types of bilingual education (Malherbe, 1943).

Resentment as a result of the appalling actions of the British towards Boer women and children during the Anglo-Boer War, and subsequent treatment by the British administrator, Alfred Milner, lasted for decades. Growing political antagonism from nationalist leaders of the Afrikaans-speaking community in combination with sympathies towards the rise of fascism in Germany in the 1930s resulted in increasing pressures to end bilingual schooling (De Klerk, 1995). The 1948 elections brought the National Party to power and introduced formal apartheid to the country. Language policy, especially in education, was to enter a new phase. The principle of MTE was expanded across each ethnolinguistic group. The logic of segregation meant that bilingual Afrikaans-English schools were actively discouraged unless there were insufficient numbers of pupils in rural areas to warrant separate schools. Apartheid was refined along territorial lines and linguistically defined groups were generally confined to different rural areas. The attraction of cheap labour, however, necessitated some Africans residing in close proximity to the urban centres. Whilst primary schools were provided for the children of urban workers in these areas, secondary schools were largely limited to the rural 'homeland' areas.[17] MTE for Africans was extended to eight years of primary school. A requirement to switch medium in secondary school to both Afrikaans and English medium (half the non-language subjects in each of these languages), in combination with what was perceived to be an unnecessary extension of MTE, led to a rebellion of students led by the Black Consciousness Movement in Soweto in 1976. Government was subsequently forced to amend its language-in-education policy in 1979, effectively reducing MTE to four years and allowing students to switch to English medium only.[18]

State language policy remained unaltered until the period of negotiations leading towards a political settlement, and the language clauses of the interim Constitution of 1993. A number of language activists in the National Language Project (NLP) had begun to initiate debates about language policy alternatives in the mid-1980s. Some of these ideas, particularly in relation to the establishment of an independent language planning body came to fruition in the Constitution, in the form of an independent Pan South African Language Board (PANSALB). However, a combination of postcolonial practices and encroaching 'governmentality' (Foucault, 1977, 1991; Pennycook, 2002a, 2002b)[19] was to result in the continuation of ethnolinguistic language planning conceived of under apartheid, and also to limit the independence of PANSALB (Heugh, 2003).

The Bill of Rights within the Constitution set language policy primarily on a language rights path. However, the debates within the country ranged from associating the multilingual character of the citizenry with 'problems', overriding resentment towards Afrikaans as a language of control, a consequential pendulum swing towards assimilation to English, and exploratory engagement with the notion of language as a resource (after Ruiz, 1984).[20] The latter consideration was a prominent feature of the Language Plan Task Group (LANGTAG) Report (DACST, 1996) to the Minister of Arts, Culture, Science and Technology.

The fragility of rights-based planning and post-colonial critiques illustrated by several authors (e.g. Blommaert, 2001; Rassool, 1998, 1999; Ricento, 2000; Stroud, 2001) and the tendency to default to earlier practices (Pennycook, 2000a, 2000b; Wiley, 2002) is evidenced in the contemporary South African situation. Although the equal status of 11 official languages was prefaced in the interim Constitution, this was diluted in the final Constitution of 1996. Instead there are now simply 11 official languages with little compulsion towards equality. This strategic weakening of the original principles has led to a situation whereby instead of two official languages operating vertically across the country as was the case under Apartheid, and instead of a shift towards better resourcing and tapping into the horizontal use of 11 languages,[21] there has been a default to one language of power, namely English. This is explained and accepted as a consequence of the resentment, by African language and English speakers towards Afrikaans as the former *de facto* language of vertical control (especially in the armed forces, the police, prison services, educational administration and civil service in general). Increasingly those who have a high level proficiency in English have come to replace Afrikaans-speakers in the civil service. Government jobs, across the country are advertised in English, very rarely in other languages. As implied above, the intention of the Constitution was to establish the principles for other legislative frameworks which would establish horizontal rather than vertical power-sharing mechanisms. What has happened linguistically is that whilst English is believed to be the horizontal language of access it has in effect become the vertical language of exclusion.

Given Table 6.2 and data illustrated above, it is obvious that key positions are being occupied by a possible 7.2% of the population, in other words, a very small elite which has Grade 12+ education plus English as their language of greatest fluency. English is thus becoming the 'dominant' if not 'predominant' language of the country (Ridge, 2000). Thus, a paradoxical situation is developing where, at present, fewer people have access to high levels of proficiency in English than they did in the pre-1994 period. First, there is a declining level of English literacy amongst young speakers of African languages. Second, there is a significant degree of emigration amongst the 25–44 year age group who has the highest level of proficiency in English. Thus, while English continues to function as the only language of access, there is a simultaneous decline in the level of ESL literacy proficiency and in the numbers of people able to use it proficiently. Thus English is fast becoming a gatekeeper rather than a language of access. Yet there is considerable denial of this process amongst senior government officials and some English-speaking academics (e.g. Asmal, 2001a; Young, 2001). Argument which demonstrates the way in which English serves (or is used to serve) exclusionary functions is mistakenly presented as 'evidence of neo-colonial attitudes' (Ridge, 2000: 166). However unintentional, the result is one where the linguistic power elite, while rapidly changing from L1 to L2 speakers of English, is shrinking rather than expanding.

Cultural, Economic and Political Factors

The following discussion presents a sketchy account of some of the factors which shape contemporary debates.[22] Both the colonial and apartheid eras spawned racism, inequity, racialized ethnicity and nationalism. 18th and 19th century European nationalism provided one of the primary influences of the white Afrikaans-speaking community where language was intricately associated with cultural, ethnic and/or national identity. An additional factor shaping Afrikaner culture and identity has been religion. The impact of the religious Reformation in Europe, which had brought about the first printed versions of the bible in Dutch and German, was clearly present in the Calvinist Dutch Reformed religion introduced to South Africa in the 17th century. Early disagreements with, and a fleeing from the Dutch East India Company, followed by British colonization, contributed to what is now called the 'laager mentality'[23] of this community.

Speakers of African languages who moved south and met Boer and English settlers, found themselves subjected to evangelizing missionary groups and were constrained, in the case of Zulu-speakers in Natal, to 'native reserves' during the 19th century.[24] Once black people found that they had been left out of the negotiations at the end of the Anglo-Boer War and again during those leading to the Union of South Africa, organized opposition to 'white' dominance slowly cohered and found expression through the medium of English under the influence of Abdurahman in 1912 (Alexander, 1989: 29; see also Chapters 3 and 4). Over the next eight decades resistance organizations (e.g. the African National Congress, the Communist Party of South Africa, the Natal Indian Congress, the Transvaal Indian Congress, the Pan Africanist Congress, the New Unity Movement, the Black Consciousness Movement, and the Azanian People's Organisation, etc.) all followed this trend. Once Afrikaner Nationalism came to entrench Afrikaans in the bureaucracy of the country and came to symbolize oppression (as manifest in the prisons and armed forces), English came to represent access to freedom (see also Chapter 4).

Early missionary competitiveness complemented tendencies towards ethnicity and nationalism. Through a process which Msimang calls the 'balkanisation' of African languages (Msimang quoted in Cluver, 1996: 16) one missionary sect would identify a language and employ a particular orthographic convention as the language was being written down; another would apply different conventions for a related language (see also Chapter 2).[25] Thus came about an artificial separation of African languages which are closely related. In a related discussion Ranger (1989) attributes the 'invention of ethnicity' to the interventions of missionaries in Africa. The logic of separate development under apartheid meant that it was convenient, for language planning purposes, to build upon the work of the missionaries and so it came about that ethnolinguistic planning is the underlying practice of most state language planning. An additional dimension under apartheid was the limited functions which ethnolinguistic planning afforded African languages *vis-à-vis* Afrikaans during the same period. The latter was developed into a modern scientific and technological language (see also Chapter 4); the former were relegated to domestic, literary and primary education functions. Uneven language development should not obscure the overall trend and effect of ethnolinguistic planning after the British colonial period came to an end. Ethnolinguistic planning, ethnicity and even in the case of the Inkatha Freedom Party, Zulu nationalism, flourished under apartheid. Although alternative integrative language planning models were proposed and thoroughly debated from the mid-1980s onwards (Alexander, 1992), it should come as no surprise therefore that an ethnolinguistic view of language planning has prevailed within a rights-based Constitution, its statutory offspring, and in the apparatus of government. This is particularly evident in an amendment to the PANSALB Act in 1999 which added ethnolinguistic representivity as an essential criterion for the appointment of board members. Instead of a horizontal view of multilingualism, a multiple version of vertical and monolingual language planning has become the point of departure within both PANSALB and the Department of Arts and Culture. The reasoning of the most senior officials in both structures was to take apartheid development in Afrikaans as the yardstick. Equal development, on a catch-up basis, should thus occur in nine other languages via parallel rather than integrated processes. One of the most obvious reasons for this to be an ill-advised strategy is that there simply are not sufficient resources to play catch-up, separately, nine times over.[26] The other is to do with nation building and integration. Separatist approaches lend themselves to narrow, fixed identities and potential ethnic conflict.

Whilst Afrikaans came to dominate the bureaucracy during National Party Rule (1948–1994), Afrikaans and English together dominated in the domestic economy, but English obviously had the international advantage and occupied diplomatic and international economic arenas. Political exiles, apart from those who went to Eastern Bloc countries, communicated through English. Thus it is perfectly understandable how it was that English has come to occupy top position on the vertical language axis of relation to power and the formal economy since the transfer of power in 1994. It needs to be mentioned that there have been a number of sociolinguistic interventions and well-intentioned consultative processes such as the LANGTAG process, and lengthy consultations over draft language policy legislation at national level spanning the years 1995–2003, and which would set in place greater functional use of more official languages. A Language Bill presented to Cabinet in 2000 eventually appeared as the National Language Policy Framework Bill which has been in the legislative queue since early 2003. Since it is now 10 years since the legislative process was first set in motion, and the bill has yet to be debated in parliament, there is little doubt that government is reluctant to alter the linguistic status quo. The significance of a clearly articulated language policy and plan which sets out guidelines for all government departments and aspects of public service cannot be underestimated. It is the absence of this legislation which facilitates the default position of a slide towards English only in the upper echelons of power. It is the absence of this legislation which effectively undermines the language policy developments in those branches of government which did attempt sectoral language policies in line with constitutional provisions, such as in education (DoE, 1997).

Language Attitudes and Choices

It is clear from the discussion above that from the perspective of speakers of African languages, negative associations with Afrikaans and the extended use of MTE as employed during the first phase of Bantu Education (to 1976), are to be expected. By default then, favourable attitudes towards English are also to be expected. A positive disposition towards English does not, however, imply the converse, i.e. negative attitudes towards African languages in general. As mentioned earlier, the PANSALB (2000) Survey provides a number of surprises. Perhaps the most significant is in relation to medium of instruction in educational institutions. Despite a series of advisory reports to the national Department of Education (e.g. Taylor & Vinjevold, 1999) and the expectations of the officials themselves, there are empirical data which show that the presumed analysis of parental and student preference for English is inaccurate. As Krashen (1996) points out, if parents are given an either/or option they are obliged to choose the language of higher status. If, on the other hand, they are given a bilingual option, they are more likely to choose this. The PANSALB Survey shows exactly this. The majority of parents (88%) prefer MTE plus English. Only 12% select an English-only option (for school and tertiary education). Too often however, what Gogolin (1997) has called the 'monolingual habitus' constrains analysis towards a false dichotomy: either African language or English (e.g. Taylor & Vinjevold, 1999; Asmal, 2001a), when neither monolingual option suffices an adequate reflection of preference or need.

On the other hand, there is a plethora of anecdotal evidence and small-scale sample studies of people close to urban and metropolitan centres who are interpreted to indicate a distinct preference for English only (e.g. Winkler, 1997; Taylor & Vinjevold, 1999). However, such studies need to be counterbalanced by a picture which includes a representative sample of contexts across the country rather than one skewed by urban-metropolitan conditions. They also need to be carefully analysed in terms of who the interviewers and respondents might be. Are the researchers able to conduct their research in African languages – fluently? Do they? Are the respondents limited to those who already speak English fluently or even the top 7.2% of the most highly educated English-speaking public? Are the respondents presented with either/or options?[27] In another context, most of the authors of a recent collection of second language acquisition (SLA) research complain that much early and contemporary 'scientific' research is seriously flawed, limited in terms inappropriate research questions, timeframes and scope (Doughty & Long, 2003). Similarly, a great many of the small-scale language attitude studies in South Africa are largely designed, albeit unwittingly, to elicit prevailing public perceptions at surface level rather than evidence of preferred alternatives at deeper levels of analysis (e.g. Probyn *et al.*, 2002). Far too few are the more nuanced studies which delve into the complex reasons why parents, for example, might choose to send their children to English medium schools as L2 learners, or what they might choose if there were viable alternatives (e.g. De Klerk, 2002a, 2002b; Desai, 2004; Plüddemann *et al.*, 2004a, 2004b).[28]

The PANSALB Survey further provides illuminating evidence of language preferences for the media, and the extent to which speakers of languages other than English and Afrikaans continue to feel marginalized under a new democratic government. The most widely read newspaper by 2000 was the English language *Sowetan*, with a mainly African readership. The second most widely read newspaper was *Ilanga*, a Zulu language newspaper, whose readership has been consistent across gender, age and education levels. Whereas the *Sowetan* is more widely read in urban areas and by people with Grade 8+ education level, Ilanga is more widely read in rural areas (PANSALB, 2000: 90). Between 40–55% of Africans would like to have more TV and radio programmes than already exists in their own languages (PANSALB, 2000: 104). People are least likely to be able to use their language in post offices and police stations (especially for written statements) (PANSALB, 2000: 43). Thirty-five percent of South Africans feel frustrated at not being able to access public signs, official notices, letters from banks, and job advertisements in their own languages. This is higher for rural people (53% of men; 48% of women) (PANSALB, 2000: 83). Forty-seven percent of people cannot or do not access public services in their own languages (PANSALB, 2000: 45); fewer than 20% of African language speakers fully understand speeches from government in English (PANSLAB, 2000: 138), while 76% of people would like languages other than English to be used by government officials (PANSLAB, 2000: 147). Finally, 58% of those whose L1 is not accommodated in job interviews feel that they are disadvantaged (PANSALB, 2001: 6).

What these data show is that the perception/hope that English might provide access to the bounty of the new democracy is not being borne out in reality. They also show trends towards growing frustration and resentment in relation to linguistic exclusion. On the other hand, the attitudes towards African languages and their use in a wide range of functions are far more positive than often otherwise acknowledged. Most astounding is the very strong preference for the continuous use of African languages, alongside English, as media of instruction through schools and tertiary institutions. The obvious need to access information in home languages is clearly evident in the readership of *Ilanga* newspaper. Interestingly, since the release of the PANSALB Survey, newspaper owners and advertisers seem to recognize the potential readership market in languages other than English or Afrikaans. There are now several bilingual (English and local African language) newspapers, such as *Vukani*, available in Cape Town townships. More significant is the very successful new Zulu language daily in one of the fastest growing urban centres of the country, Durban. *Isolezwe* is now both in print[29] and available electronically. In another development, the electronic search engine, Google.co.za, is now available in Zulu, Xhosa, Sotho and Afrikaans.

These developments are extremely promising. They illustrate the dynamism of linguistic use and the responsiveness of market forces within the private sector which appears to recognize the value of tapping into linguistic markets other than English. Government, however, continues to lag behind.

Key Human Resource Development Issues

The most significant human resource issue is undoubtedly education and training especially in relation to unemployment and poverty. On the one hand there is massive unemployment whilst, on the other hand, there are employment opportunities available for skilled labour. Vast numbers of South Africans, however, have such low levels of the skills demanded in the formal economy that they are unemployable and catastrophically, most Grade 12 school leavers are regarded as 'not trainable' (Hough, 2004; see also discussion of and discourse about 'functional' literacy above). It is common sense that improved literacy and educational levels would impact on development (NEPI, 1992; Taylor & Vinjevold, 1999) and the economy (the more years in school translates into higher earning capacity, which provides a wider tax-base, and which in turn can be fed back into improved social services and other development activities) (Bond, 2000; Grin, 2002, 2005; Legassick, 2003; Terreblanche, 2003). Yet Peron (2004) argues that after decades of independence in other developing countries, significant improvement in skills development and increased activity in higher education, poverty is not being alleviated. He argues that, in highly regulated 'interventionist economies', government practices, instead of creating openings for previously marginalized people, default to opportunities for the already highly educated elite, and very little diffusion of wealth occurs. Similar to the arguments of Bond (2000), Legassick (2003) and Terreblanche (2003), whose focus is on the economic changes in South Africa since the transfer of power, the gap between the wealthy and the poor is actually increasing during the post-colonial period, despite the overt intention of the new political elite. In South Africa, the situation may even be more exaggerated than in other countries. With the exception of official statements of the national Department of Education, most educators and key private sector analysts argue that improved educational achievement has thus far escaped the newly enfranchised South Africa. Academic achievement of students, has not, in real terms, improved (Jansen, 2004).

The discussion of literacy above indicates that the nature of a specifically narrow functional view persists in the dominant discourses about this issue in the country. What is surprising about this is that during the last years of apartheid, there was significant engagement with social and critical approaches to literacy/ies in the NGO sector[30] and evident in Prinsloo and Breier (1996). Yet, as the international debates continued elsewhere (Street, 1995; Rassool, 1998) and in relation to multilingual literacies (Hornberger, 2000; Martin-Jones & Jones, 2000) they have been largely ignored in mainstream education developments in South Africa. Their deposits have found their way into the work of early childhood concerns of the NGO sector (e.g. Bloch, 2002) rather than mainstream school education. Literacy remains neglected rather than a priority: it is seen as an illness with a remedy limited to functional, mainly ESL, literacy. The former Minister of Education, Kader Asmal, signalled his intention to mount a mass literacy campaign upon his appointment in late 1999. However there has been no such effort. Even if mass campaigns were bound to fail (see Rassool, 1998, 1999), a public commitment towards literacy would raise the level of consciousness about the issue and stimulate debate and a quest for new solutions.

Gender equality is another key human resource issue. Whilst the Bill of Rights incorporated into the Constitution gives weight to gender equality, the data provided above shows that women, especially rural women who speak African languages, continue to be marginalized. Harley (2003), as discussed above, shows that of the latest increase in numbers of adults who have not been to school, 71.5% are women. These women are in the youngest adult age group, i.e. the age group which should have had easier access to schooling and thus literacy. What is disturbing about this is that it suggests that the gender gap is widening.[31]

In sum, literacy levels are showing signs of decline which is exacerbated along geographic, urban-rural, and gender lines. The data provides an early warning signal to economists and development planners. It is effectively a litmus test which indicates increasing educational inequality and this runs counter to the overt goals of the country and its participation in the larger African arena of The New Partnership for Africa's Development (NEPAD).

Curriculum Issues, Materials and Assessment

If the discussion thus far gives the impression of a recalcitrant and irresponsible new government, then this is incorrect. One of the immediate tasks of the new government was to initiate a process of educational transformation immediately after the first democratic election. By 1995 the process of streamlining 18 different departments of education into one national Department of Education had been effected for the purpose of ensuring educational equity for all students. A new curriculum development process and a separate language-in-education policy process were underway through consultative mechanisms. In February 1997 a new outcomes-based national curriculum for schools, C2005 was announced. In July the same year a new language-in-education policy followed. Language in education was to foreground mother tongue education for as long as possible with the addition of at least one other language. Essentially it amounts to an additive bilingual approach which translates into L1 plus English for the majority of students. Provision was made for a variety of additive bilingual models and language maintenance programmes where fully-fledged bilingual models were impractical. The trialing of the new curriculum began in early 1998, but the language policy, with the exception of a preliminary mention in the curriculum documentation, was left to individual school governing bodies for implementation. By early 2000, the then Minister of Education, Kader Asmal, launched a review of the curriculum and signalled a similar process for language policy. The Revised National Curriculum Statement (RNCS) Grades R–9[32] (DoE, 2002a) was released in May 2002 including a restrictive, transitional misinterpretation of the language policy. Additive bilingual education was reduced to mother-tongue literacy to the end of Grade 3, after which the underlying assumption is that students, except for L1 speakers of Afrikaans, will switch to English. The reversion to transitional-subtractive bilingual education on paper is not simply a continuation of the latter years of apartheid education for African language speaking students; it offers reduced opportunities for L1 literacy and conceptual development than did even the last years of apartheid education when the switch to English medium on paper took place a year later, in Grade 5. Even though the Minister of Education placed great emphasis on the contribution of Edward Said's key-note address at a major DoE conference, where Said focused on the role of lifelong literacy development, reading and using several languages (Said, 2001), the department has backtracked. From Grade 4 the emphasis is on ESL literacy, and especially for the purpose of teaching mathematics and science (DoE, 2001) rather than the extensive and critical literacy experiences called for by Said. A short explanation for this turn of events lies in the hegemony of middle-class habitus, particularly as it affects key advisors[33] to government and the hierarchy of the political elite (see also Chapter 3). What is disappointing is that it follows a well-worn path of similar approaches elsewhere in Africa despite the scholarly advice of, for example, Bamgbose (2000), Mazrui (2002), Obanya (1999), Ouane (2003).

The effect of what appears to be the inevitability of a switch to English medium in the education system is that publishers cannot (will not) risk producing educational materials in African languages without guaranteed sales. Teachers cannot risk teaching more effectively through African languages since there is no material support for this. The DoE, after disposing of all the apartheid period African language text-book archives after 1994, argues that there is no terminology in African languages to make textbook production in these languages a reality (see Mahlalela & Heugh, 2002).[34] Parents from the more or less 75% majority recognize the current lack of educational materials in their languages and try to move their children into the best resourced English medium state schools (approximately 6% of schools) or the 2% of privately funded schools. The statistics demonstrate that this movement is possible only for a lucky few and the resultant pressure on the well-resourced English medium schools distorts the reality that most parents would, given the option, prefer well-resourced bilingual schools (De Klerk, 2002a, 2002b).

Assessment criteria and standards are built into the new curriculum documentation. A primary objective of educational transformation had been to dispense with norm-based and psychometric testing procedures, which were associated with advantaging middle class students with English, and Afrikaans language backgrounds. Students may repeat only one year per phase (Grades R–3, Grades 4–6, Grades 7–9, Grades 10–12). Thus, students may find themselves moved forward at times when they may not be ready to grapple usefully with the requirements of the curriculum. This is particularly unfortunate for rural children in the early years of school who may find the language mismatch too great. An award of an additional 5% to African language speaking students as compensation for writing their examinations in English, plus the introduction of continuous assessment to the value of 25% of the final mark, seriously compromise the claim for improved pass rates.

The current itemized criteria for assessment in the Languages Learning Area statement for First Additional Language (AL1, i.e. ESL, which applies to the majority of students) shows different criteria expected for each grade depending upon whether the AL1 is taken as a subject or whether it is to be used as a medium of instruction. Students who will use EAL1 as a medium have more onerous requirements for each assessment level than do those who simply take AL1 as a subject. For example, at Grade 9, if one uses EAL1 as a medium one is expected to have a reading vocabulary of 7500 words and the focus is on a narrow functional view of AL1 literacy development. If one has AL1 as a subject only, one needs only have a reading vocabulary of 6000 words, and so on (DoE, 2002b: 100–101). Thus L1 speakers of English and Afrikaans would only need to have the narrower vocabulary range at each level, since these students have L1 education throughout and do not need the additional vocabulary and linguistic proficiency required of a student studying in the L2.[35]

The essential purpose of educational transformation a decade ago was to develop a unified national system where quality education with equal access would be guaranteed. Despite promising intent, new curriculum, with its unintended assessment consequences as well as the misapplied (literacy and) language-in-education policy, is not designed to effect such change. Those who were privileged before, remain, by and large those who continue to find that the system advantages them. Despite the preference of parents for L1 maintenance in addition to ESL for the duration of the education system, the DoE pays scant regard to and makes minimal use of languages which students know best. This has seriously negative educational consequences for three-quarters of the student population. The indicators show that the educational outcomes for the previously disadvantaged have neither improved nor kept on a par with those experienced under apartheid. They are on the decline.

Teacher qualifications, supply and pedagogical implications

There are approximately 350,000 teachers in the school system at present. Of these 22% are considered, in official terms, to be under-qualified (SAIRR, 2001: 252). Strauss (1999: tables B25 and B57) provides data which record that 40% of teachers have only primary education themselves and that only 43% have three or more years of post-secondary school education. Crouch and Lewin (2000: 2, 17) estimate that there is a current annual undersupply of teachers of about 7000. If, however, the effect of the HIV-Aids pandemic on South Africa is taken into account and the needs of Aids orphans are to be addressed, then this undersupply escalates to 28,000 per year.[36]

Siebörger (2003)[37] argues that between 5000–6000 teachers exit the training facilities each year but that the education system requires about 30,000 new or additional teachers annually. Thus his estimate is of a 24–25,000 annual shortfall. The South African Institute for Race Relations (SAIRR, 2001: 275) calculates that, in particular, there is a shortage of between 4000 and 12,000 mathematics and science teachers and that one of the effects of this is that fewer than 1% of African language speaking students passed mathematics and science in the 2000 school leaving examinations.

A key feature of the Crouch and Lewin (2000: 19) study is the inefficiency of current teacher education provision and its costliness. They calculate that it costs about R80,000 to train each teacher and this would amount to R2.5 billion if 30,000 teachers were trained each year. This is unaffordable in a country like South Africa, and thus teacher training needs to become more cost-effective if any scaling-up could be facilitated. What these statistics mean, first, is that there are not enough teachers. Second, those in the system are often under-qualified. Third, the majority of those who are expected to teach through the medium of English (i.e. after Grade 3 in practice) are not themselves sufficiently proficient in English to be effective (e.g. Macdonald, 1990; Young, 1995). Fourth, the majority of those who are expected to teach through English to L1 speakers of African languages do not have the requisite training or expertise in their subject areas. Fifth, the retraining of teachers to implement outcomes-based education in the form of Curriculum 2005, and now the Revised National Curriculum Statement, relies on minimal training (between two days to two weeks) and the 'cascade' model. Such a minimalist approach cannot accomplish the transition from a content-based, rote learning and norm-based system to one that is outcomes-based and assessed through continuous and criterion-referenced approaches. The outcome of these factors is simply that the previously privileged schools can employ the best trained teachers whose linguistic skills match the needs of most of their students. The converse is that historically poorly resourced schools find themselves in a situation where teachers are now less prepared for the requirements of the new education system than they were under apartheid education. As a result, the prognosis for positive change is dismal.

If one were to look at training needs beyond the basic preparation of teachers with regard to current practice, and factor in a comprehensive reorientation towards enhanced literacy development and mother tongue and bilingual education, then one would need to consider that the implication for pre-service training is that these issues would have to receive prioritization. In addition, in order to address the poor literacy achievement in both mother tongue and ESL which currently plagues the system, comprehensive in-service education would need to follow. A rough calculation is that about 66,000 Foundation Phase teachers (Grades 1–3) require extensive training in L1 literacy development and about 260,000 teachers currently in the system need in-service programmes to equip them to use English across the curriculum.

Alternatively, if a bilingual system were in place, about half of the 260,000 teachers would require additional ESL training.[38]

Conclusion

In summary, there are a number of political, cultural, economic and educational factors which shape language policy intervention in South Africa. The main issue is how to manage the country's linguistic diversity in a way that enhances the opportunities of those who speak African languages, and ensures their ability to participate in the global cultural economy. To achieve this, South Africans need to be bilingual at least and, preferably, multilingual. This means a high level of proficiency in both the home language/s and at least one language of wider communication where this is not the L1. For domestic purposes, effective horizontal communication requires languages other than English for the majority of citizens. Aspirations of upward economic and political mobility, however, require a high level of proficiency in English. The discussion above shows, however, that current educational practices defeat these objectives.

If the exercise of citizenship within a democratic dispensation and participation in regional and global markets are to be enduring concerns, then there needs to be a reconceptualization of the role of languages in these domains. South African participation in the UN's New Partnership for Africa's Development (NEPAD) and the implications of increasing numbers of immigrants from 'Francophone', 'Lusophone' and 'Arabophone' Africa, as well as from Kiswahili and Hausa dominant regions of Africa, is that English is no longer sufficient as the only language of wider communication (LWC). It will not, on its own, guarantee access to regional or global participation. To this end, 'francophone' and 'lusophone' countries have understood that French and Portuguese need to be complemented by other LWCs in their education systems. Mozambique, for example, is investing heavily in both English and French language programmes in schools to complement the emphasis on Portuguese in that setting. Education planners recognize the importance of preparing students to participate in regional activities requiring collaboration and co-operation. The crucial difference between such countries and South Africa is that there is a fairly sophisticated understanding elsewhere that several LWCs are advisable and necessary for trade and diplomacy. South African education and development planners, on the other hand, remain time-warped in the misguided notion that global participation can only be imagined through English.

In failing to examine the entire linguistic landscape, state attention towards African languages has been limited, ineffectual and a restricted version of activities already in place during apartheid. The knock-on effect of this has been to rely on, or default to the easy option. Although the post-apartheid government promised to advance the prospects of multilingualism, protect language rights, and expand the bilingual Afrikaans-English dominance of the political, economic and educational arenas, this expansion and flattening of linguistic hegemony has not taken place. The formerly bilingual public space of the ruling minority has shrunk to an essentially monolingual one occupied by an even smaller minority. One language of greatest economic and political currency has come to dominate: it has become the sole linguistic yardstick for educational success, and since this is out of the reach of the majority it excludes participation. The literacy statistics and the PANSALB (2000) Survey attest to this. It is important to note that this situation is, however, unintentional.

> (T)he country's first national democratic elections ... presented unique opportunities to reconstruct the fragmented and deeply discriminatory education system by establishing a unified national system that is underpinned by the principles of democracy, equity, redress, transparency and participation. The social reconstruction of our education system has included the linkage to economic development in the context of global economies and competitiveness. (Asmal, 2001b: 6)

The education budget is now 22.6% of the non-interest portion of the national budget (5.4% of GDP) (Wildeman, 2005)[39] yet the return on fiscal investment is very low. The principle human resource development priority remains access to a meaningful education. Under apartheid, the source of inequality was clearly government ideology. At present, while the DoE is printing more school-leaving certificates, the catastrophic literacy and proficiency levels of students in English (now the only language of access to tertiary education, the formal economy and the civil service) means that educational transformation is an illusion.

If the early 1990s ushered in an era of hope and accommodation of alternative perspectives, this has gradually disappeared under restrictive mechanisms of excessive regulation and control (Peron, 2004). A reconceptualization of the role of literacy development and the horizontal use of African languages, to ensure access to full citizenship for ordinary people, has to be brought to the fore in education as well as in plans for national reconstruction. Language planning needs to move away from ethnolinguistic straight-jackets and become integrated into concerns of citizenship, plans for national development, and regional as well as global participation more generally. Analyses of the cost-benefit relationship between mother-tongue education plus language(s) of wider communication, and the economy are readily available to assist government to save expenditure while at the same time harness good returns to the National Treasury (see Grin, 2005). The gap between the elite and the rest of civil society will continue to widen unless such repositioning takes place. A first step would be to revisit the National Language Policy Framework Bill, revise it if necessary and complete the legislative process so that some consistent guidelines could better inform each arm and level of government service.

Notes

1. Bernstein (1996, 1999) discusses the institutionalised, class-based and hierarchical use of vertical discourse in formal settings and contrasts this with the more inclusive 'horizontal discourse' in informal contexts. I use these terms to include the deliberate use of a language for vertical exclusion and maintenance of power in contradistinction to the use of language for pragmatic purposes in informal linguistic markets. Thus a language used 'vertically' by one set of users may also be appropriated and used for horizontal purposes by another set of users. The use of Afrikaans by the military and police during apartheid in Namibia and South Africa, on the one hand, and its simultaneous use, and even reappropriation, by disenfranchised people as a vehicular, horizontal, language in this region, is one such example. The appropriation of English by Africans in East Africa is another example (see Owino, 2002).
2. Nine African languages were given national official status alongside Afrikaans and English.
3. This was known as the Department of Arts, Culture, Science and Technology (DACST) from 1994 to 2001.
4. Hot spots from which significant numbers of people have migrated over the last decade include: Angola, Côte d'Ivoire, Burundi, Democratic Republic of Congo, Equatorial Guinea, Liberia, Rwanda, Sudan, Somalia and Zimababwe.
5. It is conservatively estimated that there are 2 million refugees or migrants from African countries, although some NGOs place this figure at closer to 8 million. This is significant given that according to the 2001 Census, the total population is just under 45 million.
6. Dutch was originally declared an official language in 1910, but was replaced by Afrikaans in 1925.
7. Both Constitutions have used prefixes or the orthographic conventions of each respective Bantu language. However there is some debate about preferred conventions. There is also disagreement about which varieties are included or excluded in relation to both Northern Sotho and Ndebele in the names as they appear in the Constitutions. For these reasons, the English orthographic system will be used in this chapter.

8. For example if a state provider wanted to ensure that ordinary people had access to information about HIV-Aids and anti-retroviral medication, then one would expect that an efficient delivery plan would include a communication strategy which matched linguistic profiles and needs of the clients. If one were planning on teacher education provision one might consider the linguistic profiles of the students and attempt to match teacher recruitment with language as well as content specific criteria. If one wanted to ensure employment equity one might advertise jobs in the languages most used by the relevant communities. If one fails to take linguistic proficiency and need into account, then there is a danger of replicating old patterns where only the priviledged minority can apply for jobs, gain access to health care information, enjoy meaningful access to education, etc. The danger is that one caters only for the privileged minority and thus the economic and social empowerment of the majority remains out of reach. This is economically suicidal and is a recipe for social disaffection and cleavage over the medium to long-term.
9. This means that 25% of the 28.8% of adults over age 20, and who are the most highly educated, have English as their most fluent language – i.e. 7.2% of the population. Similarly therefore, of the 28% educated elite, 7.2% have Afrikaans as their language of greatest fluency and 5.76% have Zulu as their most fluent language (extrapolated from Census 2001; Statistics SA, 2003: 48).
10. Despite Afrikaans being the L1 of 68% of the population, followed by 21% who have Tswana and 6.2% who have Xhosa as L1, all government (local and provincial) posts were for several years after the 1994 advertised mainly in English, the L1 for 2.5% of the population (Statistics SA, 2003: 15). Local residents complained at the time that top jobs were going to people who spoke English and were 'imported' from other provinces like Gauteng. While most of these top officials speak English well, their African language speaking backgrounds do not match the language profile of the province which is Afrikaans, Tswana and Xhosa. Thus government administrators/ service providers could not match the linguistic needs of their provincial clients. Ironically, under apartheid, when the language of the administration and the dominant lingua franca, i.e. Afrikaans, were matched, service providers were better able to meet the linguistic needs of the public.
11. The increased gendered discrepancy in relation to people without any schooling referred to above, appears to be related to the traditional role of young girls/women taking on the care-giver role in families affected by HIV/Aids.
12. This research was conducted mainly in Gauteng where the technikons are located in the most highly urbanised part of the country, and where levels of English language proficiency would be expected to be highest.
13. An initial report posted on the department's website was hastily removed before researchers could access this.
14. A significant factor is that approximately 60% of L1 speakers of Afrikaans and 18% of speakers of English (i.e. 78%) of students in the Western Cape have L1 instruction. Only 22% of school pupils in this province have an African language, Xhosa, as their L1.
15. The 1999 study measured all students, except L1 speakers of Afrikaans, in English. The approximately 75% L1 speakers of African languages were expected to demonstrate literacy in English although they had switched

language medium to English only six months earlier (plus/minus 20 school weeks).

16. Researchers who were prevented from revealing their data have however indicated that the poor literacy levels are in relation to children from all linguistic communities. My own observations in early primary classrooms where most children are speakers of African languages (ALs) are that teachers are unduly affected by the washback effect of the change of medium from AL to English in Grade 4. They wonder why they should have to ensure that children can read and write in the AL when they will be required to change to English and hence have to learn to read in English only from Grade 4 onwards. Thus the principle of mother tongue literacy in the foundation years is seriously compromised.
17. Those children who wished to go to secondary school, and whose parents could afford to keep their children in school, had to be sent 'home' to the rural areas where they either lived with extended family or went to boarding schools.
18. A more detailed account of the history of language education in South Africa can be found in Heugh (2004) and du Plessis (2003).
19. Foucault (1977, 1991) and later Pennycook (2002b), note that however government is liberalized, its internal logic is towards increasing regulation, declining tolerance of external (democratic) participation, and the institutionalisation of apparatuses which render independent structures as 'docile bodies' (Foucault).
20. Richard Ruiz has offered an engaging set of conceptual tools for considering language policy and planning: 'language as a problem', 'language as a right' and 'language as a resource'. These orientations have been debated and used as points of departure in the work of many scholars of African sociolinguistics for the last 15 years.
21. There is a further layer of complexity in relation to multilingual practices within the linguistic marketplaces of ordinary people. It has to do with the way in which people use their linguistic repertoires to negotiate meaning between and across apparent linguistic divides. Fardon and Furniss (1994: 4) argue that the African lingua franca is not 'a single language but . . . a multilayered and partially connected language chain that offers a choice of varieties and registers in the speaker's immediate environment . . .'. The point here is that the public debates about language in South Africa remain narrowly circumscribed by the notion of parallel and separate language entities and the preference is towards monolingualism. Plurality in the parallel sense is difficult to accommodate and plurality in this sense, though much in horizontal evidence, has not yet been imagined in vertical discourses.
22. See Alexander (1989) for a fuller account.
23. Figuratively used to explain fearful, victim-like behaviour of a minority in relation to more powerful 'evil' forces. The most authoritative account of the history of Afrikaans can be found in Giliomee (2003b).
24. It was the British, rather than the National Party in 1948, that initiated formalised segregation.
25. See for example the different orthographic systems in use for the same language, namely, Southern Sotho in Lesotho and South Africa.

26. During PANSALB's first five-year term of office, government allocated R11 million (approximately €1 million) per year to this structure and insisted that this parallel language development should be funded from this allocation.
27. A more detailed critique of this kind of research is in Heugh (2002).
28. Siatchitema (1992) discussing language attitudes in Zambia argued for researchers to scratch a little below the surface if they want to find more enduring attitudes. My recent research in an inner-city high school involving attitude surveys shows unexpectedly high levels of tolerance of multilingual alternatives in education where access to English is not compromised.
29. The daily print circulation is the fifth highest in the country (ABC, 2005).
30. For example in the work of the Adult Learning Project (ALP) and Use Speak and Write English (USWE) from the mid-1980s to the mid-1990s.
31. The extent to which the HIV/Aids pandemic contributes to the increasing marginalisation of women requires further research.
32. R = reception/pre-school year.
33. For example, the most influential advisor on curriculum development has been Bill Spady from the US, a context where English is the numerically dominant language, and where the reality of multilingualism on the scale evident in Africa and South East Asia, is simply not regarded as a significant factor.
34. That the print media have recently increased publication in African languages demonstrates that it is both possible in terms of available terminology and profitable. What is lacking is political will.
35. On an even more fundamental level of inequality, the vocabularly range identified in the 2002 post-Apartheid education documentation for students who will learn through the L2, i.e. African students, is substantially lower than the requirements under apartheid. Almost inconceivably, this means that apartheid education offered a comparatively more enriched curriculum to African children. So instead of offering a 'better' education to black children now, the menu is more restricted and less enabling of access to higher education than before.
36. This figure was reached by using a formula which factors in a lower student–teacher ratio for orphans where teachers would have to compensate for the absence of adult guidance and supervision in the home.
37. Rob Siebörger is a senior teacher educator at the University of Cape Town. Personal correspondence, September 2003.
38. This is assuming that MTE were the principle for most of primary education, followed by a bilingual secondary school system (some subjects in L1, some in L2), rather like the European School model for children of the EU officials in Brussels.
39. Russell Wildeman, budget analyst for IDASA, e-mail correspondence March 2005.

Chapter 7

Contemporary Issues in Language, Education and Development in Pakistan

NAZ RASSOOL AND SABIHA MANSOOR

Introduction

As is discussed in Chapter 2, colonialism in India ended in 1947 with the partitioning of the country into the autonomous states of India, West and East Pakistan. Pakistan, as we know it today, came into being in 1971 in the aftermath of the civil war, which resulted in East Pakistan becoming the sovereign national state of Bangladesh. The administrative units of modern Pakistan comprise the provinces of Sindh, Punjab, Balochistan and the North West Frontier Province (NWFP) as well as the Federally Administrated Tribal Areas (FATA) which, together, are integrated into a federal national state. The capital city, Islamabad, was demarcated as a separate territory, and placed under federal jurisdiction and administration in 1981.

The ethnic dimensions of the social structure and political power in Pakistan, and the strong allegiances amongst different ethnolinguistic groups, have contributed to the fact that the debates about language have tended to be politically sensitive. The country's language-in-education policy therefore has remained problematic (see discussion below). Moreover, high levels of illiteracy throughout the country pose major problems for adequate labour supply; the general lack of cultural capital has impacted negatively on the differentiated and high skills supply needed to enable the country to compete effectively in the global labour market.

Seeking to address the political economy of language in education in Pakistan, this chapter examines some of the major issues that surround language and development within that country. This discussion is linked further to evolving labour skills demands within the global cultural economy. The discussion starts with an overview of languages that prevail within the country.

A Sociolinguistic Profile of Contemporary Pakistan

The population of Pakistan is estimated currently as 154,535,000 (Pakistan Census Organization, 2005) and is a highly differentiated ethnically, culturally and linguistically. Punjabis make up 56.6% of the population, Sindhis 23.0%, Balochis 5.0%, Pathans[1] (NWFP) 13.4%, and different tribal groupings (FATA) 2.4% (Pakistan Census Organization, 1998). Each broad ethnic group, in turn, has its own internal language and cultural differences with marked ethnic/caste/tribal sub-divisions within each group. The number of living languages listed in Pakistan is 69, a number of dialects, and Pakistan (Indian) Sign Language[2] (Sadaf Zuberi, 2005). The sociolinguistic profile of the country is summarized in Table 7.1.

Table 7.1 shows the main languages spoken in the provinces: in *Punjab* the main languages include Punjabi (75.23%) and Saraiki[3] (17.36%); in *Sindh* these include Sindhi (59.73%), Punjabi (6.99%) and Urdu (21.05%); most of the people in rural Sindh are Sindhi speakers (92.02%) whilst Urdu predominates in urban Sindh (41.48%) (see discussion below). In the *North West Frontier Province* (NWFP) Pushto (73.9%) is the language of the majority of the population whilst a range of other local languages (20.43%) predominate in rural areas. Balochi is the majority language in *Balochistan* (54.76%); its other major language is Pushto[4] (29.64%), and smaller numbers speak Sindhi (5.58%), other local languages (4.11%) and Saraiki (2.42%). The major language throughout *FATA* is Pushto (99.1%). Punjabi predominates in Islamabad (71.66%) the federal administrative capital, reflecting its geographical location. Urdu (10.11%) and Pushto (9.52%) are the most used minority languages in the capital. Alongside these languages, Deaf communities would be using Pakistan Sign Language (PSL) having its own distinct syntax and vocabulary. This, in turn, would have been adapted over the years within different cultural communities in the provinces resulting in, for example, Sindi, Urdu, Punjabi and Balochi regional varieties of PSL. Because of the vast overall population levels numerically, even relatively small linguistic groups are fairly large as compared to the linguistic minority groups in less populous countries. On this evidence then we can say that Pakistan is inherently a multilingual and multicultural society.

Table 7.1 Population by mother tongue (in percent)

Administrative unit	*Urdu*	*Punjabi*	*Sindhi*	*Pushto*	*Balochi*	*Saraiki*	*Others*
Pakistan	7.57	44.51	14.1	15.42	3.57	10.53	4.66
Rural	1.48	42.51	16.46	18.06	3.99	12.97	4.53
Urban	20.22	47.56	9.20	9.94	2.69	5.46	4.93
NWFP	0.78	0.97	0.04	73.9	0.01	3.86	20.43
Rural	0.24	0.24	0.02	73.98	0.01	3.99	21.52
Urban	3.47	4.58	0.11	73.55	0.03	3.15	15.11
FATA	0.18	0.23	0.01	99.1	0.04	—	0.45
Rural	0.18	0.18	0.01	99.15	0.04	—	0.43
Urban	0.18	1.85	*	97.00	*	—	0.96
Punjab	4.51	75.23	0.13	1.16	0.66	17.36	0.95
Rural	1.99	73.63	0.15	0.87	0.90	21.44	1.02
Urban	10.05	78.75	0.09	1.81	0.14	8.38	0.78
Sindh	21.05	6.99	59.73	4.19	2.11	1.00	4.93
Rural	1.62	2.68	92.02	0.61	1.50	0.32	1.25
Urban	41.48	11.52	25.79	7.96	2.74	1.71	8.80
Balochistan	0.97	2.52	5.58	29.64	54.76	2.42	4.11
Rural	0.21	0.43	5.27	32.16	57.55	1.87	2.51
Urban	3.42	9.16	6.27	21.61	45.84	4.16	9.24
Islamabad	10.11	71.66	0.56	9.52	0.06	1.11	6.98
Rural	2.33	83.74	0.08	7.62	0.02	0.3	5.91
Urban	14.18	65.36	0.81	10.51	0.08	1.53	7.53

*Refers to a very small population
Source: Pakistan Census Report 1998

However, over and above these diverse languages and their local varieties, English, the excolonial language has retained its high status in everyday life in Pakistan and plays an important role in all the major domains of power. For example, it is used in:

(1) The civil administration and bureaucracy, that is, in all federal and provincial government matters.

(2) The country's legal system at federal and provincial levels, although in the provincial district and session courts, Urdu is used in writing. Writing is bilingual in the lower courts, and for the superior courts i.e. the Supreme Court and High Courts the written texts are in English (Abbas, 1993).
(3) The Defence Force including the Army, Navy and Air Force. The models used for training are predominantly British, and English is the language of communication for office work. Urdu has been used to train officers and personnel in the field since 1974 when Zulfiqar Ali Bhutto came into power.
(4) The mass media, together with Urdu and the regional languages. The major television and radio stations broadcast the news both in English and Urdu. With the introduction of satellite television, viewers have access to world media in English. English and Urdu predominate in newspaper publications throughout the country, in addition to smaller numbers of newspapers in regional and local languages.
(5) The field of education (with Urdu). In all government schools Urdu is the medium of teaching and learning with English as a compulsory subject from Grade 5 or 6. In the last ten years attempts have been made by various governments to introduce English from Grade 1. English medium schools continue to flourish in the private sector.

The integration of English into the cultural, political, and economic institutions within Pakistani society means that, in practice, it represents the language of power, *par excellence*, over and above other languages within the country. As such it plays a major role in providing access to employment opportunities and, '(w)ithout knowing English one cannot enter the most lucrative and powerful jobs, both in the state apparatus and the private sector, in Pakistan' (Rahman, 2002: 2). The hegemony of English that prevails within Pakistani society relates to a complex range of circumstances including:

- the country's colonial heritage;
- the importance attached to English in the country's postcolonial national language policy (see Constitution below);
- the negligible value attached to regional and local languages within public domains;
- the predominance of English within the interactive global cultural economy (see Chapter 4).

Language lies at the heart of the state in any society and, therefore, the languages underscored by national policy will have not only their status enhanced but would also gain in political and economic value within society. A country's national language policy is usually enshrined in its Constitution, which establishes the political principles and rules by which a state supports the practices and processes of national governance. The Constitution therefore codifies the power, responsibilities and duties of each government, and ratifies the relative cultural/linguistic, political, and economic rights of people as citizens, workers and consumers of state services.

National Language Policy

Pakistan has had several Constitutions since its creation including the Constitution of 1956, the Constitution of 1962,[5] the Interim Constitution of 1972, and the Constitution of 1973. Pakistan's national language policy is enshrined in Article 251 of the 1973 Constitution. It states that:

(1) The National language of Pakistan is Urdu, and arrangements shall be made for its being used for official and other purposes within fifteen years from the commencing day.
(2) Subject to clause (1), the English language may be used for official purposes until arrangements are made for its replacement by Urdu.
(3) Without prejudice to the status of the National language, a Provincial Assembly may by law prescribe measures for the teaching, promotion and use of a provincial language in addition to the national language.

As we can see, the supremacy of Urdu as the national language is upheld in all areas. At the same time, the Constitution supports the fundamental right of all citizens to preserve and promote their language, script and culture (Article 28). However, this right is conditional; it is subject not only to the requirements of Article 251 but also to law. These conditionalities, it is argued, have strengthened the power of the central state, and through this, undermined the relative autonomy of the provinces with regard to the formal development of regional and local languages and cultures (Mansoor, 2005). Excluding Sindh province, hardly any legislation has been formulated in the provinces to promote regional languages in official spheres (Rahman, 1999; Abbas, 1993).

At meta-level, the policy statement of Article 251 of the 1973 Constitution provides insight into the complex language choices with regard to maintaining a cohesive nation whilst, at the same time, facilitating economic development by providing access to the global cultural economy. In this regard it represents the classic 'pluralist dilemma' (Bullivant, 1981). For example, as we can see, the Constitution acknowledges English as the official language (previously the colonial language) whilst, at the same time, asserting Urdu as the country's national language with the intention of integrating the (Urdu) language into official domains within a defined period. It also makes provision for the teaching and development of regional languages at provincial level. The underlying assumption at the time was that English would recede, or disappear, naturally as people over time incorporated Urdu into their everyday lives.

Significantly though, 30 years later the policy goal of transitioning to Urdu within official domains has not yet been achieved. Instead, English has retained, indeed, strengthened its position as the language of power within official domains. Thus it has been argued generally that English is the *de facto* national language of Pakistan. This has been attributed, *inter alia*, to the fact that there has been a lack of political will or any real effort to change the official language of proceedings from English to Urdu by the English speaking Pakistani elites in the country who are the products of English medium education (Mansoor, 2005). Since most of the existing official documents are in English there appears to have been little progress made towards translating these, or producing new official documents in Urdu (Rahman, 1999; Abbas, 1993). In this regard Urdu appears to be suffering from benign neglect, at least within the official domain where it remains relatively under-resourced in relation to English.

It also relates to the fact that Urdu is the mother tongue of a minority in Pakistan; it is the language of only 7.57% of the national population as opposed to 44.15% Punjabi speakers (Pakistan Census Organization, 1998). Moreover, as is discussed in Chapter 2, this linguistic minority are represented mainly by the *Mohajirs*, the diasporic community who transmigrated from India following Partition in 1947, and the civil war of 1971 and therefore did not have a social base within the province. This and the fact that the majority of the *Mohajirs* settled in Sindh Province[6] contributed to conflict between the *Mohajirs* and the Sindhi middle class who felt discriminated against, and deprived within their native region. As stated earlier, since the *Mohajirs* generally at the time tended to be more formally educated than the local Sindhi population they took up 'technical, bureaucratic, and professional jobs' (Rahman, 2000: 112). The polarization of the two groups, and competition for jobs and power between them, resulted in language riots in that province during the early 1970s. Eventually the provincial government was forced to amend the language policy to include both Urdu and Sindhi as official languages of the province (Mazari, 2002).

Urdu, religion and national identity

The hegemony of Urdu during the early days was profound, linked as it was with the founding principles of the country. The founding father of the Pakistani nation, Mohamed Ali Jinna, supported the formation of a secular state. Following his demise, the Prime Minister, Liaqat Ali Khan in 1948 in response to an amendment sought to permit the use of Bengali in the Assembly alongside Urdu and English, stated that: 'Pakistan is a Muslim state and it must have as its lingua franca the language of the Muslim nation ... it is necessary for a nation to have one language and that language can only be Urdu and no other language' (cited in Callard, 1958: 182). Pakistan became an Islamic Republic in the 1956 Constitution. Central to nationalist ideology was the view that Urdu represented a key defining principle of what it means to be a Pakistani and, *ipso facto*, of being a Muslim in Pakistan. In other words, Urdu was central to the state's view of Pakistani nationhood. Thus it had potent symbolic significance (Rahman, 2000) representing as it did a cultural variable around which the nation could be constructed. Nevertheless, whilst it became a symbol of national unity, as is discussed earlier, Urdu is not a native language of Pakistan.

Contextualizing Urdu

There are different views on how the modern Urdu language evolved. What there *is* agreement on is that the languages of the Proto-Historic Indus Valley or the present-day Pakistan are from some of the most ancient civilizations. Linguistically Pakistani languages are rooted in India; the roots of Pakistan's languages are Dravidian, Indo-Aryan and its scripts and vocabulary owe much to Arabic and Persian (Rahman, 1999). All the languages, with the exception of Brohi, are of the Indo-European family and use the Arabic-Persian script. Historically, Urdu and Hindi represent Indo-Aryan languages that originally had developed together and, except for the differences in script, are regarded by many as the same language (Rahman, 1999; Zaman, 1981; Gumperz, 1977). This language developed over centuries of mixing together Sanskrit (high status language of the elites) and the various Prakrits (low status 'root' languages of 'inferior' castes or occupations) that differed from one region to another (Rahman, 1999). Languages used by foreign rulers in the domains of power, have also enriched the indigenous languages to the extent that their vocabulary now is multilingual and varied. With the arrival of the Muslims since the 11th and 12th centuries bringing their own languages such as Arabic, Persian and Turkish as languages of state and religion, the foundations of a hybrid language called, *inter alia*, Hindi, Hindvi, Rekhta (which literally means 'a rough mixture'), Urdu (which in Turkish means 'horde' or 'army), and Hindustani[7] were laid. Modern Urdu comprises a vocabulary (at least 40%) derived from Persian and Arabic 'superimposed on a base of grammar, usages and vocabulary that it shares in common with Hindi' (http://en.wikipedia.rog/wiki/Urdu_language). Sufis and Divines such as Amir Khusro and poets including Muhammad Quli Qutub Shah, Mas'ud Sa'd Salamn and Ustad Abul Faraj Rumi (Rahman, 1999) and later, Mir, Sauda, Ghalib and Zauq popularized the Persianized Urdu language in their devotional writings and songs which mixed the languages of learning including Sanskrit, Persian and Arabic, with the local dialects.

As stated earlier, Urdu has always been a minority language in Pakistan. At the time of Partition in 1947 only 3.37% of the population in West Pakistan represented Urdu mother tongue speakers (Mazari, 2002) in comparison with large numbers of Urdu speakers residing in India (2–3%). The introduction of Urdu as national language serving as a means of securing national integration was therefore politically problematic from the beginning. In practice, it served to create long-term power imbalances within the country. First, at the level of everyday life its high status as national language served to undermine regional and local languages. However, policy meanings always exist in tension and, therefore, represent an arena of struggle for control over meaning amongst different interest groups. In this regard, the language issue became a rallying point for ethnic groups during the period of martial rule under Ayub Khan 'when all regional languages were banned in 1958 on the recommendation of the Education Commission' (Mazari, 2002: 7). Second, the Urdu-speaking *Mohajir* elite were placed at a considerable advantage with regard to education, business and jobs. As stated earlier their relatively better level of education compared to many local groups, enabled them to 'take the place of the departing Hindu middle class professionals and business groups' (Rashid and Shaheed, 1993: 2). Their domination of the central government and civil bureaucracy during the early years created power imbalances that largely still prevail within the country. Third, ethnic conflict particularly in Sindh province has been sporadic which, in turn, has contributed to ongoing social and political instability within that region. In addition to the language riots of the 1970s mentioned earlier, the 1980s also were marked by inter-ethnic riots.

Apart from Urdu and English which in practice are limited to a small proportion of the population, no language is commonly understood, that is to say, no single language can be claimed as a common mother tongue (Zaman, 1981). Urdu as national language continues to exist in tension, lending credence to the argument that the nationalist project constructed around Urdu as the common language through which an integrative national bond could be cemented has not been fulfilled.[8] As can be seen below, Pakistan remains a country divided by the language hegemonies of elite groups. The country is defined by a large literacy, knowledge and skills divide between elite groups and the majority of the population. Literacy levels within society impact on the cultural capital available within the country to support both economic and social development, as well as the development of a strong civil society. We discuss below the negative effects that the under-development of the language-in-education infrastructure as this relates to local and regional languages as well as Urdu and English, that is, the national and official languages, have had on social and economic development possibilities in Pakistan.

Language in education struggles

In our discussion so far it is evident that the formation of the sovereign state of Pakistan, in effect, represented the struggle for hegemony amongst a variety of ethnolinguistic groups. That is to say, securing the *monopoly of power within the state* by one particular ethnolinguistic group was central to the struggle for Pakistani nationhood. Some of these struggles have been mentioned above already and, moreover, are documented in depth elsewhere (Rahman, 1999, 2000; Ahmed, 1998; Mahboob, 2002). Amongst the various ethnolinguistic groups, the Urdu-speaking intelligentsia, as is evident in the words of the first Prime Minister of Pakistan, Liaqat Ali Khan mentioned earlier, claimed 'to speak for the whole nation and to represent the national essence' (Billig, 1997: 27). That they did not do so in practice is evident in the recurring ethnolinguistic conflict in Sindh province since independence. The fact that Sindhi speakers have a proud literary heritage, and their language had been the medium for teaching and learning within the province before independence, has meant that they have felt that their language was undermined by the legitimization of Urdu, the language predominantly of the refugees from India – the *Mohajirs* – as the national language, and English as the major language in higher levels of education. Moreover, the struggle against the hegemony of Urdu is not just about language, for the Sindhi speakers of Karachi it is ultimately about reclaiming cultural, political and economic power of this ethnolinguistic group within the region. As we argued earlier, this is an unequal struggle since Urdu is, fundamentally, an historical construct of Pakistani nationalism which is grounded in Islamic principles. As such, it has always been central to the political identity of the Pakistani state.

Language, religion and education

The Sharif Commission, appointed by President Ayub Khan in 1959, introduced Urdu as the language for teaching and learning in all government schools, whilst English was to be taught only as a compulsory subject, and should continue as second language for advanced study and research. This was in line with the long-term view that Urdu would ultimately replace English in education and in society as a whole. Although, as we argued earlier, Pakistan is *culturally* a multilingual society, its *political basis* is ultimately monolingual; the interpellation of Urdu as national language with Islamic identity and cultural values forms the hegemonic basis of the Pakistani national identity. These meanings were reinforced during the military regime of President Zia ul Haq which overtly and fervently pursued policies of 'Islamization' and 'Urdu-ization'. In 1978 the government advised English medium schools to shift to Urdu – or the regional language recognized by the state – thus undermining languages spoken locally in the provinces. At the same time, Arabic seen as representing the language of Islam, was introduced initially as a compulsory foreign language and, subsequently, as the language medium for teaching and learning in all government schools from Grade 1. English was not introduced until Grade 6. The introduction of Arabic as medium for teaching and learning coincided with government support for religious schools (*Deeni Madrassas*) which currently pose major pedagogical, cultural and political problems to the country. Prime Minister Nawaz Sharif gave further support to them in 1998 by recognizing their *Sanad* (Degree) as a Masters degree in Arabic and Islamiyat. Political analysts have criticized successive rulers, especially General Zia-ul-Haq and Prime Minister Nawaz Sharif, for the misuse of Islam and the ideology that underpins the Pakistani state to propagate their own views (Mansoor, 2005).

Despite the policy emphasis on Urdu as the language medium for teaching and learning, and the intention for those matriculating in 1989 to do so in Urdu which, it was hoped, would facilitate the envisaged transition to Urdu in Higher Education (Mahboob, 2002), English continued to flourish in the private sector during these periods. Later, during the first Benazir Bhutto regime, schools were given the option of adopting English as the medium for teaching and learning. English has continued to predominate in the country's national institutions and, therefore, the formal life of society. How then have these policies translated into practice in the national education system, and how do they relate to broader educational policy and existing sociocultural and economic conditions within the country?

Education in Pakistan

Pakistan is one of the largest Muslim countries in the world. It has a geographical area of approximately 803,940 square kilometres and, as stated above, comprises a culturally and linguistically diverse population. However, since the country has not benefited from a stable political base since independence (see Chapter 3), it is therefore not surprising that development in the social sector is one of the lowest in the world. With a current ranking of 142 in the UNDP Human Development Index, Pakistan features among the countries with the worst profiles on human development (UNDP, 2004). Although the country's GNP per capita income for the period 2004–2005 is $736 having risen from $579 in 2002–2003, at least a quarter (27.3%) of the population live below the poverty line (Government of Pakistan Economic Survey, 2003–2004). This is compounded by a high population growth rate; the population has grown by at least 2% since 2000–2001 making Pakistan now the seventh most populous country in the world (Government of Pakistan Economic Survey, 2004–2005). This factor impacts in a significant way on resource provision in education.

Literacy and education levels

The literacy rate in 2003–2004 was estimated at 53%, with 66.25% for males and 41.75% for females (Government of Pakistan Economic Survey, 2003–2004). In 2002–2003 the country spent 1.7% of its GNP on education compared with 2.5% in 1996–1997 (Government of Pakistan Economic Survey, 2004–2005). Pakistan is one of only 12 countries spending less than 2% of its GNP on education, and according to the UNDP (2004) Human Development Report the country has the lowest 'education index' of any country outside Africa. Pakistan lags behind the other South Asian Countries in elementary, secondary and tertiary education. Table 7.2 provides insight into the levels of education in the country based on information obtained from the Labour Force Survey of 2003–2004.

Table 7.2 Percentage distribution of population by age, sex, literacy and level of education

Age groups		*Total*	*Illiterate*	*Literate*	*Level of education* *No Formal Educ*	*K.G. but below Primary*	*Primary but below Middle*	*Middle but below Matric*	*Matric but below Intermediate*	*Intermediate but below Degree*	*Degree and Post Grad PhD*
Both Sexes	All Ages	100.00	60.31	39.69	.47	8.73	11.40	7.01	6.74	2.70	2.63
Male	All Ages	100.00	51.81	48.19	.54	10.26	13.33	8.98	8.47	3.22	3.39
Female	All Ages	100.00	69.24	30.76	.41	7.13	9.37	4.95	4.92	2.15	1.83

Source: Compiled from table 3 Labour Force Survey 2003–2004, Federal Bureau of Statistics, Pakistan (pp. 56) (literacy measurement based on definition of being literate in relation to a person's ability to read a newspaper and write a simple letter in any language)

Table 7.2 shows that more than 60% of the population is still illiterate, with women lagging behind men. This gender disparity is reflected also in the cross-phase levels of education. Although the literacy figures for 2004–2005 shows a significant improvement from 39.69% the previous year, to 53% (Pakistan Census Organization, 2004–2005), the national literacy level nevertheless remains low in comparison with other countries in the region. Moreover, 70% of the total population works in the informal sector (Government of Pakistan Economic Survey, 2004–2005) signalling an unequal distribution of the labour force across sectors with the majority employed in low or unskilled and, therefore, underpaid jobs. This suggests that there is a mixed language economy in action within the overall labour market – especially at the lower end – with a sizable proportion of the workforce relying on local or regional languages in their various employment environments. There also are quite big variances in the literacy levels of the different provinces as is evident in the more developed Punjab (51.8%) and Sindh (54.9%) provinces, and lower literacy levels in the under-developed provinces of Balochistan (33.5%) and the North Western Frontier Province (39.3%) (Government of Pakistan Economic Survey, 2004–2005). However, because of the way in which the literacy statistical data are collected there is no indication of literacy levels in particular languages. This is a highly significant point and will be discussed again later in relation to research.

The generally low educational profile suggests that the country has massive under-employment problems particularly in relation to the requirement for highly skilled workers within the global cultural economy as is discussed in Chapter 4. This is significant since the burgeoning information technology and telecom sector of the economy represents major job opportunities for educated unemployed young people 'in the wide range of areas (such as) call centers, telecom engineering, telecom sales, customer services, finance, accounting and jobs through franchises of the telecom companies' (Government of Pakistan Economic Survey, 2004–2005: 45, information in brackets added). As part of its poverty reduction strategy, the country has since 2001 increased investment in human resource development with a major emphasis on Higher Education.

Higher education

Currently in Higher Education which includes undergraduate and postgraduate studies, the participation rate is only 2.63% as compared to the average 50% participation rate in industrialized countries (Pakistan Labour Force Survey, 2004). There are 964 Arts and Science colleges with an enrolment of 801,746 students, and 382 Professional colleges with an enrolment of 163,852 students throughout the country. The number of teachers in Arts and Science colleges is 27,911, and 9841 in Professional colleges (Government of Pakistan Economic Survey, 2003–2004). The country has 29 universities, and eight degree awarding institutions in the public sector with a total enrolment of 126,870 students; as well as 30 universities, and 15 degree awarding institutions in the private sector with an enrolment of 16,410 students (Pakistan Ministry of Education, 2004).

Higher Education is regarded as a capital investment which benefits the individual as well as the economic and social development of the country. As such it has received special attention in various educational policies and Education Commission and Committees Reports since independence. Issues identified and addressed in these reports range from lack of dedication amongst faculty staff and student discipline (Karachi University Enquiry Committee, 1956–1957), to concerns related to language medium (Sharif Report, 1959; Zia ul Haq, 1979), and the need to improve the quality of education through administrative reforms (Zia ul Haq, 1979; Nawaz Sharif, 1998; General Musharraf, 2000–2002). A thorough revision of the duration of the BA and BSc Degree from a three-year Honours Degree was advocated (Nawaz Sharif, 1998), to a recommended four year degree by the Task Force on Higher Education (General Musharraf, 2002). The emphasis on Computer Education and Information Technology initiated by President Nawaz Sharif in 1998 has been strengthened by the General Musharraf regime in recent policy announcements (National Education Policy, 1998–2010). The Education Sector Reforms introduced by the General Musharraf Government in 2001, have focused on the areas of basic education and literacy, Higher Education, public–private partnership, and good governance. This reinforced the recommendations made previously by the Zulfiqar Ali Bhutto government in its education policy of 1972 to promote free and universal education, and followed by the Nawaz Sharif government in its education policy of 1988 to achieve universal literacy in 15 years. At the moment the emphasis is on human resource development and modernization in order to meet the demands of the global cultural economy. In line with this, the long-term aims of the National Education Policy (1998–2010) are 'to make Pakistan's Education system more meaningful and relevant, aiming to create a knowledge-based society, designed to support economic growth and poverty alleviation' (Government of Pakistan Economic Survey, 2004–2005: 137). Improving national levels of literacy and education are central to the fulfilment of these goals. These factors highlight the need to take a closer look at the overall significance of language with regard to boosting educational achievement *per se*. In turn this raises questions about the place of mother tongues or regional languages in education, especially in relation to the important role that these languages play in the learning process, and the acquisition of knowledge. At the same time, there is also a need for language-in-education policy to take account of the relationship between language and the national, and international, labour market. This is the case, especially in relation to the job opportunities presented by information technology, and the expansion of the telecommunications industry mentioned earlier, and the opportunities offered thus for the labour force to compete effectively in the global labour market. Adequate supplies of skilled workers who can readily be absorbed into the modern labour market could, implicitly, support the diversification of the country's economy placing it in a more competitive position within the international global cultural economy. Together, these factors have implications for the way in which education is organized, and the language policies that underpin educational provision.

Research and development

As is indicated earlier, there currently appears to be no link between existing policy and educational or sociolinguistic research in the country. At the moment policy, seemingly, is 'handed down', that is to say, it appears to be formulated without consultation with stake holders including educational planners and practitioners, sociolinguists, educational economists – and parents. Language policies informed by empirical research into patterns of language use, and the demography of literacy levels in the country, are important in relation to the organization and delivery of education as well as its long-term effectiveness in sustaining economic and social development. There are several policy issues to consider in this regard.

First, it is important that the collection of educational data in national census and labour force surveys takes account also of *language use within particular domains*. For example, which languages are used by whom, where and when, and for what purposes? What are the levels of fluency in particular languages – amongst which communities? How literate are people in these languages? Literacy statistics that do not reflect how different languages are used within the country, provide a limited perspective of formal language use especially in relation to literacy levels in the national, official and regional languages (see also Chapter 6). This, in turn, has implications for the strategic channelling of resources in education. Literacy mapping and cross-country sociolinguistic surveys could therefore play a major role in informing strategic policy making, for example, with regard to developing the educational infrastructure in rural areas within the different provinces (see Chapters 5 and 6).

Second, information on language use and levels of literacy in different languages is important also in relation to documenting language skills needs within the emerging technologically driven labour market discussed earlier (see Chapter 4) as well as employment possibilities and their language requirements locally, regionally and within the global terrain (see Chapter 4). In this regard, the mapping of workplace literacies and language use would play a significant role in informing educational policy, thus potentially creating a more balanced match between changing labour market skills demands and educational planning.

Third, it is by now a commonly accepted view in education grounded in research that fluency in learners' first language facilitates the acquisition of a second or third language, and that they learn more easily in their first language than they do in a language that does not feature naturally in their everyday lives (Cumings, 1976; Skutnabb-Kangas, 1981). These factors have implications for national educational achievement levels and, therefore, the possibility of improving the country's overall educational profile. This, in turn, impacts on employment possibilities within the formal labour market and, ultimately, economic development. These factors also have implications for language in educational policy frameworks as these relate to the language mediums for teaching and learning within different provinces and how these combine with a cohesive nationhood.

The discussion here highlights the significance of sociolinguistic research past, present and future, including national research studies to be conducted to inform policy and practice, and thus to contribute to effective and sustainable human resource development. As stated earlier, together these factors impact on economic possibilities nationally and globally. Overall, the issues identified here underscore the significance of including sociolinguistic data in macro-educational planning focused on preparing learners adequately for a modernizing labour market relying increasingly on communication skills including intercultural and multilingual skills (Rassool, 1999). Taking these arguments into account, it therefore is debatable whether political ideologies necessarily provide a useful basis for decisions about language in education. The next section revisits some of the main political discourses that have surrounded national language issues in Pakistan.

Political Discourses about Language and Nation

It is evident earlier in the discussion that the state's declared policy since independence has been to promote Urdu as a national language, and as a symbol of national identity and integration, thus to ensure social cohesion. Although the political discourse has not been overtly pro-English, English nevertheless continues to flourish and remains the official language of Pakistan. This fact prompts political analysts to infer that the support given to Urdu is rhetorical; that there appears to be an inherent contradiction between Pakistan's stated official policy of promoting Urdu as the national official language of Pakistan, 'and the real policy where the status quo is maintained and English remains the language of power' (Rahman, 1995: 17). The ruling elites, that is, all those with power and influence in Pakistan such as the bureaucracy and military, have command in English through their English medium education. English is not only the language of the upper classes in Pakistan; it also provides access to the best jobs in the governmental, non-governmental and international bureaucracy. Seemingly then all these groups would have a vested interest in maintaining English as the language in which formal affairs and business are done and therefore continue to support English as the official language and, therefore, the language of Higher Education learning. In this regard English represents a potent form of cultural capital, implicitly devaluing local and regional languages.

Within the context of Higher Education, in *all* educational policies and reports of education commissions and committees set up between 1957 and 1998, the official policy has been to maintain English as the medium of teaching and learning. It is important to note that this policy continues to be regarded as an interim arrangement. Although Urdu was declared the official medium of instruction for schooling (Grades 1–12) in the public sector soon after the country's independence, the period assigned to the transfer from English medium to Urdu medium in Higher Education has varied in different government reports. This includes 15 years in the Report of the Sharif Commission in 1959, and five to seven years in the Report of the University Grants Commission in 1982. Despite endorsement of this policy by every subsequent regime, the problems regarding learners' language difficulties in the English medium, or developing sufficient and quality materials in Urdu for Higher Education have not been addressed adequately (Mansoor, 2005). This argument is reinforced by the fact that the Report of the Education Sector Reforms (2001) and the Task Force on Higher Education (2002) set up by General Musharraf, have not addressed the issue of language policy in higher education.

Regional languages in higher education

Furthermore, although there is Constitutional provision for the Provincial Assembly to promote the regional language in education, it is implied in the Constitution that no measure should be adopted to promote the regional language at the cost of the status of the national language, Urdu. This requirement raises fundamental questions about language and the early learning experiences of students in schools. It is also a politically sensitive issue revolving around concerns about loyalty and national identity. Consequently, in all provinces, except Sindh,[9] hardly any legislation has been passed to promote the regional languages in official spheres or to integrate it as a medium for teaching and learning in the education system (Rahman, 1999; Abbas, 1993). Most of the state funded 'schools in Punjab, Azad Kashmir, Balochistan and the N.W.F.P use Urdu as the medium of instruction' (Rahman, 2002: 3), a language not necessarily used in their everyday lives. At the same time, the North Western Frontier Province also has a good selection of schools using different languages including Urdu (13,556), Pashto (10,731 up to Grade 5) and English (3995) medium schools (Rahman, 2002). However, although they use Pashto as a language medium of teaching and learning within some schools in NWFP, many of these are distributed amongst the parallel system of education represented by the *Deeni Madrassas* (religious schools) which mainly use Arabic. Urdu predominates in Balochistan where there are at least 9939 Urdu-medium schools and 465 English-medium schools. The same applies to the Punjab where there are, on average, 67,490 Urdu-medium schools and 22,855 English-medium schools (Rahman, 2002). English medium schools are dominated by children of the military and government elite as well as elites of the provincial state institutions including the Railways, Customs, Telecommunications, Police Departments who run their own schools (Rahman, 2002).

Language Issues in Higher Education

English is a compulsory subject at graduate level, whilst Urdu is not. As we indicated earlier, this raises important questions related to the quality of students' learning experience at Higher Degree level as well as the potential quality of the university output. For example, what is the level of proficiency in English amongst all students by the time that they start their Higher Education studies? At the moment English language is compulsory from Grade VI to first degree level in all educational institutions except in Sindh province and Punjab, where English is compulsory from Grade 1. In these instances, an emerging graduate therefore would have studied English for at least nine years. However, what does this mean in relation to their English language ability to study at under-graduate or postgraduate level? How do students experience their studies through English as medium for teaching and learning? What systems are in place within universities to support further development of English for Academic Purposes? What is the quality of the learning and teaching materials in English? What are the levels of fluency in English amongst teachers? To what extent do teachers and students rely on Urdu/regional/local languages as a means of facilitating knowledge acquisition? What educational support systems are in place for the development of Urdu as well as regional languages at Higher Education level? How valid is the policy emphasis on English as the language of Higher Education with regard to sustaining (a) the development of a cohesive and culturally integrated Pakistani nationhood and (b) the development of the nation's cultural capital that would enable learners, as citizens, to participate meaningfully in the democratic process as well as (c) to participate effectively in the competitive global cultural economy? What are the implications of this policy for facilitating equal life chances for students completing their degrees and entering the labour market? Who benefits? Who loses out? How does this impact on national development possibilities? In 2001 the Federal Minister for Education announced the intention to introduce English as a compulsory subject from Grade 1 (Mansoor, 2005). This policy has not yet been implemented. There is therefore much slippage between policy rhetoric and policy formulation that includes guidelines for implementation and, moreover, the resources required for successful implementation.

A recent large scale qualitative and quantitative study[10] (Mansoor, 2005) focusing on English in Higher Education in Pakistan found that there are significant differences in provision for English language teaching between private and public institutions. The study also found that the majority of students in private educational institutions tended to be those who had been educated in English throughout their schooling, and therefore could operate with confidence in a language environment with which they are largely familiar. The families of these students would also have been imbued with social capital including having access to books, equipment and other English language resources that ultimately benefited their children. Many of these students would have grown up in an English/regional/national language environment. These students therefore tended to achieve better examination results than those students who had been educated in Urdu, or the regional languages, in the public school sector. One of the students interviewed in the study argued that:

> ... we are talking about Higher Education but 70% of our population live in rural areas and whose parents also are not literate. Our families are educated so we can study English. But nobody cares about that 70%

> of the population. In the 8th Grade 90% (of the) students fail just because they cannot pass the English subject. Then when they reach matriculation level 90% or 80% (of the) students fail because English is compulsory. If English compulsory was not there, the students might have studied further perhaps till FA or BA. English should therefore be just an elective language. (Mansoor, 2005: 252)

This student raises important issues related to the ways and extent in which the *habitus* of particular communities and the cultural capital of parents impact on students' educational attainment. Since the language medium for teaching and learning in Higher Education is English, this means that students, who had been educated predominantly in Urdu or the regional languages, would operate at a distinct disadvantage compared to those whose home languages included English – and had been educated in English throughout their schooling. English in Higher Education thus serves as a screening mechanism; it excludes the majority from access to Higher education.

Regional languages and students' mother tongues play a negligible role in education in general in Pakistan – the latter, if they are local languages, do not feature in any educational policy frameworks. Where regional languages *are* used, they lack adequate teaching materials and a progressive pedagogical base; much emphasis remains on formal didactic approaches and rote learning (see also below). As a result of the lack of emphasis on regional languages in language-in-education policy students do not regard the study of their regional language or mother tongue as important. Consequently, many Punjabi speakers, for example, choose to develop their competence in Urdu and English instead (Mansoor, 2005).

Significantly, Mansoor's (2005) study reported a lack of adequate resource supply and appropriate teaching methodologies in *all* the languages used in Higher Education including English, Urdu and the regional languages. Moreover, a perceived general lack of proficiency in English amongst teachers posed a major problem in relation to the quality of students' learning experience. Many students in Mansoor's study continued to rely on rote-learning as the means of passing examinations. This confirms Rahman's findings that at secondary level, most Matriculants 'from vernacular-medium schools cannot speak English and can barely read their textbooks which they tend to memorize' (Rahman, 2002: 2). Students in Mansoor's (2005) study reported having major difficulties in following lectures, making presentations, examinations and understanding texts in English. This meant that many of them did not necessarily have a full grasp of the concepts and ideas that underpin their subject knowledge. For some, full literacy in *any* of the languages sanctioned by state policy remains problematic. This is the case especially for those who come from rural areas who speak local languages and dialects, and where a non-literate *habitus* prevails except perhaps where this involves the reading of the Quran.

Despite massive inputs into the teaching of English the national results generally are abysmally poor in education (Abbas, 1993). Since English is a compulsory subject, failure in English means failing the entire University examination (Mansoor, 2005). Seemingly then the requirement for English language in Higher Education presents major difficulties to many students, especially those with a native language background. This raises another set of questions revolving around the levels of literate engagement in Urdu the national language and the regional languages amongst different sections of the population and, particularly, those who are within (or are about to enter) the labour market. This confirms the earlier argument that the 'language-blind' literacy statistics collected in the national census are not helpful to analyses of specific areas of need in education. For example, what are the levels of literacy in each of the languages used in education? This data could serve an important means of comparison with the language demands within different sectors of the labour market. Moreover, what is the relative exchange value of different languages within the national, regional and international labour market? This has implications for the quality of the labour force in relation to meeting the complex language demands of the regional and national as well as the global cultural economy discussed in Chapter 4.

Conclusion

This chapter situated Pakistan's language-in-education policy within the broader framework of the country's political development since independence. The sustained low literacy rates nationally, and the high levels of under-employment within high skills areas call into question the effectiveness of the country's language-in-education policy in supporting adequate levels of skilled labour supply to make the country competitive in the global labour market. The discussion has shown that Pakistan's language-in-education policy is fraught with problems on both a conceptual and practical level. This reflects the ever-shifting policy landscape related to ongoing political struggles amongst different interest groups within and around the state. As political regimes have changed shifts often have taken place in policy emphases leaving unresolved political tensions between the role of English, Urdu and Regional Languages in education. This is a macro-political problem that has its genesis in the founding of the Pakistani state, and has remained unresolved as a result of sustained political instability since independence.[11] Moreover, the envisaged transition from English to Urdu within official domains has not taken place, and the lack of policy support and provision for the development of regional languages in education has contributed to the tension that has prevailed in Sindh province with its strong ethno-cultural identity base. Of major significance is the silence on the use of local languages in education as a means of building literate communities from grassroots level within both rural and urban areas, with other major languages added at key stages, thus laying the basis of a cumulatively multilingual, multi- or at least a bi-literate social base (see also Chapter 8). The implications of this for a differentially skilled labour market are immense.

Important questions arose in the discussion throughout the chapter. For example, given the mismatches between learner needs and resource provision as well as the under-developed English language ability and pedagogical competencies of teachers, how effectively does the existing language-in-education policy in Pakistan serve the needs of a professed modernizing state and economy in relation to: (a) labour and business competition within the global cultural economy; and (b) serving the needs of maintaining an integrated nationhood?

How does federalism articulate with the formulation of language-in-education policy? That is to say, what is the level of relative autonomy vested in provincial governments as this relates to the ability to choose the language medium for teaching and learning – and investment in the development of regional languages? Why are regional languages not developed as resources for learning? How does language research inform language-in-education policy?

In essence, Pakistan reflects the general picture in many postcolonial developing countries. Most of these countries are defined by developmental gaps as their histories had been interrupted and deformed, sometimes for centuries, by colonialism. In other words, the cultural hegemony of colonialism grounded in linguistic imperialism, the displacement of historically derived national identities and the destruction of local cultures have led to cultural alienation particularly amongst elite groups (see Chapter 3). These groups choose to self-identify with 'non-native' cultural values, mores, beliefs and cultural means of communication. In this regard, elite groups in Pakistan approximate not only the linguistic behaviours but also the cultural aspirations of elite groups elsewhere in the 'developing world' (see Chapter 4). For these groups international lingua franca, notably excolonial languages, become important social markers 'and serve as models for the aspiring masses' (Agheyisi, 1977; see Chapter 3). While these practices remain intact, and language-in-education policy stays entirely within the political domain and therefore uninformed by existing linguistic and educational research, it will remain subject to change according to the ideological projects of particular political regimes in power. The lack of progression in language-in-education policy and educational practice is a major contributing factor to educational under-achievement and, therefore, the under-developed human resource base in Pakistan. Ultimately, the success of any policy relies not only on a set of ideological principles; it also needs to be accompanied by a comprehensive set of guidelines to frame implementation as well as adequate resource allocation to support teaching and learning in all phases of education. This includes translation of key texts, literary texts as well as subject related textbooks, supporting materials such as dictionaries in different languages, adequately trained language teachers, audio-visual equipment, adequate assessment frameworks, processes and procedures, and coherent educational leadership. In addition, classroom practice needs to be grounded in established and enabling language pedagogies grounded in process-based learning. This means that pedagogy has to be framed by a set of educational principles grounded in pedagogies that empower students, as learners, and as future citizens. Together these elements highlight the significance of incorporating language provision into the educational planning and policy process.

Ultimately, to enable a meaningful link between language education and national development within the broader framework of the global cultural economy to be established, language-in-education policy needs to be disengaged from party politics. To this end pursuing an interdisciplinary and cross-political party approach grounded in multilevelled consultation amongst different stake holders could potentially be empowering. In the process it could engender economic development benefiting society by strengthening its human resource base to compete more effectively within the global cultural economy. In essence then, within the much vaunted 'knowledge economy' the emphasis should be on facilitating national transformation cognitively, linguistically, economically as well as politically, with regard to engagement in the political process for all citizens. The global cultural economy is interdependent and, despite the dominant position occupied by English, in practice, it has an organically interactive multilingual base. A narrow monolingual nationalism, an under-resourced educational system as well as unequal access to English as international lingua franca, therefore, is counter-productive to national growth. Such a limited policy framework would undermine the country's possibilities to participate effectively within the highly competitive international labour market. These issues are discussed again in Chapter 8.

Notes

1. Pathans in practice refer to the Pashtun/Pakhtun/Afghan ethnic group, they are Pashto speakers; Balochistan is also written as Baluchistan; they are Baluchi/Balochi speakers. Punjabi is also written as Panjabi.
2. The country has an estimated 243,683 deaf population (7.40% of the whole population); there are 55 institutions for the deaf. Amongst the nation, 265,398 (8.06% of the whole population) are registered blind. There are 73 educational institutions nationally catering for the visually impaired populations (Sadaf Zuberi, 2005).
3. Sometimes also written as Seraiki.
4. Sometimes also written as Pashto.
5. Both Bengali and Urdu became the country's national languages in the Constitution of 1962. This changed in 1971 when, at least in part, due to the pressures exerted by the Bengali Language Movement, East Pakistan became the autonomous state of Bangladesh adopting Bengali as its national language.
6. By 1951 the Muhajirs comprised 51% of Sindh's urban population (Mazari, 2002).
7. A covering term for the languages spoken by both Hindus and Muslims in Northern India (Rahman, 2000).
8. Urdu is currently spoken mostly in and around urban Karachi, Lucknow, Lahore and Hyderabad.
9. There are at least 36,750 Sindhi medium schools in Sindh Province (Rahman, 2002).
10. The sample comprising 2136 students and their parents was drawn from the capital cities of Punjab (Lahore and Taxila) and Sindh (Karachi and Hyderabad), Balochistan (Quetta) as well as the Federal Capital (Islamabad), and the N.W.F.P (Peshawar). The data were collected in pre-coded questionnaires sent to students and parents, and semi-structured interviews were conducted with 121 subject and English teachers from all provinces except Balochistan. Only 63 parent questionnaires were received from Punjab and Sindh, and no response was received from parents of students from the other two provinces and Islamabad, the Federal Capital. For the quantitative data a two-stage cluster sampling plan was implemented; purposive sampling was used for the qualitative data (for further information on methodology see Mansoor, 2005).
11. 'There have been five periods of full or partial martial law, lasting 18 years, six abortive coups and three periods under state emergency. Only one president has completed his term, Prime ministers have been dismissed eight times, one Prime Minister was assassinated, one executed and eight parliaments have been prematurely dissolved.' (C. Thomas in *The Times* of 14 August 1997, 'Pakistan loses faith in democracy as dream turns sour').

Part 3

Globalization and Linguistic Diversity

Chapter 8

Postcolonial Perspectives: Issues in Language-in-Education and Development in the Global Cultural Economy

Decolonization and the emergence of postcolonial states took place in an atmosphere of optimism and hope for the future. This was to be given expression in integrative nation-building including self-defined socio-political, economic and cultural change and development. The 1960s were defined by high levels of investment in education since most post-colonial societies placed language and education at the centre of their development plans. At least 50 years later, many postcolonial societies throughout sub-Saharan Africa, and South Asia, have remained under-developed economically and politically. Since independence, many of these societies have experienced long periods of sustained political and social instability as result of, *inter alia*, coup d'états, military dictatorships, inter-ethnic violence, sustained political corruption, and natural disasters. In some instances, countries have experienced all of these situations. Education cannot flourish in unstable situations, and lack of education contributes to an under-skilled labour supply unable to access all sectors of the labour market. Consequently, these societies are caught in a cycle of under-development. In particular, the under-education of colonized peoples, a curriculum based on the metropolitan elite education model, chronic under-funding of education, the educational divide between rural and urban education provision, the heritage of colonial languages in education, and the lack of educational infrastructure to sustain adequate levels of human resource development, generated long-term development problems in these societies. The status accorded, historically, to colonial 'mother tongues', combined with contemporary changes taking place within the global cultural economy, have left an enduring dilemma with regard to language planning and language policy in developing countries.

Central concerns in this book have been the constraints presented by unresolved language problems, to the availability of appropriately skilled human resource power needed to enable postcolonial countries, in Sub-Saharan Africa, and South Asia to compete more effectively in national and international labour markets. The argument was, first, that most of these unresolved language problems have their origins in colonialism. Second, that at macro-societal level there are intertextual links between the language relations of colonized societies and those that now prevail in postcolonial countries. Chapters 1 and 2, discussed the demographic shifts that occurred as a result of the arbitrary geographic borders instituted in Sub-Saharan Africa at the 1885 Berlin Congress, followed later by the Partitioning of India in 1947. Both of these historical events resulted in forced transmigration of vast numbers of people. In both Sub-Saharan, and South Asian, regions many ethnolinguistic populations were scattered across the newly and, in the case of Sub-Saharan Africa, arbitrarily created countries. These historically displaced peoples have been joined by more recent transmigrations, as a result of political, economic and social instability within their countries of origin. Many, both symbolically, and physically, reside on the margins of different societies.

The discussion throughout the book has highlighted the fragmentation of ethnolinguistic communities across various national borders throughout countries in the Sub-Saharan African, and South Asian regions. In the case of Sub-Saharan Africa, for example, the Mandingo people were dispersed across six countries including Senegal, Guinea, Mali, Ivory Coast, Gambia and Sierra Leone (see further examples in Chapters 1 and 2). Existing as they do in the interstices between two or more countries and, therefore, two or more dominant cultures and languages, most of these displaced peoples, live in-between lives. This involves them, on the one hand, in having to make dilemmatic language choices in relation to cultural maintenance, and on the other hand, integration and economic access within mainstream society. Language and social/economic development in these contexts therefore exist in tension.

Of significance too is the fact that missionaries, during both precolonial and colonial periods, had a major cultural impact on African societies. Notwithstanding its proselytizing ideological base, missionary education played a significant role in the development of literacy and reading materials in African languages. Missionaries also became important actors in the growth of formal education, and played a key role in the implementation of the colonial state's policy. However, their long-term legacy lies in the idiosyncratic translation of African languages which contributed significantly, to the evolution of different spelling systems amongst what, in many instances, was effectively the same language. This and the dispersal of peoples across different regions, contributed to the idea of Africa as a veritable Tower of Babel (see Chapter 2). In practice, many African languages share commonalities, and are mutually understandable (Prah, 2000).

In South Asia, the partitioning of India in 1947 also created new national boundaries, resulting in the dispersal of different ethnolinguistic groups across India as well as in the newly created Pakistan. As is discussed in Chapter 7, the transmigration of Urdu speakers to Pakistan has generated sporadic conflict articulated around language, particularly, in Sindh province. Together these factors indicate that the linguistic complexity of countries in these regions, and the unresolved language problems that prevail can, to a significant extent, be said to have been artificially created. Colonialism left behind a legacy of linguistic, cultural and often social inequalities throughout excolonized states. It also resulted in the alienation of subjugated people, individually, and en masse, from their own cultural/linguistic traditions and social mores. As could be seen in the discussion throughout the book, this was, and continues to be, perpetuated by the proto-elite. In addition, colonialism also made use of indentured labour, which resulted in vast numbers of colonized people transmigrating from, for example, India to work in the sugar-cane industry of South Africa, Kenya, and Uganda (see Chapters 1 and 3). Arising from these transmigrations, and those that took place within Sub-Saharan Africa and India/Pakistan, colonialism has left a legacy of multiple, or rather, multilayered cultural/linguistic identities.

Different language markets prevail in everyday life, each, in turn, associated with specific social roles linked with both private and public spheres of interaction. These two spheres are hierarchically organized in everyday social life; the public sphere is associated traditionally with languages and discourses of power. As is discussed throughout the previous chapters, most postcolonial societies have retained excolonial languages as the language of economic, social and institutional power. This predominance of the excolonial language as official language has helped to preserve colonial cultural hegemony. In some instances, this has contributed to a lack of legitimacy of national languages chosen by postcolonial governments as an important element of nation hood. As is discussed earlier, in Pakistan Urdu is, in effect, a minority language associated with transmigration as well as the proto-elite. This is also the case, to some extent, with Kiswahili in Tanzania and Kenya. Seeking within this broad framework, to examine some of the major issues that surround language-in-education and development in post-colonial societies in Sub-Saharan Africa and South Asia, the discussion throughout the book attempted to address some of the main questions related to:

- the long-term impact of colonial cultural/linguistic hegemony on the social *habitus* and, therefore, language-in-education policy choices;
- the role that colonial and postcolonial language-in-education policies have played historically in sustaining low societal literacy rates;
- the impact of this on human resource development and therefore on the labour market;
- the relationship between this and under-developed postcolonial economies.

The underlying intention was to examine the complex relationship that exists between language-in-education policy and the economy, culture and society. In this regard, the political economy of language-in-education policy in postcolonial societies in Sub-Saharan Africa and South Asia represented the main theme throughout the discussion in the book.

The Political Economy of Language-in-Education Policy

Chapters 1 and 2 focused on the central role that language played in the hegemonic and, indirectly, the political projects of the colonial state. Looking for intertextual links, Chapters 3 and 4 mapped the contemporary global cultural economy and highlighted the centrality of language to the technological labour process, its relationship with human resource development, and the national and international labour market as well as its significance in the cultural terrain. This multi-disciplinary discussion presented the view that language-in-education policy lies at the centre of the development project of the state – ideologically, economically, socioculturally and politically. Key issues related to this, are discussed in the sections below.

Ideological function

The choice of particular language(s) for teaching and learning plays a major role in defining the ethno-cultural basis of the politically constructed nation. Language-in-education policy underscores the literary canon, and forms of knowledges legitimated in social policy as hegemonic cultural capital. In doing so it plays a significant role in imbuing learners with the sets of beliefs, mores, traditions and values embedded in the dominant culture, and through this serves to shape the cultural norms of society as a whole. As could be seen in Chapter 2, British colonial policy allowed the teaching of local mother tongues at least for the first few years of schooling. This provided learners with the opportunity to develop their first-language skills which, in turn, would have facilitated learning and their access to knowledge. However, secondary and tertiary education took place in colonial languages. British colonial language-in-education policy therefore was not integrative; ultimately, it was grounded in a transitional model of bilingualism. It eventually coincided with the assimilationist orientation of French, Spanish and Portuguese colonialism. The significance in teaching through the medium of colonial languages lay in the major role that it played in colonial governmentality; it served the dual function of domination and self-discipline. In other words, the colonies could not be governed without incorporating the colonized into the colonial state's political, hegemonic and economic project. First, as could be seen in the Introduction and Chapter 1, colonial languages provided the racist categories of description central to the legitimation in colonial discourse of the idea of the inherent superiority of the rulers (see Lord Macauley's discourse in Chapter 2). This, in turn, served to justify the paternalist role of the ruler as against the (forced) subservience of the colonized. Second, colonial languages incorporated into institutions of power situated colonized peoples as subjects, and penetrated their social experience. Third, associated with high social status, colonial languages secured a captive clientele especially amongst the local proto-elites. Through these processes colonial languages performed a major hegemonic function; embedded in educational practices and processes they were instrumental in shaping the aspirations, expectations, dreams and desires of learners, aspirant workers and consumers of culture. The colonial *habitus* thus shaped, played a central role in influencing postcolonial language-in-education policy choices.

The case-studies of Pakistan and South Africa provided good examples of the high status that English has maintained within education (see Chapter 7), and the extent to which it continues to influence popular expectations and aspirations. Thus continuity between colonial cultural hegemony and postcolonial language relations has been consolidated.

Whilst colonial language-in-education policies played a significant role in shaping colonial subjectivities, they also served to frame levels of access to the labour market. In other words, those who were literate and fluent in colonial languages, which represented the languages of power, would have had better access to jobs than those who did not meet this requirement (see case-study of Mali, Chapter 5). Language-in-education policies play an important role in facilitating access to life chances; as such, it also has a significant economic role.

Economic functions: Postcolonial dilemmas

Emerging postcolonial societies were catapulted into a highly competitive international financial, commodity and labour market in which they had to compete. The association of colonial languages with social status, economic power and societal modernization provided a powerful rationale for their inclusion in language-in-education policies. The assumption was that the adoption of colonial languages as official languages, would facilitate international trade and, through this, economic development.

The high status of ex-colonial languages has been reinforced by the significance that they, and particularly, English, have assumed in the interactive global cultural economy. Chapter 4 highlighted the fact that ex-colonial languages, and particularly, English:

- have become central elements in human resource development and therefore have a high exchange value in the international labour market;
- are central to the interactive global financial market – as means of communication, as information, and as cultural commodities;
- have primary significance in international information flows, amongst which the cultural industries occupy an important position.

Since languages serve to mediate versions of reality grounded in their associated cultures, excolonial languages, and especially English, through the mass media continue to be instrumental in shaping the aspirations, dreams and desires of large numbers of people living in discrete polities. Incorporated into global economic and cultural processes, excolonial languages, and particularly, English also have become a powerful means of legitimating a 'free-market' consumer, and international worker hegemonic consciousness. In other words, the interactive nature of the global cultural economy has boosted the economic, political and cultural currency of historically powerful excolonial languages. The case-studies of Pakistan, Mali and South Africa, provide insight into the extent to which excolonial languages still dominate language-in-education policies of postcolonial societies. They also offer insights into the dilemmas that surround language choice within these contexts. For example, despite South Africa's admirable language policy framework, which gives parity to 11 languages, and the existence of various internal lingua franca and cross-border languages in the country, in practice, it valorizes English by incorporating it into formal structures of the state. Here then, English has been divested of its colonial heritage; it has been reinterpreted and given new meaning. Repositioned as a powerful 'world' language within the interactive global cultural economy, it features centrally in a development framework centred on modernization.

The fact that English has replaced Afrikaans, which was dominant during the apartheid regime, as the preferred official language is significant. As is argued earlier in Chapter 6, the imposition of Afrikaans as medium for teaching and learning provided the catalyst to the unrest that started in 1976, and continued until the end of apartheid. Nevertheless, Afrikaans cannot be discounted; it is the first language of at least 18% of the country's population. Postcolonial South Africa's policy emphasis on 11 official languages is undermined by the fact that it is exclusively, English, and not one or more African languages and English that lie at the centre of the country's economic and political life (see Chapter 6). As is evident in the case studies of Pakistan, and to a more limited extent, Mali, this is replicated across the postcolonial landscape in Sub-Saharan Africa and South Asia.

In most postcolonial societies, excolonial languages continue to operate as languages of vertical control (see Chapter 6). As such, they serve as powerful exclusionary mechanisms by which those who cannot operate effectively in these languages are prevented from accessing the high skills sector of the labour market, and therefore also high political office, nationally and internationally. Power positions constructed in this way remain occupied, and are reproduced, by small intellectual/language/political elite groups. Thus the effects of habituated state practices outlive the lifespan of governments (see Chapter 6). The case study of postcolonial Pakistan (see Chapter 7) provided a good example.

The importance of pursuing multilingual language-in-education policies is supported by the fact that, in practice, a mixed language economy generally prevails in the labour market, regionally, and nationally in most societies. Whilst international business and trade would rely on multilingual (which include English) and highly skilled labour, other sectors of the economy would continue to depend on skilled and unskilled labour fluent in regional and/or local languages (Graddol, 1997, 2006). This complexity in linguistic needs and demands within the economic terrain, and their association with human resource development, is often not considered in language-in-education policy. This is regrettable, because a strategic multilingual education policy is likely to boost literacy levels in different languages, and thus provide access to knowledge. Together, this has the potential to contribute significantly to human resource development which, in turn, would facilitate access to the labour market. Moreover, using local and/or regional languages in different subjects, would naturally develop subject registers, and thus contribute to the modernization of these languages.

Sociocultural issues

The third function of national language-in-education policy is *socio-cultural* in that it frames the cultural knowledges to be learned. This includes not only legitimized scientific and technological knowledges, literary canons, and historical accounts but also the beliefs, values, aspirations and expectations embedded in the idea of citizenship. Representation of different groups of people, their languages, cultures and their social roles play an important role in educational processes and practices. This book has argued that, historically, they have played an important role in shaping the colonial *habitus* of colonized peoples (see for example, the discussion of Dr Abdurahman in South Africa in Chapters 2 and 6). The importance of excolonial languages in economic and political life, both nationally, and internationally, have contributed significantly to ambiguity, a cultural 'double-ness', or 'janus-like' orientation of postcolonial language-in-education policy. Historically, this relates, on the one hand, to the fact that emerging postcolonial societies, needed to adopt language(s) that could provide a means through which a cohesive national awareness could be generated. At the same time, they also needed to be able to participate effectively in the expanding global economy of the 1950s and 1960s. The drive for modernization which depended on higher literacy rates, and more skilled employment, contributed to a significant extent to the fact that emerging postcolonial societies opted to retain their excolonial languages within the formal institutional arena. Human capital arguments therefore underscored the importance of adopting excolonial languages. Within a multilingual context, these policy choices generated dilemmas related, on the one hand, to cultural and linguistic maintenance amongst people whose languages were not catered for in language-in-education policy, and on the other hand, the importance for them to be able to access the labour market. It is evident in the case-studies in Chapters 5, 6 and 7 that this dilemma remains and, in effect, has intensified within the framework of the global cultural economy.

The world has undergone rapid and high levels of technological development that, in turn, have effected major cultural, economic and political changes. As has been argued throughout the book, multilingual and multi-layered communication skills represent important cultural capital in the interactive global cultural economy.

Human resource development

Language then lies at the centre of the neoliberal concept of 'employability'. At the same time, it also occupies a key position in the interactive information-based cultural terrain, and is central to the global processes of finance capital (see Table 3.1). Language and communication, therefore, represent key human resource development variables in contemporary models of modernization. The dominant emphasis is on English as a 'world' language, to the exclusion of the use, and development, of regional languages. Whilst regional languages have been incorporated into human resource development frameworks throughout Sub-Saharan Africa, this is not the case in South Africa; neither is it in Pakistan where with the exception of Sindh province, and Siraiki in Balochistan, regional languages do not feature in the educational framework in a major way.

If account is taken of the centrality of language and communication to economic and political life, then the fact that national language-in-education policy frameworks, in many postcolonial societies, have remained largely unlegislated and unregulated, or as is the case of South Africa, and Paskistan, is largely unimplemented, is significant. The organic relationship between language, literacies, knowledge acquisition and human resource development – and ultimately – the labour market, underscores the need for a coherent national language-in-education policy framework that is holistic and:

- takes account of local, regional and national employment needs and possibilities;
- takes account of local, regional and national development issues;
- is mindful of the differentiated linguistic landscapes within society;
- is coherently and realistically linked to educational policy aims grounded in pedagogies that empower learners;
- is formalized, and financed;
- has an adequate range of appropriate resources that can support its implementation; and
- is monitored and evaluated.

Language-in-education policy therefore has to form an integral part of educational policy, and planning, aimed at political and economic modernization, and long-term development goals centred on poverty alleviation, whilst at the same time, also maintaining social equilibrium, as well as an integrative, cohesive citizenship (see also Chapter 6). By this definition, language-in-education policy has to orient itself towards differential language markets nationally and internationally, and should be aimed at improving the quality of life of all peoples within society. As can be seen in the discussion later, this aim is central to UNESCO's perspective on the relationship between language and development.

Language-in-education policies and cultural and symbolic capital

Language-in-education policies legitimize the languages in which learners should acquire knowledge that, ultimately, would be assessed at different levels of education. Those who have been educated, and are assessed in languages that they know and understand and use in their everyday lives, have a distinct advantage over others who are assessed in languages that they do not know, or in which they lack fluency as is evident in the case studies of Pakistan and, to some extent, South Africa; or those who speak non-standard forms of the language(s) in which they are assessed. Levels of literacy in the languages, supported by education policy, facilitate access to jobs and cultural resources within society, since these are necessarily imbued with cultural and economic power. Literacy, in languages sanctioned by educational policy, also provides citizens living within liberal/social democratic societies, the opportunity to acquire skills necessary to take an active part in the democratic process. This is the case since official information, including laws and regulations as well as sources of information, would be accessible in languages sanctioned by policy.

For those not living in democratic societies, it has the potential to provide citizens with the subject registers, the intellectual tools with which to interpret and deconstruct their individual, group and social experience – and through this to engage in a process of reflexive self-definition (Giddens, 1991). The significance of this lies in the fact that thinking develops through cultural mediation, and education grounded in the mother tongue, in the cultural idiom, facilitates deeper levels of sociocultural understanding. Used critically, this represented the essence of Paulo Freire's approach to adult literacy learning in South America during the 1970s (Freire, 1972). These processes, practices and opportunities, facilitated by language, are necessarily empowering. By the same token, speakers whose languages are not included in national policy frameworks, or who occupy a subsidiary position within society are disempowered culturally, educationally and economically. Not only are they incorporated into the hegemony of the dominant cultural/linguistic group, they also are limited in their opportunities to access high skilled jobs in the national and international labour market. This is the case particularly in rural communities where disparities in language provision prevail (see also below).

In some societies, that regard themselves to be democratic, civic information and knowledge are interpreted, and disseminated by community leaders who deal with legal issues on behalf of the people. As a result, although most of the people might be literate in the official language and/or their mother tongue, they do not necessarily know their full rights as citizens, nor do they directly engage with the democratic process – other than in voting – and even here their choices are often those made by the community leaders. This highlights the significant role that language and politics play in the distribution of power and resources. There are also societies where the majority of people cannot speak, nor are they literate, in the languages in which the laws governing them are written (e.g. at least 47% of the population in South Africa, see Chapter 6, and also Pakistan in Chapter 7). This phenomenon probably is widely spread in many postcolonial societies.

At the same time though, this is not to argue that there is no contestation, that people are neatly sutured into static positions within society, that excolonial languages inevitably engender cultural alienation. There is evidence in small-scale studies, emphasizing ways in which excolonial languages are used in instrumental ways. They do so consciously, often strategically, as a means towards specific ends, without necessarily compromising local cultures; that is, language users being incorporated into the belief system of the dominant culture in which the particular excolonial language is embedded (Canagarajah, 2005; Mansoor, 2005; Kachru, 1982). Furthermore, excolonial languages also have played a key role in counter-hegemonic discourses as was evident in the nationalist struggle in India prior to Partition. Similarly, as is discussed in Chapters 2 and 6, English played an important symbolic role in the struggle against apartheid hegemony in South Africa. English has retained its high status within that society, despite the policy emphasis on multilingualism incorporating 11 languages. Some of this could be attributed to the empowering meanings, historically associated with English in the struggle against the ideology of white-supremacy that was attached to Afrikaans, as well as the lack of teaching and learning resources in African languages. It could also be related to the fact that the emerging post-apartheid state coincided with an interactive global cultural economy in which English represents important cultural capital. This has been an influential factor in language-in-education policy as well as in relation to parental choice of language medium for their children. Again, this echoes the policy and parental language choices in education within other societies emerging from colonialism. Here then English as the excolonial language, can be seen to have been incorporated into a different ideological framework, in which it was imbued with power grounded in a reflexive process of self-definition. However, as is argued in Chapter 6, the reliance of English only as a means of access to the international labour market is restrictive, especially, in relation to cross-regional economic opportunities. Many countries in Southern Africa have opted for a multilingual approach that includes several languages of wider communication (see Chapter 6).

This book has argued that within culturally plural societies a national language policy that is multilingual and culturally integrative, necessarily accords equal status to, and/or acknowledges formally all languages and cultures within society. They therefore make adequate provision for the teaching of these languages in the curriculum. A monolingual national language policy rooted in the idea of one common language, on the other hand, secures a particular cultural vision of citizenship and, in the process, marginalizes the languages, cultures and, therefore, speakers of other linguistic groups. The concept of 'common' languages so central to the concept of post-Enlightenment nationhood discussed in Chapter 2, invariably, represents languages of power within society. As such, they represent the languages of powerful groups within society. Incorporated into the official institutional domains such as the Church, political administration, Defence Force, Business, and the Media, they serve to mediate the dominant worldview. Thus language-in-education policy circumscribes the relative access to power that different groups in society might have. Overall, this means that a national/excolonial language policy orientation also demarcates a power divide, not only culturally and linguistically, but also economically, socially and politically. Those whose languages are supported by policy (or who have access to the colonial language) have better access to cultural resources as well as education and therefore, implicitly, also to job opportunities within the labour market. This is the case, since they have as their starting point, the appropriate form of linguistic capital through which they can access the education market, and also operate, more effectively, linguistically within the various institutions of the state – including education. In these circumstances:

> ... language is a means for rationing access to jobs with high salaries. Whenever people must learn a new language to have access to education or to understand classroom instruction (teaching), language

is a factor in creating and sustaining social and economic divisions. (Tollefson, 1991a: 8–9)

Again, this supports earlier arguments that language not only has potent symbolic power in relation to what it signifies, but also material value, that is, its exchange value/currency within the labour market. Language-in-education policy therefore can play a significant role in the subjugation and displacement of some languages, undermining cultural landscapes, and contributing thus to the demise of cultural ways of knowing, and ways of doing. The narrative of nationalism that has underpinned postcolonial development, constructs an ideal vision of society that is imbued with the meanings and cultural knowledges associated with language(s) sanctioned by the state. As could be seen in the discussion throughout the book, this has largely been in the interest of excolonial languages which serve as official languages. In the case of Pakistan, Urdu, the national language, occupies a secondary position to English which is the official language; as such its power is mainly symbolic. This is the case in many postcolonial societies where the excolonial language represents the official language. Consequently, people learn to sublimate their cultural knowledges, and to unlearn their cultural pasts. Clearly then, the quest for modernization comes at a perilous cost to linguistic minority groups in such contexts. This reinforces the argument in Chapter 6, that the ethnolinguistic orientation of many national language policies in postcolonial societies is fundamentally problematic.

The discussion throughout this book has argued that language-in-education policy interacts with culture, politics, and economy regionally, nationally and internationally, and that in the case of postcolonial developing societies, it has to be seen also in relation to the historical dynamic from which it emerged. Postcolonial development therefore cannot be seen as a discrete phenomenon; it is rooted in the modernist development regimes constructed under colonial rule, and the languages, cultural, economic and political structures and social practices inherited in the process of decolonization. Within the contemporary world, it has to be viewed also in relation to the economic, cultural and political processes that define the global cultural economy.

Contemporary Language and Development Issues in Postcolonial Societies

The task of government, traditionally, has been to plan, and manage, the economy in the interest of the national population. The interactive and competitive nature of the global cultural economy has altered this linear relationship between economy and the people; governments now have to manage not only in the interests of the national economy, they also have to secure advantage within the global economic market. National policy frameworks, therefore, need to have, not only a national orientation, but also need to take account of external demands; they have to be considered in relation to discursive power relations that extend beyond the boundaries of the national state. In particular, the relationship of language to postcolonial development has to be viewed in relation to the ways in which postcolonial polities, on the one hand, are enmeshed in global cultural organizations such as UNESCO and, on the other hand, the regulatory processes of the World Bank/IMF, as well as international trade agreements within the framework of the World Trade Organization (WTO).

UNESCO

As is argued in Chapters 2 and 3 since the publication of its influential report *The Use of Vernacular Languages in Education* in 1953, the focus in UNESCO has been on the relationship between literacy, basic education and development. During the late 1960s and early 1970s this was incorporated into its mass literacy campaigns with their focus on adult and work place literacies. This has been sustained and developed in UNESCO initiatives since that time; currently the focus is on endangered languages, linguistic diversity, multilingual education and development, advocating additive bi- or multilingualism (UNESCO, 2003). Recent reports have emphasized the importance of, for example, (a) mother tongue instruction in the first few years of education as providing a sound basis for future learning; (b) multilingual education as a means of preserving cultural identities, developing communication skills and the ability to dialogue; (c) and foreign language learning within the framework of intercultural education as a means of promoting a deeper understanding between communities and nations (UNESCO, 2003). Much of the discourse emphasis within UNESCO currently is on the linguistic rights of indigenous peoples, and mapping endangered languages. As stated earlier, UNESCO's *Initiative B@bel* centres on facilitating access to knowledge and information, and therefore supports linguistic diversity at all levels of education as well as universal language access on the Internet (see example of this in South Africa in Chapter 6). These developments are positioned within the broader framework of human rights, individual and group empowerment, and social development and have been highly influential across developing countries.

World Bank

The World Bank, since the early 1990s, also has incorporated support for indigenous languages into its strategy for poverty reduction and sustainable development. It aims to ensure 'that the development process fully respects the dignity, human rights, economies, and cultures of Indigenous Peoples[1] (World Bank, 2005b). The significance of the World Bank's support for language diversity in education, relates mainly to its association with human capital development. Its emphasis therefore is particularly on maximizing learning, decreasing repetition rates as well as levels of learner drop-out from full-time education. In this regard, acknowledging linguistic diversity in education, and including indigenous languages in World Bank educational projects, is framed by the neoliberal ideology of economy, effectiveness, and efficiency. At the same time, however, there is a duality here. Countries can, potentially, benefit from this approach especially since the use of indigenous languages in education can promote learning of content subjects. It could also have long-term benefits with regard to developing scientific language and discourse in indigenous languages. Through this it could support the development of language infrastructure within aid-receiving countries. Theoretically then, postcolonial developing societies stand to gain from the multilingual policy approach advocated by both UNESCO and the World Bank.

Regrettably though, many of these policy intentions have been undermined by the effects of the World Bank/IMF's structural adjustment policies, on the social and economic base of developing countries, catapulting them into cycles of poverty. As could be seen in the case-study of Mali, the SAPs have impacted on education provision which, in turn, has limited the scope for language policy implementation. Moreover, neoliberal ideology that underpins World Bank policy advocates decreasing the size of the state and reducing the role of the state in the social sphere. The incorporation of these meanings into the conditionalities of the SAPs has contributed to under-investment in education in borrowing countries. This, in turn, has undermined maintenance of school buildings, and resulted in large class sizes, and ill-equipped classrooms (see Mali in Chapter 5). As could be seen in the case-studies in Chapters 5, 6 and 7 many postcolonial countries have an under-supply of well-trained teachers and under-developed teacher education and in-service training infrastructure. This differs significantly from education and development in industrialized societies. Table 8.1 summarizes some of the major differences between industrialized and under-developed economies.

Table 8.1 Differences between developed and under-developed national economies

Developed national economies	*Under-developed national economies*
• High levels of education • High literacy rates • High levels of retention in education • Well-established economic, social, political, technological and educational infrastructure • Sustained political stability • Coherent education policies linked with the economy • Well-qualified cross-phase teacher supply • Integrative national language policy • Coherent language-in-education policy • Adequate educational resources • Differentiated economy with adequately skilled labour supply	• Low levels of education • Low literacy rates • High school dropout rates • Under-developed economic, social, political, technological and educational infrastructure • Sustained political instability • Lack of coherent education policies • Under-supply of qualified teachers • Non-integrative national language policy – often excolonial language is official language • Language-in-education policy often only symbolic re local languages – often excolonial language prevails • Lack of educational resources • Often undifferentiated economy – high reliance on agriculture, raw materials • Under-skilled labour supply

As can be seen in Table 8.1, under-developed national economies lack the necessary language, social, political and economic infrastructure to support the development of a skilled labour supply which represents a prerequisite to participate effectively in the global labour market.

WTO/GATS

These constraints to development run the risk of intensifying as a result of trade agreements within the framework of the World Trade Organization (WTO). The WTO underscores liberalization of trade and investment, including the deregulation of markets which, according to neoliberal ideology, leads to greater competition and market efficiency. Much of this is to the advantage of already 'developed' countries. In the discussion here, the focus is particularly on the potential impact of the General Agreement in Trade in Services (GATS) on education in developing countries. The GATS represents one of the major agreements of the WTO and advocates the deregulation, the liberalization of trade in services. The notion of 'freedom of trade' is grounded in the neoliberal concept of the 'free-market' and is oriented towards 'the opening up of public services to corporate capital ... it aims to create a "level" playing field so that there is no discrimination against foreign corporations entering the services market' (Rikowski, 2002). In practice, it operates to the advantage of economically advanced societies that make agreements in their own favour, thus restricting access to markets for developing countries. As such, they undermine the development process within these societies and are, therefore, instrumental in reinforcing already existing poverty. Ultimately, GATS in educational services are geared towards maximizing corporate profits; it is underscored by the neoliberal principles of competition, cost-benefit analysis and demand/supply issues. Education, within this ideological framework, features as a commodity as well as an investment as opposed to the traditional liberal/social democratic view of education as being a social good, and a human right. Education services within the context of the WTO/GATS include primary education, secondary education including technical and vocational education, higher education (tertiary) and adult education (literacy) and also educational support services. Postcolonial developing countries would be greatly disadvantaged in the event that GATS succeeds. Removing the limitations on trade would run 'the risk of converting education from a subjective public right into a process of simple commercialisation of educational packages' including the distribution of textbooks, maps, evaluation and certification systems, uniforms (de Sigueira, 2005: 1). This, in turn, would impact on the possibility for postcolonial countries to implement language-in-education policies that are centred on local languages. For example, within societies where there is already a shortage of textbooks *per se* and, moreover, a dearth of textbooks in African and South Asian languages, the courses, textbooks, literature, curricula, teaching programmes, tests, etc., exported and implemented, would more likely be in the languages of countries that have the capacity to produce and export them on a large scale. These resources are therefore likely to be published in excolonial languages. In this regard, globalization, through the processes and practices of the WTO, represents a powerful constraint in relation to the ability of countries to sustain cultural and linguistic diversity. It is fundamentally oriented towards homogenization. This contrasts sharply with common views on the fluidity of cultural exchanges within, and the multilingual nature, of the global cultural economy.

Nevertheless, this is not to argue that language and educational inequalities in postcolonial societies are attributable exclusively to the residual effects of colonialism, or exclusionary practices and processes that inhere within international agencies. Problems inherent in the policy frameworks of postcolonial societies as well as a range of other factors also play a major role in continued under-development within these societies.

Internal development constraints

In addition to the constraints discussed above, continuing under-development and social inequalities in postcolonial societies have been exacerbated also by poor governance. Many postcolonial societies have experienced coup d'états frequently resulting in long periods of military rule – we saw evidence of this in the case-studies of Mali and Pakistan in Chapters 5 and 7. In addition, many have been governed by successive corrupt political administrations and/or charismatic rulers who issue edicts based on whim, often negating existing policy. Many also have had a long history of civil wars which destroyed the limited social and educational infrastructures that had been inherited from the colonial occupiers. As could be seen in the case-study of Mali, educational infrastructure is poor generally, and as could be seen in the discussion of displaced peoples in postcolonial societies in Chapter 3, in some instances, it is non-existent. Sustained political instability has contributed to the fact that many postcolonial societies' development trajectories have been altered and/or were interrupted and, in some instances, reversed as has been the case, for example, in Democratic Republic of Congo. One of the major additional contributing factors in these situations has been debt inheritance; that is, transferring debt from one regime to another; from one generation to another. Cumulatively, these factors impact significantly on development possibilities; they undermine educational goals and undermine important debates on language-in-education policies and their relationship with human resource development.

Conclusion

At independence most postcolonial societies placed language at the centre of their development priorities. Most modified the language policies that they had inherited from the colonial regimes by making the excolonial language the official language, and choosing a major local language as the national language. Others, such as South Africa, adopted 11 languages used by major linguistic groups as official languages. However, whilst policy rhetoric has been strong, and as is the case in South Africa, policy intentions are aimed at integration, these have not been followed by successful implementation. The case study of Mali highlighted the importance of national language institutions involved exclusively with the development of languages including, for example, corpus planning centred on the development of standardized orthographies, developing bilingual dictionaries and terminologies, strategic status planning especially as this relates to local and regional languages, and acquisition planning involving developing strategies and incentives for people to learn targeted languages. Recent initiatives in 'developed' countries in this regard are, for example, in the devolved states in the UK, the institution of Language Boards for the development of Welsh, Irish and Scottish-Gaelic, and elsewhere in Europe, which centre on the development of society's language infrastructure. In countries throughout Sub-Saharan Africa where there are cross-border languages and, especially, where there are mobile groups of people, it is important that transnational and inter-regional linguistic co-operation with regard to language development, be encouraged. In Mali, this role is fulfilled by the Institute of Languages (*l'Institut des langues Abdoulaye BARRY* [ILAB]) following restructuring in 2001 (see Chapter 5). The drive for the intellectualization of African languages is ongoing currently throughout Africa and, particularly, within the framework of the African Union (AU), especially the African Academy of Languages (ACALAN) initiative as well as in the work of the Centre for Advanced Studies of African Languages (CASAS) with its pan-African focus on language harmonization and standardization. In this regard 2006 has been declared the 'Year of African Languages' which represents a pan-African project centred on the implementation of the AU official language policy which is based on the Language Plan of Action for Africa adopted in Addis Ababa in 1986 (Alexander, 2005).

All three cases studies emphasized the need for sociolinguistic research to inform language policy. Policy would then be based on actual needs rather than projections, especially where there is movement of large groups of people internally, from rural to urban areas, and amongst different regions as well as cross-border regions. Moreover, language in-education policies to be decided at school level, as is the case with Mali, and South Africa, would require accurate and up-to-date data on language use and parental choice. Although, on the surface, such policies appear democratic, in practice, they are problematic. In essence, they have a static view of school populations which change according to demographic changes taking place within society. Such policies require close monitoring. Moreover, in South Africa with its history of separatism amongst different, and often arbitrarily created, ethnic groups this approach could result in creating new ethnic enclaves within communities. In general, language policies, as is the case with all policies, need to be evaluated at regular intervals to assess their effectiveness, relevance and, within a situation of high people mobility, the changing linguistic landscape.

Research then necessarily needs to be central to the policy process. Whilst at the level of the individual, learning languages for their own sake, needless to say, is admirable, in policy terms, emphasis purely on providing for the linguistic diversity within society, provides an inadequate rationale for bi- or multilingualism. Policy needs to define the social groups for which it caters as well as the *purposes* of learning particular languages. That is to say, the question of what learners need *to do* with these languages within mainstream society needs to be incorporated into the policy framework. This includes, for example, the relationship between particular languages and the ability that they would provided to access jobs in the labour market, the opportunity/need to use the language as a means of everyday communication (written and oral), as a cultural resource as well as the ability that it would provide learners to achieve a better understanding of society and the wider world, and their place within it. These factors are central to fostering active citizenship which, in turn, relies on access to information, an ability to make discriminating choices regarding available information, a critical knowledge base as well as the ability to articulate issues in the language appropriate to the particular situation. That is to say, the ways in which particular languages would be incorporated into the social infrastructure and how they would empower people within everyday life need to be made evident. This means that the particular model of bi- or multilingualism, and the types and levels of literacy to be acquired in these languages, the pedagogies as well as the range of resources to be made available, would have to be clarified in the policy framework. Languages need to be seen as actively serving economic, social, political and cultural interests, that is to say, they must be seen to have exchange value for them to gain status amongst individuals and communities. As is the case in Wales where, as part of promoting the Welsh language, this also involves creating a visible bi- or multilingual social environment including, for example, bi- or multilingual road signs, official communications, names of public buildings, leaflets and brochures used in everyday life, and shop signs. Furthermore, learning the languages of the community in which people work should be a requisition of public professional positions, and could be incorporated into professional and vocational courses (Webb, 2005). The dominant language regime would therefore have to undergo fundamental transformation, to be able to incorporate a bi- or multilingual ethos, and to put in place the requisite language infrastructures. This, in turn, would influence the way in which these languages in society are viewed by people and, ultimately, attitudes and behaviours are altered. These factors endorse the earlier argument that languages need to be developed consciously and systematically. Again, this is especially the case if account is taken of the powerful impact that colonialism had on the sociocultural and economic base of these societies and, moreover, the continuing powerful position occupied by excolonial languages formally in everyday life.

However, as is argued throughout this chapter, the policy implementation process is much more complex; it does not mean that these developments would necessarily take place even as part of a coherent policy. This book has emphasized the fact that these developments do not take place within a social, political, ideological and power vacuum. They are dependent on national state development policy priorities which, in turn, are linked to a discursive range of external agencies that pursue their own economic and political interests. How the economic, political and cultural constraints generated in the interaction between these domains are addressed, is of major significance in relation to the formulation, and implementation, of national language-in-education policies. Even the best policies cannot flourish within a social context defined by sustained bad governance, and political, social and economic instability. Moreover, change starts from within, from a critical awareness of the inherent weaknesses and contradictions in society, and a self-defined programme of change geared towards poverty reduction and development. Changing the disabling political ethos and ethics of governance in many postcolonial societies within the Sub-Saharan Africa and South Asia regions is, therefore, imperative. How languages are taught should play an important part in achieving these goals. The struggle for control over language and meaning within society, ultimately, is the struggle for self-defined democratic engagement involving communities, individuals and power institutions. National policy geared towards societal development should, therefore, incorporate languages for different purposes. This includes planning for a horizontal integration of languages for, national unity, cultural identity, economic development as well as individual and community empowerment. The essence of this is a coherent multilingual policy, embedded in a systematically developed language infrastructure. Language and literacy development should feature centrally in economic and social development policy and planning.

Postcolonial developing countries need to be enabled to make the transition from subsistence based economies, to the differentiated, internationalized, service economy. In this regard, the 'colonial habitus' needs to be fractured as this relates to language policy choices in educational, societal and political institutions within postcolonial developing countries. A mixed language economy, adequately supported by social, political and linguistic infrastructure nationally – reinforced by more equitable social and economic policies within global power ensembles – are needed to enable citizens and workers in countries throughout sub-Saharan Africa and South Asia, to participate in the constantly evolving cultural, economic and language markets globally. Literacy, as an indicator of national development, cannot be sustained outside a consideration of cultural, political and economic relations within the global arena. It is imperative that the political economy of language, education and development is addressed within dominant discourses of empowerment centred on capacity building, and poverty alleviation, in countries throughout the sub-Saharan Africa and South Asia regions. Language as medium of communication as well as a cultural, economic, and political commodity lies at the centre of the interactive global cultural economy.

Note

1. The World Bank defines the term 'Indigenous People' to refer to 'a distant, vulnerable, social and cultural group' based on their self-identification as a distinct cultural group, their collective attachment to geographically distinct habitats or ancestral territories, distinct cultural institutions and an indigenous language often distinct from the official language of the country or region (World Bank, 2005b).

References

Abbas, S. (1993) The power of English in Pakistan. *World Englishes* 2(2), 147–56.

ABC (2005) Urban daily newspapers. Average net sales analysis. July 2004–December 2004. Rev 1–21/2/05. On WWW at http://www.biz-community. com/ Article/196/15/5847.html.

Abdulaziz, M.H. (1971) Tanzania's national language policy. In Whiteley, W.H. (ed.). *Language Use and Social Change*. London: Oxford University Press.

Ade Ajayi, J.J. (2003) New trends and processes in Africa in the nineteenth century. In Adhikari, M. (ed.). *Africa in the Nineteenth Century Until the 1880s* (Vol. VI) (pp. 1–10). J.F.A.

Adhikari, M. (ed.) (1996) *Straatpraatjies. Language, Politics and Popular Culture in Cape Town, 1902–1922*. Cape Town: J.L. van Schaik.

Adu Boahen, A. (1985a) Africa and the colonial challenge. In Boahen, A. (ed.). *Africa Under Colonial Domination 1880–1935* (Vol. VII) (pp. 1–18). General History of Africa. London, Paris, Berkeley: Heinemann Educational Books Ltd., UNESCO, University of California Press.

Adu Boahen, A. (1985b) Colonialism in Africa: Its impact and significance. In Adu Boahen, A. (ed.). *Africa Under Colonial Domination 1880–1935* (pp. 782–809). General History of Africa. London, Paris, Berkeley: Heinemann Educational Books.

Adu Boahen, A. (2003) New trends and processes in Africa in the nineteenth century. In Ajayi, J.F.A. (ed.). *Africa in the Nineteenth Century Until the 1880s* (Vol. VI) (pp. 15–20). General History of Africa. Glosderry: New Africa Books.

Advanced Workplace Associates (2002) Paper 9 Going Offshore. On WWW at http://www.advanced-workplace.com.

Afigbo, A.E. (1985) The social repercussions of colonial rule: The new social structures. In Boahen, A.A. (ed.). *Africa Under Colonial Domination 1880–1935* (Vol. VII) (pp. 487–507). General History of Africa. London, Paris, Berkeley: Heinemann Education with UNESCO and the University of California.

Agheyisi, R. (1977) Language interlarding in the speech of Nigerians. In Der-Houssikian, P.F.A.K.a.H. (ed.). *Language and Linguistic Problems in Africa*. (pp. 97–110). Columbia, SC: Hornbeam.

Ahmad, I. (2004) Islam, democracy and citizenship: An examination of the social studies curriculum in Pakistan. *Current Issues in Comparative Education: Literacy, Education and Development* (Vol. 7) (pp. 1–11).

Ahmed, F. (1998) *Ethnicity and Politics in Pakistan*. Oxford: Oxford University Press.

Ajayi, UNESCO General History of Africa. Glosderry: New Africa Books.

Akintoye, S.A. (1976) *Emergent African States*. London: Longman.

Alexander, N. (1989) *Language Policy and National Unity in South Africa/Azania*. Cape Town: Buchu Books.

Alexander, N. (1992) Harmonising Nguni and Sotho. In Crawhall, N. (ed.). *Democratically Speaking: International Perspectives on Language Planning* (pp. 56–68). Cape Town: National Language Project.

Alexander, N. (2000) *English Assailable but Unattainable: The Dilemma of Language Policy in South African Education*. Cape Town: Project for Alternative Education in South Africa (PRAESA).

Alexander, N. (2005) *The Intellectualisation of African Languages*. Cape Town: Project for the Study of Alternative Education in South Africa (PRAESA).

Alexander, N. and Heugh, K. (1999) Language policy in the New South Africa. In Zegeye, A. and Kriger, R. (eds). Cultural Change and Development in South Africa. Special Issue 1998–9, *Culturelink*, 9–33.

Allan, S. and Thompson, A. (1999) The time-space of national memory. In Brehony, K. and Rassool, N. (eds). *Nationalisms Old and New* (pp. 35–50). Basingstoke: Macmillan Press.

Amadio, M. (ed.) (2001) Mali. In *IBE World Data on Education* (IV edn). Geneva: IBE (CDROM).

Anderson, B. (1991) *Imagined Communities: Reflections on the Origin and Spread of Nationalism*. London: Verso.

Anonymous. (2005) History. On WWW at http://users.aber.ac.uk/jbb1/history.htm. Accessed 3.06.05.

Anthes, E. (2002) Classes on Arabic see large rise in popularity. In *Yale Daily News*. On WWW at http://www.yaledailynews.com/article.asp?AID+19783. Accessed 11.05.05.

Appadurai, A. (1993) Disjuncture and difference in the global cultural economy. In Chrisman, L. and Williams, P. (eds). *Colonial Discourse and Post-Colonial Theory: A Reader* (pp. 324–39). London: Harvester Wheatsheaf.

Arnove, A.K. and Arnove, R.F. (1997) A reassessment of education, language, and cultural imperialism: British colonialism in India and Africa. In Cummings, W. and McGinn, N. (eds). *International Handbook of Education and Development: Preparing Schools, Students and Nations for the Twenty-First Century* (pp. 87–101). Oxford: Elsevier Science Ltd.

Asmal, K. (2001a) Responses to the PANSALB Education sub-committee's Presentation to the Education Portfolio Committee, National Assembly, Parliament, 20 February.

Asmal, K. (2001b) Message from the minister. *Education Africa Forum Fifth Edition: Delivering Africa's Education Renaissance in South Africa* (pp. 6–7). Pinegowrie: Education Africa.

Associates, Advanced Workplace (2002) Going Offshore, advanced working papers. Advanced Workplace Associates Ltd. On WWW at http://www.advanced-workplace.com. Accessed 2.01.04.

Bakwesegha, C.J. (2000) Keynote address on 'the rise of the ethnic question'. In *Facing Ethnic Conflicts*. Bonn, Germany: Center for Development Research (ZEF Bonn).

Ball, S. (1984) Imperialism, social control and the colonial curriculum in Africa. In Goodson, I.F. and Ball, S.J. (eds) *Defining the Curriculum: Histories and Ethnographies* (pp. 117–47). London: The Falmer Press.

Bamgbose, A. (2000) *Language and Exclusion: The Consequences of Language Policies in Africa*. Münster, Hamburg and London: Lit Verlag.
Bartlett, L. (2003) Social studies of literacy and comparative education: Intersections. *Current Issues in Comparative Education: Literacy, Education and Development* 5, 1–10.
Basu, A. (1974) *The Growth of Education and Political Development in India, 1898–1920*. Delhi, Bombay, Calcutta: Oxford University Press.
Beetham, D. (1990) *The Legitimation of Power*. Basingstoke: Macmillan Press.
Berlin Conference Background. Vol. 2004: Thinkquest E-Diplomacy. On WWW at http://library.thinkquest.org. Accessed 14.03.04.
Berman, B.J. (1998) Etnicity, patronage and the African state: The politics of uncivil nationalism. *African Affairs* 97, 305–41.
Bernstein, B. (1996) *Pedagogy, Symbolic Control and Identity: Theory, Research and Critique*. London: Taylor and Francis.
Bernstein, B. (1999) Vertical and horizontal discourse: An essay. *British Journal of Sociology of Education*, 20(2), 157–73.
Bernstein, H. (1983) Development. In Thomas, A. and Bernstein, H. (eds) *The Third World and Development*. Milton Keynes: The Open University Press.
Betts, R.F. (1985) Methods and institutions of European domination. In Boahen, A.A. (ed.) *Africa Under Colonial Domination 1880–1935* (Vol. VII) (pp. 312–31). General History of Africa. London, Paris, Berkeley: Heinemann Educational Books Ltd, UNESCO and University of California.
Beyene, B. (1998) The historical genesis of the juridical concept of terra nullius. On WWW at http://www.ethiopiafirst.com/. Accessed 26.07.04.
Bhabha, H. (1994) *The Location of Culture*. London: Routledge.
Billig, M. (1997) *Banal Nationalism*. London: Sage Publications.
Blaut, J.M. 1993. *The Coloniser's Model of the World: Geographical Diffusionism and Eurocentric History*. New York: The Guilford Press.
Bloch, C. (2002) A case study of Xhosa and English biliteracy in the foundation phase versus English as a 'medium of destruction'. *Perspectives in Education* 20(1), 65–78.
Blommaert, J. (2001) The Asmara Declaration as a sociolinguistic problem. Reflections on scholarship and linguistic rights. *Journal of Sociolinguistics* 5(1), 131–55.
Bond, P. (2000) *Elite Transition: From Apartheid to Neoliberalism in South Africa*. London: Pluto Press.
Bourdieu, P. (1977) The economics of linguistic exchanges. *Social Science Information* 16, 645–68.
Bourdieu, P. (1991) *Language and Symbolic Power*. Adamson, G.R.a.M. (trans.). Cambridge: Polity Press.
Bourdieu, P. and Wacquant, L. (1992) *An Invitation to Reflexive Sociology*. Chicago: Chicago University Press.
Brock-Utne, B. (2000) *Whose Education For All? The Recolonisation of the African Mind*. New York and London: The Falmer Press.
Brutt-Griffler, J. 2004. *World English: A Study of its Development*. Clevedon: Multilingual Matters.
Buck, V. (2002) One world, one language? International Association of Conference Interpreters (AIIC). On WWW at http://www.aiic.net/ViewPagecfm/page732.html. Accessed 22.05.05.

Bullivant, B. (1981) *The Pluralist Dilemma: A Cross-Cultural Study*. London: Allen and Unwin.
BusinessWeek. The New Global Job Shift. 3, February 2003.
Buthelezi. M. (2002) Speech by Minister of Home Affairs, Dr Mangosuthu Buthelezi on the Second Reading of the Immigration Bill [B79], National Assembly, 17 May.
Buthelezi, M. (2003) Introductory Speech by Mangosuthu Buthelezi, MP, Minister of Home Affairs, during Home Affairs Budget Debate, National Assembly, Cape Town, 19 May.
Caldwell, J.C. (1985) The social repercussions of colonial rule: Demographic aspects. In Boahen, A. (ed.) *Africa Under Colonial Domination 1880 to 1935* (Vol. VII) General History of Africa (pp. 458–86). London, Paris, Berkeley: Heinemann Educational Books Ltd.
Callard, K. (1958) *Pakistan: A Political Study*. London: Allen and Unwin.
Canagarajah, A.S. (1999) *Resisting Linguistic Imperialism in English Teaching*. Oxford: Oxford University Press.
Canagarajah, A.S. (2005) *Reclaiming the Local in Language Policy and Practice*. New Jersey: Lawrence Erlbaum Associates.
Canvin, M. (2003) *Language and Education in Mali: A Consideration of Two Approaches*. Unpublished PhD thesis, University of Reading, United Kingdom.
Castells, M. (1993) The informational economy and the new international division of labour. In Carnoy, M.C.M., Cohen, S. and Cardoso, F. (eds) *The New Global Economy in the Information Age: Reflections on our Changing World* (pp. 15–44). Basingstoke: Macmillan Press Ltd.
Castells, M. (1996) *The Rise of the Network Society. The Information Age: Economy, Society and Culture Volume 1*. Oxford: Basil Blackwell.
Chambas, G., Combes, J., Guillaumont, P., Guillaumont Jeanneney, S. and Laporte, B. (2000) *Mali: les facteurs de croissance à long terme*. OCDE programme de recherche sur l'Afrique émergente. On WWW at http://www.oecd.org/.
Charlick, R., Wing, S. and Kone, M. (October 1998) *The Political Economy of Educational Policy Reform in Mali: A Stakeholder Analysis. A Report in Partial Fulfillment of IQC: AEP-5468-I-00-6060-00 DO 806 (MSI Project 3224–023)*. Washington: Management Systems International (personal copy by kind permission of R. Charlick).
Chatterjee, P. (1986) *Nationalist Thought and the Colonical World: A Derivative Discourse?* London: Zed Press.
Chatterjee, P. (1993) *Colonical and Postcolonical Histories*. Princeton: Princeton University Press.
Chossudovsky, M. (1997) *The Globalisation of Poverty: Impacts of IMF and World Bank Reforms*. London: Zed Books Ltd.
Cliff, M. (1985) *The Land of Look Behind*. Ithaca, New York: Firebrand Books.
Cluver, A. (1996) Language development in South Africa. A report for the Language Plan Task Group (unpublished mimeo).
Coulibaly, N.G. (2003) Communication du Mali. *Atelier régional de mise en commun des expériences en matière des langues nationales dans les pays de l'Afrique de l'Ouest du 19 au 21 novembre 2003 à Bamako*. Bamako: Ministère de l'Education Nationale.
Coulmas, F. (1992) *Language and Economy*. Oxford: Basil Blackwell.
Crouch, L. and Lewin, K. (2000) Turbulence or orderly change? Teacher supply and demand in South Africa – current status, future needs and the impact of

HIV/Aids. Discussion Paper 26. MUSTER (Multi-Site Teacher Education Research Project. Centre for International Education, University of Sussex Institute of Education. On WWW at http://www.sussex.ac.uk/usie/muster/lisst.html.

Cumings, J. (1976) The influence of bilingualism on cognitive growth: A synthesis of research findings and explanatory hypotheses. *Working Papers on Bilingualism* 9, 1–43.

DACST (1996) *Towards a National Language Plan for South Africa. Final Report of the Language Plan Task Group (LANGTAG)*. Pretoria: Department of Arts, Culture, Science and Technology (DACST).

Das Gupta, J. (1970) *Language Conflict and National Development*. Berkeley and Los Angelos: University of California Press.

Datta, R. (2004) Worker and work – a case study of an international call centre in India. *International Labour Process Conference April 5–7*. Amsterdam Institute for Advanced Labour Studies.

Davis, H., Hammond, P. and Nizamova, L. (2000) Media, language policy and cultural change in Tatarstan: Historic vs. pragmatic claims to nationhood. On WWW at http://www.aiic.net/ViewPagecfm/page732.html. Accessed 28.06.05.

De Klerk, G. (1995) Bilingualism, the devil and the big wide world. In Heugh, K., Siegrühn, A. and Plüddemann, P. (eds) *Multilingual Education for South Africa* (pp. 53–62). Johannesburg: Heinemann.

De Klerk, V. (2002a) Language issues in our schools: Whose voice counts? Part 1: The parents speak. *Perspectives in Education* 20(1), 1–14.

De Klerk, V. (2002b) Language issues in our schools: Whose voice counts? Part 2: The teachers speak. *Perspectives in Education* 20(1), 15–27.

de Sigueira, A.C. (2005) The regulation of education through the WTO/GATS. *Journal for Critical Education Policy Studies*. (Vol. 3). On WWW at http://www.jceps.com/?pageID=articleandarticleID=41. Accessed 28.06.05.

de Varennes, F. (1996) *Language, Minorities and Human Rights*. The Hague: Kluwer Law International.

Desai, Z. (2004) Starting a research project. In Brock-Utne, B., Desai, Z. and Qorro, M. (eds) *Researching the Language of Instruction in Tanzania and South Africa*. Cape Town: African Minds.

Diakité, D. (2000) La crise scolaire au Mali. *Nordic Journal of African Studies* 9(3), 6–28.

Dixon, C. and Heffernan, M. (1991) *Colonialism and Development in the Contemporary World*. London: Mansell Publishing Limited.

DNAFLA (1981) *Règles d'orthographe des langues nationales*. Bamako: DNAFLA.

DNAFLA (1993) *Alphabets et règles d'rthographe des langues nationales*. Bamako: DNAFLA.

DNSI (2001) *Perspectives de la population, Mali, 1987–2022*. Bamako: DNSI.

Docquier, F. and Marfouk, A. (2004) Measuring the international mobility of skilled workers (1990–2000). *Policy Research Working Papers 3381*. Washington: The World Bank.

Docquier F., Lohest, O. and Marfouk, A. 2005. *Brain Drain in Developing Regions (1990–2000), IZA Discussion Papers 1668*. Bonn: Institute for the Study of Labor (IZA).

Docquier, F. and Rapoport, H. (2004) *Skilled Migration: The Perspectives of Developing Countries* (pp. 38). Washington: The World Bank.

DoE (1997) *Language-in-Education Policy.* Pretoria: Department of Education.
DoE (2001) *Language-in-Education Policy Implementation Plan.* Pretoria: Department of Education.
DoE (2002a) *Revised National Curriculum Statement Grades R-9 (Schools) Policy: Overview.* Pretoria: Department of Education.
DoE (2002b) *Revised National Curriculum Statement Grades R-9 (Schools) Policy: Languages – English First Additional Language.* Pretoria: Department of Education.
Donald, J. (1993) How English is it? Popular literature and national culture. In Carter, E., Donald, J. and Squires, J. (eds) *Space and Place: Theories of Identity and Culture* (pp. 165–86). London: Lawrence Wishart.
Doughty, C. and Long, M. (eds) (2003) *The Handbook of Second Language Acquisition.* Malden, MA and Oxford: Blackwell.
Doumbia, A.T. (2000) L'enseignement du bambara selon la pédagogie convergente au Mali: théorie et pratiques. *Nordic Journal of African Studies* 9(3), 98–107.
Du Plessis, T. (2003) Multilingualism and language-in-education policy in South Africa – a historical overview. In Cuvelier, P., du Plessis, T. and Teck, L. (eds) *Multilingualism, Education and Social Integration. Studies in Language Policy in South Africa.* Pretoria: Van Schaik.
du Plessis, T. (2003) Commentary on the Report of the Ministerial Committee appointed by the Minister of Education in September 2003: *The Development of Indigenous African Languages as Mediums of Instruction in Higher Education.* Unit for Language Facilitation and Empowerment. Bloemfontein: University of the Free State.
Dumestre, G. (1994) Mali: Language situation. In Asher, R.E. (ed. in chief), Simpson, J.M.Y. (coordinating editor). *The Encyclopedia of Language and Linguistics* (Vol. 5) (pp. 2353–54). Oxford: Pergamon Press Ltd.
Dzvimbo, K.P. (2003) The International Migration of Skilled Human Capital from Developing Countries, World Bank, HDNED. A case study prepared for a Regional Training Conference on *Improving Tertiary Education in Sub-Saharan Africa: Things That Work!* Accra, 23–25 September, 2003.
Easton, P. and Peach, M. (1997) *The Practical Applications of Koranic Learning in West Africa.* (Nonformal Education Working Group, Research Studies Series no. 8). London: ADEA (IWG/NFE.GTI/ENF). On WWW at http://www.adeanet.org/.
Echu, G. (1999) Colonialism and linguistic dilemmas in Africa: Cameroon as a paradigm (revisited). *Quest: An African Journal of Philosophy* XIII, 19–26.
Elaigwu, J. and Mazrui, A. (2003) Nation-building and changing political structures. In Mazrui, A. and Wondi, C. (eds) *General History of Africa* (Vol. VIII) (pp. 435–67). Africa Since 1935, Glosderry, South Africa: UNESCO and National Africa Education.
Engardio, P., Bernstein, A. and Kripalani, M. (2003) "Is your job next?" *Business Week,* 3 February (pp. 50–60).
Engineer, A.A. (2000) The problematique of nation building in South Asia: the case of Pakistan. Institute of Islamic Studies and Centre for Study of Society and Secularism. On WWW at http://www.ecumene.org/IIS/CSS29.html. Accessed 2.01.05.
Evans, S. (2002) Macaulay's Minute Revisited: Colonial language policy in nineteenth-century India. *Journal of Multilingual and Multicultural Development* 23, 260–81.

Fafunwa, A. (1982) *Education in Africa; A Comparative Survey*. London: George Allen and Unwin (publishers) Ltd.
Fanon, F. (1967) *Black Skin, White Masks*. London and Sydney: Pluto Press.
Fardon, R. and Furniss, G. (1994) *African Languages; Language and Languages; Language Policy; Language Planning; Political Aspects*. London: Routledge.
Foucault, M. (1977) *Discipline and Punish: The Birth of a Prison*. Sheridan, A. (trans.). New York: Pantheon Books.
Foucault, M. (1980). *Power/Knowledge: Selected Interviews and Other Writings 1972–1977*. Gordon, L.M.C., Mepham, J. and Soper, K. (trans.) Brighton: The Harvester Press.
Foucault, M. (1991) Governmentality. In Burchell, G., Gordon, C. and Miller, P. (eds) *The Foucault Effect: Studies in Governmentality* (pp. 87–104). Hemel Hempstead: Harvester Wheatsheaf.
Freire, P. (1972) *Pedagogy of the Oppressed*. London: Penguin.
Friedman, M. (1982) *Capitalism and Freedom*. Chicago: University of Chicago.
Gee, J.P. (1996) *Social Linguistics and Literacies: Ideology in Discourses*. London: Taylor and Francis.
Gellner, E. (1988) *Nations and Nationalism*. Oxford: Basil Blackwell Publishers.
Giddens, A. (1984) *The Constitution of Society: Outline of the Theory of Structuration*. Cambridge: Polity Press in association with Blackwells.
Giddens, A. (1991) *Modernity and Self Identity: Self and Society in the Late Modern Age*. Cambridge: Polity Press.
Giddens, A. (2002) *Where Now for New Labour?* Cambridge: Polity Press.
Giliomee, H. (2003a) The rise and possible demise of afrikaans as a public language. PRAESA Occasional Papers No 14.
Giliomee, H. (2003b) *The Afrikaners: Biography of a People*. Charlottesville: University of Virginia Press.
Gordon, R.G. Jr. (ed.) (2005) *Ethnologue: Languages of the World* (15th edn). Dallas, TX: SIL International.
Gogolin, I. (1997) The 'monolingual habitus' as the common feature in teaching in the language of the majority in different countries. *Per Linguam*, 13(2), 38–49.
Gordon, R.G. Jr. (ed.) (2005) *Ethnologue: Languages of the World*. Dallas, TX: SIL International.
Government of Pakistan, Statistics Division (2004) *Labour Force Survey 2003–2004*. Islamabad: Federal Bureau of Statistics.
Graddol, D. (1997) *The Future of English*. London: The British Council.
Graddol, D. (2006) *English Next. Why Global English may Mean the End of 'English as a Foreign Language'*. London: The British Council.
Gramsci, A. (1971) *Selections from the Prison Notebooks*. Edited and translated by Hoare, Q. and Nowell Smith, G. London: Lawrence Wishart.
Green, A. (1990) *Education and State Formation: The Rise of Education Systems in England, France and the USA*. New York: St Martin's Press.
Grin, F. (2002) *Using Language Economics and Education Economics in Language Education Policy. Guide for the Development of Language Education Policies in Europe: From Linguistic Diversity to Plurilingual Education*. Strasbourg: Council of Europe.
Grin, F. (2005) The economics of language policy implementation: Identifying and measuring costs. In Alexander, N. (ed.) *Reports on Mother-Tongue Based Bilingual*

Education in Southern Africa. The Dynamics of Implementation. Proceedings of a PRAESA Symposium, funded by the Volkswagen Foundation, held at the University of Cape Town, 16–17 October 2003. Cape Town: PRAESA.
Guibernau, M. (1996) *Nationalisms: The Nation State and Nationalism in the Twentieth Century*. Cambridge: Polity Press.
Guibernau, M. (2000) *Nations Without States. Political Communities in a Global Age*. London: Polity Press.
Guigan, L.H. and Gann, P. (1977) Introduction. In Guigan, L.H. and Gann, P. (eds) *The History and Politics of Colonialism, 1870–1914* (Vol. 1) (pp. 1–26). Cambridge: Cambridge University Press.
Gumperz, T.J. (1977) Language problems in the rural development in North India. *Journal of Asian Studies* 16, 251–59.
Haïdara, Y. (1998) *Etat des lieux de la Pédagogie Convergente: Forum sur la Pédagogie Convergente*. Bamako: Comite charge des stratégies d'utilisation des langues nationales et de la Pédagogie Convergente/Ministère de l'Education de Base.
Hall, S., Critcher, C., Jefferson, T., Clarke, J. and Roberts, B. (1978) *Policing the Crisis: Mugging, the State and Law and Order*. London: Macmillan Education.
Hall, S. (1990) The state in question. In Held, D., Hall, S. and McLennan, G. (eds) *The Idea of the Modern State*. Buckingham: Open University Press.
Hall, S. (1993) Cultural identity and diaspora. In Williams, P. and Chrisman, L. (eds) *Colonial Discourse and Post-Colonial Theory: A Reader*. London: Harvester Wheatsheaf.
Hall, S. (1996) When was 'the post-colonial'? Thinking at the limit. In Chambers, I. and Curtis, L. (eds) *The Post-Colonial Question: Common Skies, Divided Horizons* (pp. 242–60). London: Routledge.
Hameso, Seyoum Y. (1997) The language of education in Africa: The key issues. *Language, Culture and Curriculum* 10, 1–13.
Harley, A. (2003) Census 2001: What do the statistics have to say about adult literacy? *Talking Adult Learning* (pp. 10–11). November 2003. Cape Town: Adult Learning Network.
Harrison, M. (2004) Why teachers should support the market. National Business Review. Accessed 21.05.04.
Hayek, F. (1978) *The Mirage of Social Justice*. London: Routledge and Kegan Paul.
Hegel. G.W.F. (1975) *Lectures on the Philosophy of World History, Introduction: Reason in History*. Nisbet, H.B. (trans.). Cambridge: Cambridge University Press.
Held, D. (1992) The development of the modern state. In Gieben, S.H.a.B. (ed.) *Formations of Modernity*. Oxford: Polity in association with the Open University Press.
Held, D. and McGrew, A. (2003) The great globalization debate. In Held, D. and McGrew, A. (eds) *The Global Transformations Reader*. Cambridge: Polity Press.
Henevald, W. and Craig, H. (1996) *Schools Count: World Bank Project Designs and the Quality of Primary Education in Sub-Saharan Africa*. Washington, DC: World Bank.
Heugh, K. (2002) The case against bilingual and multilingual education in South Africa: Laying bare the myths. *Perspectives in Education*, 20(1), 171–96.
Heugh, K. (2003) Can authoritarian separatism give way to language rights? *Current Issues in Language Planning* 4(2), 126–45.

Heugh, K. (2004) A re-take on bilingual education in and for South Africa. In Fraurud, K. and Hyltenstam, K. (eds) *Multilingualism in Global and Local Perspectives. Papers from the 8th Nordic Conference on Bilingualism, November 1–3, 2001, Stockholm*. Rinkeby. Stockholm: Centre for Reserch on Bilingualism, Stockholm University and Rinkeby Institute of Multilingual Research.

HM Treasury, UK (2005) *UK Writes Off Multilateral Debt and Consults on Commission for Africa proposals in Mali* (press release, 14 February 2005). London: HM Treasury. On WWW at http://www.hm-treasury.gov.uk/newsroom_and_speeches/press/2005/press_17_05.cfm.

Hoogvelt, A. (2001) *Globalization and the Postcolonial World: The New Political Economy of Development*. Basingstoke: Palgrave Macmillan.

Hooks, B. (1989) *Talking Back: Thinking Feminism – Thinking Black*. Boston, London: Sheba Feminist Publishers.

Hornberger, N. (2000) Multilingual literacies, literacy practices, and the continua of biliteracy. In Martin-Jones, M. and Jones, K. (eds) *Multilingual Literacies* (pp. 353–67). Amsterdam/Philadelphia: John Benjamins.

Horne, T. (2001) Education and language transferees. Education Africa Forum Fifth Edition. *Delivering Africa's Education Renaissance in South Africa* (pp. 40–45). Pinegowrie: Education Africa.

IMF (1999) *Mali: Enhanced Structural Adjustment Facility Medium-Term Policy Framework Paper 1999–2002, prepared by the Government of Mali in collaboration with the International Monetary Fund and World Bank Staff* July 12 1999. Bamako: Government of Mali/IMF. On WWW at http://www.imf.org/.

IRIN (2004) MALI: Sponsorship scheme launched to get kids in schools. In *IRIN News, 28th September 2004*. On WWW at http://www.irinnews.org/report.asp?ReportID=41939andSelectRegion=West_AfricaandSelectCountry=MALI.

James, P. (1996) *Nation Formation: Towards a Theory of Abstract Community*. London: Sage Publications.

Jansen, J. (2004) Matric quick-fixes miss the mark. *Sunday Times*, 4 January, p. 15.

Jeater, D. (2001) Speaking like a native: Vernacular languages and the state in Southern Rhodesia, 1890–1935. *Journal of African History* 42, 449–68.

Jules Ferry. (1897) Speech before the French Chamber of Deputies, March 28, 1884. In Robiquet, P. (ed.) *Discourse et Opnions de Jules Ferry*, Paris: Armand Colin and Cie. On WWW at http://www.fordham.edu/halsall/mod/1884ferry.html. Accessed 9/01/04.

Kachru, B. (1982) *The Other Tongue: English Across Cultures*. Urbana: University of Illinois Press.

Kané, S. (2000) Manuels utilisés dans l'enseignement de la langue dans les écoles à pédagogie convergente: Disponibilité et utilisation. *Nordic Journal of African Studies* 9(3), 66–79.

Kautsky, K. (1907) Socialism and Colonial Policy (Vol. 2004) Translated by Angela Clifford, December 1975. On WWW at http://www.athol-st.dircon.co.uk/index.html. Accessed 4.03.04.

Kellas, J. (1991) *The Politics of Nationalism and Ethnicity*. London: Macmillan Publishers.

Kemshall, H. (2002) *Risk, Social Policy and Welfare*. Milton Keynes: Open University Press.

Khor, M. (2001) *Rethinking Globalization: Critical Issues and Policy Choices*. London: Zed Books.

King, C. (1999) *One Language, Two Scripts: The Hindi Movement in Nineteenth Century North India*. India: Oxford University Press.
Krashen, S. (1996) *Under Attack: The Case Against Bilingual Education*. Cluver City, CA: Language Education Associates.
Kromah, A. (2002) Geo-political tracks of the liberian mandingoes. Liberian Orbit. On WWW at http://www.liberiaorbit.org/lonewsgeopol.manding.html. Accessed 4.03.04.
Lange, M. and Diarra, S. (1999) Ecole et démocratie: l'explosion scolaire sous la III République au Mali. *Politique Africaine*, 76(décembre), 164–72.
Larrain, J. (1989) *Theories of Development: Capitalism, Colonialism and Dependency*. Cambridge: Polity Press in association with Basil Blackwell.
Leclerc, J. (2003) *Mali*. On WWW at http://www.tlfq.ulaval.ca/axl/afrique/mali.html.
Leftwich, A. (1995) Governance, democracy and development in the Third World. In Corbridge, S. (ed.). *Development Studies: A Reader* (pp. 427–47). London: Edward Arnold.
Legassick, M. (2003) Ominous threat to our young democracy: The poor have become poorer in the most unequal society – South Africa. *Cape Times*, 28 February, p. 9.
Lockheed, M. (1993) The condition of primary schooling in developing countries. In Levin, H. and Lockheed, M. (eds) *Effective Schools in Developing Countries*. London: Falmer.
Lowell, L.B. and Findlay, A. (2003) *Migration of Highly Skilled Persons from Developing Countries: Impact and Policy Responses* (p. 46). Geneva: International Labour Office, International Migration Branch.
Macdonald, C. (1990) *Crossing the Threshold into Standard Three. Main Report of the Threshold Project*. Pretoria: Human Sciences Research Council.
Mahboob, A. (2002) No English, no future: Language policy in Pakistan. In Obeng, S. and Hartford, B. (eds) *Political Independence with Linguistic Servitude: The Politics About Languages in the Developing World*. New York: NOVA Science.
Mahlalela, B. and Heugh, K. (2002) Terminology and schoolbooks in Southern African languages: Aren't there any? PRAESA Occasional Papers No. 10.
Malaquias, A. (2000) Ethnicity and conflict in Angola: prospects for reconciliation. In Cilliers, J. and Dietrich, C. (eds) *Angola's War Economy: The Role of Oil and Diamonds*. Pretoria: Institute for Security Studies.
Malherbe, E. (1943) *The Bilingual School*. Johannesburg: CNA.
Mali, Republic of (1992) *The Constitution of the Republic of Mali*. University of Richmond, School of Law. Craver, J. (trans.) (2000). On WWW at http://oncampus.richmond.edu/~jjones//confinder/Mali.html.
Mali, République du (1999) *Portant loi d'orientation sur l'éducation, LOI No 99–046/du 28 décembre 1999*. Presidency of the Republic (personal photocopy of original document signed by the President of Mali).
Mali, République du (2001a) *Ordonnance No. 01-044/P-RM du 19 septembre 2001. Portant création de l'Institut des Langues*. Bamako: Secrétariat générale du gouvernement.
Mali, République du (2001b) *Décret No. 01-516/P-RM du 22 octobre 2001. Fixant l'organisation et les modalités de fonctionnement de l'Institut des Langues*. Bamako: Secrétariat générale du gouvernement.

Mallikarjun, B. (2004) Indian multilingualism, language policy and the digital divide. *Language in India* (Vol. 4). On WWW at http://www.LanguageinIndia.-com. Accessed 30.03.04.
Manning, P. (1988) *Francophone Sub-Saharan Africa 1880–1985*. Cambridge: Cambridge University Press.
Mansoor, S. (2005) *Language Planning in Higher Education: A Case Study of Pakistan*. Oxford: Oxford University Press.
Mansour, G. (1993) *Multilingualism & Nation Building*. Clevedon: Multilingual Matters.
Marouni, M. and Raffinot, M. (2004) *Perspectives on Growth and Poverty Reduction in Mali*. Paris: DIAL/Unité de Recherche CIPRÉ.
Martin-Jones, M. and Jones, K. (2000) Multilingual literacies. In Martin-Jones, M. and Jones, K. (eds) *Multilingual Literacies* (pp. 1–15). Amsterdam/ Philadelphia: John Benjamins.
Massey, D. (1999) Imagining globalization: Power geometries of space-time. In Hickman, M., Mac an Ghaill, M. and Brah, A. (eds) *Global Futures: Migration, Environment and Globalization* (pp. 27–44). London: Macmillan.
Mateene, K. (1999) OAU's strategy for linguistic unity and multilingual education. *Social Dynamics* 25, 164–78.
May, S. (2001) *Language and Minority Rights: Ethnicity, Nationalism and the Politics of Language*. London and New York: Longman.
Mazari, S. (2002) Ethnicity and political process: The Pakistani experience. *Conference on South and South East Asia in Perspective – 20th and 21st Centuries*. Lisbon, Portugal.
Mazrui, A. (1980) *The African Condition*. London: Heinemann.
Mazrui, A.A. (1997) The World Bank, the language question and the future of African education. *Race and Class* 38, 35–48.
Mazrui, A. and Mazrui, A.A. (1998) *The Power of Babel: Language and Governance in the African Experience*. Oxford: James Currey.
Mazrui, A. (2002) The English language in African education: Dependency and decolonization. In Tollefson, J. (ed.). *Language Policies in Education: Critical Issues* (pp. 267–81). Mahwah, NJ: Lawrence Erlbaum Associates.
Mbah, S. and Igariwey, I. (2001) *African Anarchism: The History of a Movement*. Tucson, Arizona: Sharp Press.
McNamara, T. (2000) *Language Testing. Oxford Introductions to Language Study*. Oxford: Oxford University Press.
Mesthrie, R. (2002) South Africa: A sociolinguistic overview. In Mesthrie, R. (ed.) *Language in South Africa* (pp. 1–26). Cambridge: CUP.
Ministère de l'Education, République du Mali (2001) *Rapport présenté à la 46è session de la conférence internationale de l'éducation sur la thème: contenus de l'éducation et stratégies d'apprentissage pour vivre ensemble au XXIème siècle: Problèmes et solutions, Genève, 5–7 septembre 2001*. Bamako: Commission nationale Malienne pour l'UNESCO/IBE, UNESCO.
Ministère de l'Education de Base, République du Mali (1999) *Note sur les éléments de politique des langues du Mali, Plan d'action triennal 2000–2002*.
Ministère de l'Education Nationale, République du Mali (2004a) *Rapport du Mali, Quarante septième session de la conférence internationale de l'éducation, Thème: Education de qualité pour tous les jeunes: Défis, tendances et priorités,*

Genève, 8 au 11 Septembre 2004. Bamako: Secrétariat Général, Ministère de l'Education Nationale.

Ministère de l'Education Nationale, République du Mali (2004b) Actes du Forum. *Forum National sur la Généralisation du curriculum de l'Enseignement Fondamental, Bamako 9 et 10 septembre 2004*. Bamako: Ministère de l'Education Nationale et Centre National de l'Education Division Nationale de l'Education de Base.

Ministère de l'Education Nationale, République du Mali (2005a) *Etude de cas sur la qualité de l'éducation: La pédagogie convergente (PC) comme facteur d'amélioration de la qualité de l'éducation de base au Mali: Analyse du développement de l'innovation et perspectives*. Bamako: Ministère de l'Education Nationale, République du Mali/Association pour le Développement de l'Education en Afrique/ ROCARE-MALI.

Ministère de l'Education Nationale, République du Mali (2005b) *Tableaux statistiques du C.F.E.P.C.E.F. 2005*. Bamako: Centre National des Examens et Concours de l'Education, Ministère de l'Education Nationale.

Ministry of Economy and Finance, Republic of Mali (2002) *Final PRSP, Poverty Reduction Strategy Paper, Document prepared and adopted by the Government of Mali, May 29th 2002*. Bamako: Ministry of Economy and Finance. On WWW at http://poverty.worldbank.org/.

Monare, M. (2003) Grade 3 flunkers sound a warning about our schools. *Sunday Times*, 22 June 2003. On WWW at http://www.sundaytimes.co.za/2003/06/22/insight/in05.asp.

Montagnes, I. (2000) *Textbooks and Learning Materials 1990–1999*. Paris: Unesco, World Education Forum, Education for All 2000 Assessment.

Morley, L. and Rassool, N. (1999) *School Effectiveness: Fracturing the Discourse*. London: The Falmer Press.

Morris, J. (1968) *Pax Britannica: The Climax of an Empire*. London: Faber and Faber.

Mühlhäusler, P. (1996) *Linguistic Ecology: Language Change and Linguistic Imperialism in the Pacific Region*. London: Routledge.

Myers-Scotton, C. (1993) *Social Motivations for Code-switching: Evidence from Africa*. Oxford: Clarendon Press.

Nayyar, D. (2002) Towards global governance. In Nayyar, D. (ed.) *Governing Globalization: Issues and Institutions*. Oxford: Oxford University Press.

Nederveen, J. (1990) *Empire and Emancipation*. London: Pluto Press.

NEPI (National Education Policy Investigation) (1992) *Language*. Cape Town: National Education Co-ordinating Committee and OUP.

Ngcongco, J.D. (2000) *Nineteenth Century until the 1880s* (Vol. VI) Ade, Ajayi, J.J. (ed.). General History of Africa. Glosderry: New Africa Books.

Ngcongco, L.D. (1989) The Mfecane and the rise of new African states. In Ade Ajayi, J.J. (ed.) *Africa in the Nineteenth Century Until the 1880s* (Vol. VII) (pp. 90–123). General History of Africa. London, Paris, Berkeley: Heinemann International; UNESCO, University of California Press.

Ngũgĩ wa Thiongo (1993) The language of African literature. In Williams, P. and Chrisman, L. (eds) *Colonial Discourse and Post-colonial Theory: A Reader*. (pp. 435–56). London: Harvester Wheatsheaf.

Norton, B. (1998) Accountability in language assessment. In Clapham, C. and Corson, D. (eds) Language testing and assessment, *Encyclopedia of Language and Education* (Vol. 7) (pp. 7313–22). Dordrecht: Kluwer Academic.

Obanya, P. (1998) Language education in Africa. Fafunwa Foundation Internet Journal of Education. On WWW at http://www.fafunwafoundation.tripod.com. Accessed 4.03.04.

Obanya, P. (1999) *The Dilemma of Education in Africa*. Dakar: UNESCO Regional Office.

Obeng, S. and Adegbija, E. (1999) Sub-Saharan Africa. In Fishman, J.A. (ed.) *Handbook of Language and Ethnic Identity* (pp. 353–68). Oxford: Oxford University Press.

OPEC (2000) *OPEC Fund Supports Education in Mali with US$5 Million Loan* (Press release, 29 February 2000). Vienna: OPEC. On WWW at http://www.opecfun.org/.

Organization for African Unity (OAU) (1969) Pan-African cultural manifesto. *First All Africa Cultural Festival*. Algiers: OAU.

Organization for African Unity (OAU) (1976) Cultural charter for Africa. *Organization of African Unity Meeting in its Thirteenth Ordinary Session*. Post Louis, Mauritius: OAU.

Organization for African Unity (OAU) (1979) Proceedings of the meeting of experts on the use of the regional or subregional African languages as media of culture and communication with the continent. *African Languages*. Bamako, Mali: OAU.

Ouane, A. (1995) Mali. In Postlethwaite, T.N. (ed.) *International Encyclopedia of National Systems of Education* (2nd edn) (pp. 615–22). Oxford: Pergamon Press.

Ouane, A. (2003) Introduction: The view from inside the linguistic jail. In Ouane, A. (ed.) *Towards a Multilingual Culture of Education* (pp. 1–22). Hamburg: UNESCO Institute for Education.

Owino, F. (2002) Conquering the conqueror. The empowerment of the African languages casts a shadow over English in Africa. *Perspectives in Education* 20 (2), 197–212.

Pakistan Census Organization (1998) 1998 Census Report. Pakistan Census Organization, Government of Pakistan. On WWW at http://www.statpak.pk. Accessed 2.06.05.

Pakistan Census Organization (2005) Population statistics. Pakistan Census Organization, Government of Pakistan. On WWW at http://www.statpak.pk. Accessed 2.06.05.

Pakistan, Government of (1973) The Constitution of the Islamic Republic of Pakistan. On WWW at http://www.statpak.pk. Accessed 2.06.05.

Pakistan, Government of (2003–2004) Economic Survey. Islamabad: Federal Bureau of Statistics. On WWW at http://www.finance.gov.pk/survey/chapter/11-education pdf. Aaccessed 6.07.04.

Pakistan, Government of (2004–2005) Economic survey. Islamabad: Federal Bureau of Statistics. On WWW at http://www.finance.gov.pk/survey/chapter/11-education pdf. Accessed 6.07.04.

Pakistan Ministry of Education (2004) *Higher Education Sector Reforms Plan 2001–2004*. Ministry of Education: Islamabad.

Paku, N. (1996) Colonialism and Sub-Saharan identities. In Renwick, J. and Krause, N. (eds) *Identities in International Relations*. London: Macmillan.

PANSALB (2000) Omnibus February 2000. *Language Issues Frequencies*. Pretoria: MarkData (Pty) Ltd.

PANSALB (2000) *Language Use and Language Interaction in South Africa: A National Sociolinguistic Survey*. Pretoria: Pan South African Language Board.

PANSALB (2001) *Language Use and Language Interaction in South Africa: A National Sociolinguistic Survey Summary Report*. Pretoria: Pan South African Language Board.

Parsons, N. (1999) Kicking the hornet's nest: A third view of the Cobbing controversy on the Mfecane/Dificane. University of Botswana. On WWW at http//www.thuto.org/ubh/ac/mfec.htm. Accessed 15.04.04.

Pecheux, M. (1982) *Language, Semantics and Ideology*. Nagpal, H. (trans.). London: Macmillan.

Pennycook, A. (1998) *English and the Discourses of Colonialism*. London: Routledge.

Pennycook, A. (1995) English in the world/the world in English. In Tollefson, J. (ed.) *Power and Inequality in Language Education* (pp. 34–58). The Cambridge Applied Linguistics Series. Cambridge: Cambridge University Press.

Pennycook, A. (2000a) Language ideology and hindsight: Lessons from colonial language policies. In Ricento, T. (ed.) *Ideology, Politics and Language Policies: Focus on English* (pp. 49–65). Amsterdam: John Benjamins Publishing Co.

Pennycook, A. (2000b) English, politics, ideology: From colonial celebration to postcolonial performativity. In Ricento, T. (ed.) *Ideology, Politics and Language Policies: Focus on English* (pp. 107–19). Amsterdam: John Benjamins Co.

Pennycook, A. (2002a) Language policy and docile bodies: Hong Kong and governmentality. In Tollefson, J. (ed.) *Language Policies in Education: Critical Issues* (pp. 91–110). Mahwah, NJ: Lawrence Erlbaum Associates.

Pennycook, A. (2002b) Mother tongues, governmentality, and protectionism. *International Journal of the Sociology of Language* 154, 11–28.

Peron, J. (2004) Education alone DoEs not stimulate growth and reduce poverty. *Cape Times*, 14 January, p. 9.

Phelps-Stokes Commission, African Education. (1922) *Education in Africa* (a study of West, South, and Equatorial Africa, conducted under the auspices of the Phelps-Stokes Fund and foreign mission societies of North America and Europe). Prepared by Thomas Jesse Jones, Chairman. (pp. 323). New York: Phelps-Stoke Fund.

Phillipson, R. (1992) *Linguistic Imperialism*. Oxford: University of Oxford Press.

Phillipson, R. (1993) *Linguistic Imperialism*. Oxford: Oxford University Press.

Phillipson, R. (1997) Realities and myths of linguistic imperialism. *Journal of Multilingual and Multicultural Development* 18, 238–47.

Phillipson, R. (2003) *English-Only Europe? Challenging Language Policy*. London: Routledge.

Piore, M. and Sable, C. (1984) *The Second Industrial Divide: Possibilities for Prosperity*. New York: Basic Books.

Plüddemann, P., Braam, D., Broeder P., Extra, G. and October, M. (2004a) Language policy implementation and language vitality in Western Cape primary schools. PRAESA Occasional Papers No. 15.

Plüddemann, P., Braam, D., October, M. and Wababa, Z. (2004b) Dual-medium and parallel-medium schooling in the Western Cape: from default to design. PRAESA Occasional Papers No. 17.

Pool, J. (1969) National development and language diversity. *La Monda Lingvo Problemo* 1, 140–56.
Potter, D. (1997) Colonial rule. In Allen, T. and Thomas, A. (eds) *Poverty and Development in the 1990s* (pp. 273–90). Oxford: Oxford University Press in association with the Open University.
Prah, K.K. (1999) African Renaissance or Warlordism? In Makgoba, M.W. (ed.) *African Renaissance – The New Struggle*. Cape Town: Tafelberg Publishing.
Prah, K.K. (2000) *Language for Scientific and Technological Development in Africa*. Cape Town: The Centre for Advanced Studies of African Society (CASAS).
Prah, K.K. (2002a) Education, mother-tongue instruction, Christianity and development of an African culture. Paper presented at the *International Conference on Visionen fur das berufliche Bildungssystem in Africa*. Loccum, Germany: Centre for Advanced Studies of African Society (CASAS).
Prah, K.K. (2002b) Language, the African development challenge. In *TRIcontinental*, No. 150. Havana, Cuba. On WWW at http://www.casas.co.za.
Prinsloo, M. and Breier, M. (1996) *The Social Uses of Literacy*. Cape Town. Amsterdam: Sached/John Benjamins.
Probyn, M., Murray, S., Botha, L., Botya, P., Brooks, M. and Westphal, V. (2002) Minding the gaps – an investigation into language policy and practice in four Eastern Cape districts. *Perspectives in Education* 20(1), 29–46.
Rahman, T. (1995) The Siraiki movement in Pakistan. *Language Problems and Language Planning* 20(2) (Spring), 1–25.
Rahman, T. (2000) *Language and Politics in Pakistan*. Oxford: Oxford University Press.
Rahman, T. (2002) Language teaching and power in Pakistan. *World Congress on Language Policies*. Barcelona, Spain.
Rama Rao, V.V.B. (2002) 20th century language visionaries. *Language in India* (Vol. 2). On WWW at http://www.LanguageinIndia.com. Accessed 2.05.04.
Ramesh, R. (2004) The last thing on their minds. *Guardian Unlimited*, London.
Ranger, T. (1989) Missionaries, migrants and manyika: The invention of ethnicity in Zimbabwe. In Vail, L. (ed.). *The Creation of Tribalism in Southern Africa* (pp. 18–150). London/Berkeley and Los Angeles: James Currey/University of California Press.
Rangila, R.S., Thirumalai, M.S. and Mallikarjun, B. (2001) Bringing order to linguistic diversity: Language planning in the British raj. *Language in India* 1. On WWW at http://www.LanguageinIndia.com. Accessed 2.05.04.
Rashid, A. and Shaheed, F. (1993) *Pakistan: Ethno-politics and Contending Elites* (p. 65). Geneva: United Nations Research Institute for Social Development (UNRISD).
Rassool, N. (1993) Post-Fordism? Technology and new forms of control: The case of technology in the curriculum. *Journal of Education Policy* 14(3), 227–44.
Rassool, N. (1998) Postmodernity, cultural pluralism and the nation-state: Problems of language rights, human rights, identity and power. *Language Sciences* 20(1), 89–99.
Rassool, N. (1999) *Literacy for Sustainable Development in the Age of Information*. The Language and Education Library 14. Clevedon/Philadelphia: Multilingual Matters.
Ricento, T. (2000) Historical and theoretical perspectives in language policy and planning. In Ricento, T. (ed.). *Ideology, Politics and Language Policies: Focus on English* (pp. 9–24). Amsterdam: John Benjamins Publishing Co.

Ridge, S. (2000) Mixed motives: Ideological elements in the support for English in South Africa. In Ricento, T. (ed.) *Ideology, Politics and Language Policies: Focus on English* (pp. 151–72). Amsterdam: John Benjamins Publishing Co.

Rikowski, G. (2002) *Globalisation and Education* (pp. 12). London: House of Lords Select Committee on Economic Affairs Inquiry into the Global Economy.

Roy, M. (1994) Englishing India: Reinstituting class and social privilege. *Social Text* 39. On WWW at http://www.LanguageinIndia.com. Accessed 4.05.04.

Roy-Campbell, Z.M. (2001) *Empowerment Through Language: The African Experience: Tanzania and Beyond*. Trenton NJ and Asmara, Eritrea: Africa World Press, Inc.

Ruiz, R. (1984) Orientations in language planning. *Journal of the National Association for Bilingual Education* 8, 15–34.

Rule, P. (2003) 'The time is burning': The right of adults to basic education in South Africa. Paper presented at the Education Rights Project Forum, 1 July. University of Witwatersrand, Johannesburg, South Africa.

Sadaf Zuberi, N.S. (2005) Pakistan Sign Language – A Synopsis (Vol. 2005). Sustainable Development Networking Programme, Pakistan and IUCN – The World Conservation Union. On www at http://www.special.net.pk/htm. Accessed 22.07.05.

Said, E. (1983) *The World, the Text, and the Critic*. Cambridge, MA: Harvard University Press.

Said, E. (1993) *Culture and Imperialism*. London: Chatto and Windus.

Said, E. (2001) The confluence of civilizations: The book, critical performance, and the future of education. Keynote address. In *DOE Saamtrek: Values, Education and Democracy in the 21st Century. Conference Report of the National Conference, Kirstenbosch*, 22–24 February 2001. Pretoria: Department of Education.

SAIRR (2001) *South Africa Survey 2001/2002*. Johannesburg: South African Institute for Race Relations.

SAIRR (2002) *Hard Lessons*. Fast Facts No11/November 2002. On WWW at http://www.sairr.org.za/publications/pub/ff/200211/lessons.htm.

Sartre, J.P. (1977) *Colonialism and Neocolonialism*. London: Routledge & Kegan Paul.

Saul, J. (1986) The state in post-colonial societies: Tanzania. In Held, J.A.D., Gieben, B., Hall, S., Harris, L., Lewis, P., Parker, N. and Turok, B. (eds) *States and Societies* (pp. 457–74). Oxford: Basil Blackwell in association with the Open University.

Schultz, T. (1963) *The Economic Value of Education*. New York: Columbia University Press.

Seligman, A.B. (1995) *The Idea of Civil Society*. Princeton, New Jersey: Princeton University Press.

Shukla, S.P. (2002). From the GATT to the WTO and Beyond. In Nayyar, D. (ed.) *Governing Globalization: Issues and Institutions*. Oxford: Oxford University Press.

Siatchitema, A. (1992) When nationism conflicts with nationalist goals: Zambia. In Crawhall, N. (ed.). *Democratically Speaking* (pp. 17–21). Cape Town: National Language Project.

Sieborger, R. (2003) Personal communication.

Skutnabb-Kangas, T. (1981) *Bilingualism or Not: The Education of Minorities*. Clevedon: Multilingual Matters.

Skutnabb-Kangas, T. (2000) *Linguistic Genocide in Educaiton or Worldwide Diversity and Human Rights?* Mahwaw, NJ: Lawrence Erlbaum Associates, Inc.

Skutnabb-Kangas, T. and Phillipson, R. (1995) Linguistic human rights, past and present. In Skutnabb-Kangas, T. and Phillipson, R. (eds) *Linguistic Human Rights: Overcoming Linguistic Discrimination*. Berlin and New York: Mouton de Gruyter.

Smith, A.D. (1983) *State and Nation in the Third World*. Brighton: Harvester Wheatsheaf Books Ltd.

Sonntag, S. (2002) Minority language politics in North India. In Tollefson, J.W. (ed.) *Language Policies in Education* (pp. 165–78). Mahwah, New Jersey and London: Lawrence Erlbaum Associates, Publishers.

Spencer, J. (1974) Colonial language policies and their legacies in Sub-Saharan Africa. In Fishman, J.A. (ed.) *Advances in Language Planning* (pp. 163–75). The Hague: Mouton.

Statistics S.A. (2003) *Census 2001: Census-in-Brief*. Pretoria: Statistics SA.

Stiglitz, J. (2002) *Globalization and its Discontents*. London: Penguin Books.

Strauss, J. (1999) *Results of the Monitoring Learning Achievement (MLA) Project*. Bloemfontein: University of the Free State and Department of Education.

Street, B. (1995) *Social Literacies: Critical Approaches to Literacy Development, Ethnography and Education*. London: Longman.

Stroud, C. (2001) African mother-tongue programmes and the politics of language: Linguistic citizenship versus linguistic human rights. *Journal of Multilingual and Multicultural Development* 2(4), 339–55.

Taylor, N. and Vinjevold, P. (eds). (1999) *Getting Learning Right. Report of the President's Education Initiative Research Project*. Johannesburg: The Joint Education Trust.

Terreblanche, S. (2003) *A History of Inequality in South Africa 1652–2002*. Pietermaritzburg: University of Natal Press.

"The Scramble for Africa." On WWW at http://en.wikipedia.org/w/wiki.phtml. Accessed 22.07.04.

Thirumalai, M.S. (2003) Macaulay. *Language in India* (Vol. 3). On WWW at http://www.LanguageinIndia.com. Accessed 2.05.04.

Thirumalai, M.S. (2005) Language policy of the Indian National Congress during the pre-partition period 1939–1946. *Language in India* (Vol. 6). On WWW at http://www.LanguageinIndia.com.

Thomas, C. (1997) Pakistan loses faith in democracy as dream turns sour. In *The Times*, 14 August 1997, London.

Tilly, C. (1990) *Coercion, Capital and European States, AD 1990–1992*. Oxford: Blackwell Publishers.

Tollefson, J. (1991a) *Planning Language, Planning Inequality*. Harlow: Longman Group.

Tollefson, J.W. (1991b) *Planning Language, Planning Inequality: Language Policy in the Community*. London and New York: Longman.

Tomaney, J. (1990) The reality of workplace flexibility. *Capital and Class* 40, 29–60.

Toure, A. (1982) Education in Mali. In Fafunwa, A. and Aisiku, J. (eds) *Education in Africa: A Comparative Study* (pp. 188–204). London: George Allen and Unwin.

Touval, S. (1999) *The Boundary Politics of Independent Africa*. San Jose, New York, Lincoln, Shanghai, Cambridge, MA: Harvard University Press.

Traoré, S. (2001a) *La Pédagogie Convergente son expérimentation au Mali et son impact sur le système éducatif (Monographies innodata – 6)*. (Educational Innovations in Action Series). Geneva: UNESCO/IBE.

Traoré, S. (2001b) Convergent teaching in Mali. *Prospects: Quarterly Review of Comparative Education*, XXXI *(3) September 2001* (pp. 353–71).

UNESCO (1976) *Mali. The Experimental World Literacy Programme: A Critical Assessment*. Paris: The UNESCO Press/UNDP.

UNESCO (1981) African languages: Proceedings of the meeting of experts on the transcription and harmonization of African languages, Niamey, Niger, 17–21 July 1978. Paris: UNESCO. On WWW at http://www.bisharat.net/.

UNESCO (1985) *African Community Languages and Their Use in Literacy and Education*. Regional Office for Education in Dakar: Unesco.

UNESCO (2000) *World Education Report 2000. The Right to Education, Towards Education for All Throughout Life*. Paris: UNESCO.

UNESCO (2002) Initiative B@bel. UNESCO. On WWW at http://www.unesco.org/webworld/multilingualism. Accessed 4.07.05.

UNESCO (2003) *Education in a Multilingual World*. Paris: UNESCO.

UNESCO (2005) *Community Multimedia Centres*, a website about community centre use of ICTs for the poor. On WWW at http://portal.unesco.org/ci/en/ev.php-URL_ID=12594andURL_DO=DO_TOPICandURL_SECTION=201.html.

UNESCO/CLT/BALING (1966) Final report. Réunion d'un groupe d'experts pour l'unification des alphabets des langues nationales, Bamako, Mali, 28 février–5 mars (1966). Paris: UNESCO. On WWW at http://www.bisharat.net/.

United Nations Development Programme (UNDP) (1999) *Human Development Report 1999*. Oxford: UNDP/Oxford University Press.

United Nations Development Programme (UNDP) (2001) *Human Development Report 2001*. New York: United Nations. On WWW at www.undp.org. Accessed 4.07.05.

United Nations Development Programme (UNDP) (2002) *Human Development Report 2002*. Oxford: UNDP/Oxford University Press.

United Nations Development Programme (UNDP) (2004) *Human Report 2004*. Oxford: UNDP/Oxford University Press.

United Nations High Commissioner for Refugees (UNHCR) (2000) *The State of the World's Refugees: Fifty Years of Humanitarian Action*. Oxford: Oxford University Press.

United Nations High Commission for Refugees (UNHCR) (2002) *Statistical Year Book 2002*. Geneva: United Nations High Commissioner for Refugees.

United Nations High Commissioner for Refugees (UNHCR) (2003) Population Data Unit/PGDS with the assistance of the Education Unit/HCDS, Division of Operational Support. 2003. *Refugee Education in 2002/3: Indicators and Standards for 66 Camp Locations*. Geneva: United Nations High Commissioner for Refugees (UNHCR).

United Nations High Commissioner for Refugees (UNHCR) (2004a) *2003 Global Refugee Trends: Overview of Refugee Populations, New Arrivals, Durable Solutions, Asylum-Seekers and Other Persons of Concern to UNHCR*. Geneva: United Nations High Commissioner for Refugees (UNHCR).

United Nations High Commissioner for Refugees (UNHCR) (2004b) *Refugee Trends 1 January–30 September 2004*. Geneva: United Nations High Commissioner for Refugees (UNHCR).

United Nations High Commissioner for Refugees (UNHCR) (2004c) Executive Committee of the High Commissioner's Programme. *Protracted Refugee Situations*. Geneva: UNHCR.
Uzoigwe, G.N. (1985) European partition and conquest of Africa: An overview. In Boahen, A.A. (ed.). *Africa Under Colonial Domination 1880–1935* (Vol. VII) (pp. 19–44). General History of Africa VII. London, Paris, Berkeley: Heinemann Educational Books Ltd, UNESCO, University of Califorina Press.
Webb, V. (2002) *Language in South Africa: The Role of Language in National Transformation, Reconstruction and Development*. Amsterdam: John Benjamins.
Webb, V. (2003) *Language in South Africa: The Role of Language in National Reconstruction and Development*. Amsterdam/Philadelphia: John Benjamins.
Webb, V. (2005) LOTE as languages od science in mulitlingual South Africa. A case study at the University of Pretoria. Paper presented at the conference on bi and multilingual universities – challenges and future prospects. University of Helsinki.
Whitehead, C. (1992) British Colonial Policy in India 1858–1921. On WWW at http://www.aare.edu.au/92pap/whitc92.496. Accessed 2.01.04.
Wildeman, R. (2005) Personal communication, e-mail 10 March.
Wiley, T. (2002) Accessing language rights in education: A brief history of the U.S. context. In Tollefson, J. (ed.) *Language Policies in Education: Critical Issues* (pp. 39–64). Mahwah, NJ: Lawrence Erlbaum Associates.
Williams, R. (1961) *The Long Revolution*. Harmondsworth: Penguin in association with Chatto and Windus.
Williamson, J. (1993) Development and the "Washington Consensus". In *World Development* (Vol. 21) (pp. 1239–336). Washington, DC: Institute for International Economics.
Winkler, G. (1997) The myth of the mother tongue: Evidence from Maryvale College, Johannesburg. *Southern African Journal of Applied Language Studies* 5(1), 29–41.
World Bank (1999) Education and Koranic literacy in West Africa. *IKNotes*. Washington: World Bank. On WWW at http://www.worldbank.org/.
World Bank (2005a) World Development Indicators 2005. CD-ROM, Washington DC.
WorldBank (2005b) The World Bank Operational Manual: Operational Policies: Operational manual OP 4.10. On WWW at http://wbln0018.worldbank.org/Institutional/Manuals/OpManaual.nsf/B52929624EB2A35. Accessed 14.01.06.
WSIS (2002) African Languages and Internet Workshop. Bamako 2002 Conference. World Summit on the Information Society. On WWW at http://www.uneca.org/aisi/Bamako2002/report_afrlang_en.htm.
WSIS (2005) Background document. *Multilingualism for Cultural Diversity and Participation of All in Cyberspace UNESCO WSIS Thematic Meeting Bamako, Mali, 6–7 May 2005*. World Summit on the Information Society. On WWW at http://portal.unesco.org/ci/en/ev.php-URL_ID=17688andURL_DO=DO_TOPICandURL_ SECTION= 201.html.
Yan, X. (2004) HRD soft-skills technology transfer in higher education: A case study of one US university to two Chinese universities and one corporate university in China. Unpublished PhD thesis, Institute of Education, The University of Reading, United Kingdom.
Young, C. (1988) The colonial state and post-colonial crisis. In Louis, P.G.a.W. (ed.) *Declonization and African Independence: The Transfers of Power, 1960–1980*. New Haven and London: Yale University Press.

Young, C. (1994) *The African Colonial State in Comparative Perspective*: New Haven: Yale University Press.
Young, D. (1995) Preparing teacher trainees to teach in multilingual classes. In Heugh, K., Siegrühn, A. and Plüddemann, P. (eds) *Multilingual Education for South Africa* (pp. 107–112). Cape Town: Heinemann.
Young, D. (2001) Why Applied Language Studies and not Applied Linguistics? In Ridge, E., Makoni, S. and Ridge, S. (eds). *Freedom and Discipline. Essays in Applied Linguistics from Southern Africa* (pp. 221–62). New Dehli: Bahri Publications.
Young, R. (2001) *Postcolonialism: An Historical Introduction*. Oxford: Blackwell.
Zaman, U.S. (1981) *Banners Unfurled: A Critical Analysis of Developments in Education in Pakistan*. Karachi: Quereshi Art Press.
Zastoupil, L. and Moir, M. (eds). (1999) *The Great Indian Education Debate: Documents Relating to the Orientalist-Angliscist Controversy, 1781–1843*. Richmond: Curzon Press.
Zono, A. (2002) *La pédagogie convergente en Afrique, plaidoyer pour son adaptation aux réalités du milieu*. Bandiagara: GTZ.

Index